YEOVIL

5|17

CANCELLED

Please return/renew this item by the last date shown
on this label, or on your self-service receipt.

To renew this item, visit **www.librarieswest.org.uk**
or contact your library.

Your Borrower number and PIN are required.

LibrariesWest

VINTER'S   TEER

G000245223

CANCELLED

4 1 0514410 1

VINTER'S **RAILWAY** GAZETTEER

A GUIDE TO BRITAIN'S OLD RAILWAYS THAT YOU CAN WALK OR CYCLE

JEFF VINTER

GREAT WESTERN RAILWAY.
NOTICE.
ALL PERSONS ARE WARNED NOT TO TRESPASS
UPON THE LINES OF RAILWAY OF THE COMPANY,
AND NOTICE IS HEREBY GIVEN THAT PURSUANT
TO THE PROVISIONS OF THE COMPANY'S ACTS
EVERY PERSON WHO TRESPASSES UPON ANY OF
THE LINES OF RAILWAY RENDERS HIMSELF LIABLE
TO A PENALTY OF FORTY SHILLINGS, AND IN DEFAULT
OF PAYMENT TO ONE MONTH'S IMPRISONMENT
FOR EVERY SUCH OFFENCE.
BY ORDER.

The
History
Press

For Nigel Willis and the members of Railway Ramblers – still the best possible intelligence network for a project like this.

The plume of smoke below Tresmeer has gone.
The porter and the ticket clerk have flagged the final train.
Their neatly tended flowerbeds, abandoned, run to seed.
Their station windows weep Atlantic rain.

From 'A Cornish Lament'
Author

Cover illustrations
Front, from top: Carnon Viaduct near Truro, with the old Redruth & Chacewater Railway below (Author); Overbridge north of Marlborough (Author). *Back, from top*: Clydach Viaduct and station near Brynmawr (Phil Earnshaw); Middleton Top Engine House, Derbyshire (Peter Martin).

First published 2011
This edition published 2017

The History Press
The Mill, Brimscombe Port
Stroud, Gloucestershire, GL5 2QG
www.thehistorypress.co.uk

© Jeff Vinter, 2011, 2017

The right of Jeff Vinter to be identified as the Author of this work has been asserted in accordance with the Copyright, Designs and Patents Act 1988.

All rights reserved. No part of this book may be reprinted or reproduced or utilised in any form or by any electronic, mechanical or other means, now known or hereafter invented, including photocopying and recording, or in any information storage or retrieval system, without the permission in writing from the Publishers.

British Library Cataloguing in Publication Data.
A catalogue record for this book is available from the British Library.

ISBN 978 0 7509 6976 5

Typesetting and origination by The History Press
Printed in China

CONTENTS

FOREWORD

When I joined Sustrans as Chief Executive in June 2016, following Malcolm Shepherd's retirement, I was immediately introduced to this extraordinary gazetteer, written and updated by Jeff Vinter. Jeff's breadth and depth of knowledge of the history, folklore and current usage of Britain's old railways clearly positions him as the leading authority in the field.

Whether you are interested in the history of our disused railways, have a love of Britain's unique countryside fauna and flora, are looking to open up these often overlooked gems for greater use by the public, or just want to embark on safe walks or cycle rides with friends and family, then this is the book for you.

Vinter's Railway Gazetteer provides the most comprehensive and accessible information on some of our most valuable and under-used heritage assets. Delving through its pages, planning many and varied expeditions and outings, will provide you with a lifetime of enjoyment.

The first edition of this book was published in 2011, after many years of patient research and record keeping. This latest edition brings us right up to date with the many developments of the intervening years – the result is invaluable.

Xavier Brice
Chief Executive, Sustrans

Sustrans is the charity that's enabling people to travel by foot, bike or public transport for more of the journeys we make every day. Our work makes it possible for people to choose healthier, cleaner and cheaper journeys, with better places and spaces to move through and live in.

ACKNOWLEDGEMENTS

Many individuals in many organisations have taken the time to answer enquiries, which have helped me to assemble this gazetteer. In particular, I extend my thanks to the staff of Sustrans Ltd (especially Malcolm Shepherd, Xavier Brice, Huw Davies and John Lauder), Railway Paths Ltd, the former Countryside Commission, various National Park Authorities and countless local councils, especially Devon County Council whose Graham Cornish was immensely helpful. Amongst the many individuals who have contributed Tim Chant and the late Ralph Rawlinson deserve particular credit for the sheer range and volume of information supplied, while Tony Jervis, Chris John, Duncan McLeish and Keith Potter supplied a mass of detail about railway walks in Scotland. Keith Holliday deserves a special mention for his prescient encouragement, which led me to start this new edition before the publisher's letter arrived and in the later stages of the project he helped with the proofreading. The many books on disused railways were a great help, but none more so than Rhys ab Elis's *Railway Rights of Way*, which comprised a main report and three supplements published by the Branch Line Society between 1985 and 1989. Rhys has now brought his work up to date, with the BLS republishing it in CD format in 2013. The many photographers represented in this book are credited alongside their work, but I thank them again for helping to give this book its visual impact.

Since the first edition of the gazetteer appeared in 1997, new information has been supplied by the following: Jonathan Aston, Martyn Babb, Richard Bain, Chris Bedford, Greg Beecroft, Barra Best, Graeme Bickerdike, Maurice Billinton, J. Blenkin, Stephen Bragg, Colin Brown, Tim Chant, Jonathan Dawson, Bob Delaney, Hugh Dougherty, Mike Ellison, Phil Earnshaw, John Elson, John Everest, Tom Ferris, John Fisher, Kenneth Goddard, John Grimshaw, Tim Grose, Bill Harrow (Dumfries & Galloway Council), Tim Hewett, Bob Hipgrave, Keith Holliday, Andy Hutchings, Tony Jervis, Chris John, Mark Jones, Philip Kirk (Savills for The Edward James Foundation), Graham Lambert, Richard Lewis, Stephen Lewis, Brian Loughlin, Ian Lund, Roger Mayo, Duncan McLeish, Andrew McLintock, Stuart McNair, Bob Morgan, Bryan Nicholls, Chris Parker, David Pedley, Lionel and Zita Pilbeam, Keith Potter, Ralph Rawlinson, Derek Richards, Peter Richards, Dave Roberts, Brian Russell, Matt Skidmore, Paul Smith, Liam Standing, Ron Strutt, Robin Summerhill, John Swan, David Thompson, Keith Turner, Robin Wade and Phil Wood. I am very grateful to all of the above, for they are my countrywide network of 'disused trackbed spies' who help me to keep abreast of railway path developments throughout the UK.

INTRODUCTION

This gazetteer lists all known railway paths in the British Isles, i.e. disused railway lines over which one may walk (and sometimes cycle) with official sanction. As a general rule, it excludes (a) short routes of less than 2 miles, and (b) routes which have been proposed but are not yet open, although exceptions have been made for short trails, which meet one or more of the following criteria:

- Features a large engineering structure, e.g. the ½m section of NCN66 at Stamford Bridge, Yorkshire, which includes a fine viaduct over the River Derwent.
- Is close to a longer railway path, e.g. Upper Gartness to Croftamie, near Loch Lomond, which is near the longer Gartness to Blanefield trail.
- Is in a county with few, if any, other railway paths, e.g. Abingdon to Radley in Oxfordshire.
- Is on a line where one might have expected nothing at all to be accessible, or to have even survived, e.g. parts of the former Hundred of Manhood & Selsey Tramway in West Sussex, which closed in January 1935.

Old railways that have been turned into roads are excluded on the grounds that few will wish to walk them, especially when the road is a motorway or dual carriageway as is the case at Swindon (M4) and Newbury (A34).

In recent years, increasing numbers of old railways have been opened as multi-use trails as the Sustrans-inspired National Cycle Network has expanded. It is not surprising that Sustrans has been active in Northern Ireland since the 'six counties' form part of the UK, but now the government of the Republic has become interested in developing a network of safe routes for cyclists as well. What is noticeable about many of the new breed of paths is how much former railway land has been reused over the years, resulting in the path builders having shorter mileages of continuous disused trackbed to work with. As a result, many 'new build' schemes cleverly string together what remains of an old railway, using anything that comes to hand as an inter-railway connection – canal towpaths, riverside paths, farm tracks, bridleways, quiet lanes, etc. An example of such a path will be found between Garmouth and Cullen in Grampian (modern Moray). On the other hand, very occasionally part of an old railway will be reinstated. Users of the North Dorset Trailway travelling north from Blandford Forum to Stourpaine will cross a section of trail near Manor France Farm where the trackbed once existed for trains; then was closed, removed and incorporated in a field, but in 2013 was reinstated for the trail.

With the exception of Ireland, six-figure grid references have been provided for all entries using the Ordnance Survey's online OS Maps service. Due to the small number of railway paths in Ireland, I have not added grid references to the entries for that country, although Ordnance Survey Ireland (OSi) have released a product called Trail Master – an interactive mapping tool on DVD which might make this task achievable in the future with only a single purchase. (Even then, will OSi show details of railway paths? Our own OS did not do so consistently until fairly recently.) Anyway, economic constraints prevailed. I love Ireland, but not enough to buy dozens of OSi maps which I can use for only a week a year when visiting the country.

As great as it is to have all of these railway walks to explore, it is clearly too much for one person to go out and check all of them personally, so I appealed to members of Railway Ramblers for their help, and they were very generous with their assistance. If you know of a route that I have missed or which has been extended, please let me know (see 'Contact Me' section). However, do remember that any nominated route must be at least 2 miles long (or more), and officially open to the public.

I acknowledge that the amount of detail published for each county does vary, this being partly a by-product of where I live (on the south coast), where I travel, and where I walk. It is not difficult for me to visit, say, Bath or Bournemouth, but Edinburgh and Carlisle are a different proposition. Fortunately, since 2012, my voluntary work as a director of Railway Paths Ltd has enabled me to sample a good selection of trails in what, for me, are the further flung parts of the country. Using printed and online sources, I have added a thumbnail description of every route but, if you have further significant details that should be added, do please get in touch.

From its first self-published edition back in 1997, this gazetteer made it obvious which counties had done little with their disused railways, and this is still the case. As the years go by, the laggards become more and more apparent, although it must be said in defence of counties like Kent and Surrey that they escaped lightly when railway cuts were being made. Nowadays, it is generally recognised that old trackbeds, like canal towpaths, offer many recreational and travel opportunities for walkers and cyclists alike; even government planning guidance has made this point in recent years. However, these opportunities can be lost if the local council lacks imagination or the will to act decisively. If the potential of a railway line is ignored when it closes, that line will be infinitely more difficult to reuse when it has been left for a decade to fly tippers, property developers and so on.

Finally, I must emphasise that this gazetteer is not intended to emulate Rhys ab Elis's *Railway Rights of Way*, which is comprehensive to the point of listing sections of old railway that were barely 100yds long. Useful though such detail is for the 'completist', it produces a confusing picture for the ordinary walker who has to sift through lengthy listings to discern those routes that are long enough to warrant a visit. Hopefully, this guide will provide a practical remedy to this problem and encourage more people to get out and explore one of this country's once neglected resources – its stock of disused railway lines. Happy railway rambling!

THE TROUBLE WITH COUNTIES

Administrative counties tend to pop in and out of existence like soap bubbles … Welsh and Scottish counties are separately complicated.

Bill Bryson

In his book, *The Road to Little Dribbling*, Mr Bryson pokes gentle fun at the chaos which has grown out of British local authority boundaries. He reckons that there are five categories, but we can exclude 'Duchy' because it contains only one entry – Cornwall. Fortunately, the River Tamar has helped to ensure that Cornwall's boundary with Devon hasn't been pushed back and forth in recent years to a range of arbitrarily drawn lines between, say, Looe–Tintagel and Kingsbridge–Lynton. Other parts of the country have not been so lucky. Take Bath as an example. Historically the city belonged to Somerset but in 1974 the Heath government placed it in the invented county of Avon, and since 1995 it has belonged to a unitary authority called 'Bath & North East Somerset'.

I started work on the gazetteer in 1988, by which time the major local authority changes of 1974 had bedded in. Like many at the time, I assumed that these new boundaries would last a lifetime, or more, as had the old boundaries before them. Unfortunately, Mr Heath and his Cabinet had let the genie out of the bottle, and, ever since, once stable administrative boundaries have become increasingly unstable. In its annual *Good Beer Guide*, the Campaign for Real Ale has given up on this nonsense and imposed administrative divisions of its own, such as 'Mid Wales', 'North West Wales' and 'Greater Glasgow and Clyde Valley', a solution which must require a lot more in the way of mapping resources than I can afford.

Accordingly, this latest version of the gazetteer continues to use the 1974 boundaries, which became familiar during my student years at the University of Exeter. While I could reorganise its contents into a more modern sequence, it would be a cosmetic exercise that would add nothing material to the book, and in any case another government could change everything again in a few years' time. By comparison, how sensible and sane seems Ireland's retention of its long-standing status quo: County Donegal is still County Donegal, County Cork is still County Cork, and the same applies to every Irish county in between.

In the 1940s, we removed all signs from the UK in order to confuse a potential invader. I sometimes wonder if a few rounds of bureaucratic boundary changes might have been even more effective. To reinforce Bill Bryson's point about soap bubbles, while investigating this subject I came across television reports published between 2010 and 2015 calling for Bristol City, South Gloucestershire, Bath & North East Somerset and North Somerset councils to be merged into a re-formed Avon County Council. Local businessmen point out that all four unitary authorities are working closely together already, and that a merger would offer better value for money to the public by reducing the number of chief executives (and every other post) from four to one. On 14 December 2015 Local Government Secretary Greg Clark confirmed that he had 'no intention of reintroducing Avon by the back door, front door or side door' – but that's just this minister in this government talking.

Railway Paths and Rights of Way

Please be aware that many railway walks and cycle trails are not, and never have been, public rights of way. Many are owned by local authorities which have chosen not to 'dedicate' them in order to simplify procedures when the routes need to be closed, e.g. for resurfacing or other maintenance. Some of these routes have major engineering features on them, and even a humble road-over-rail bridge represents a maintenance liability on a scale rarely encountered on a traditional field path.

In addition some of the new railway paths (i.e. those opened since c. 2000) depend on licences negotiated with local landowners. There are sometimes restrictions on these routes, such as dogs not being permitted in order to avoid disturbing wildlife or livestock (typically sheep). If you come across such restrictions, please comply with them since the landowner is entitled to withdraw access if members of the public do not comply with the licence's terms. It would be a great pity if, having waited many years for access to old railways to be improved, that access were withdrawn due to the thoughtlessness of a minority. Over the years, many have complained that Britain's old railways were scrapped with scarcely a thought for their reuse. Now that this is being put right, let's work together with local authorities and landowners to make 'rail trails' a success.

Contact Me

If you put my name into Google, you will find my personal website which contains an email link. (The website's address may change so is not included here.) Should you need an alternative, please use the 'Contact' page on the Railway Ramblers' website (railwayramblers.org.uk).

Please note that, normally, I will not enter into correspondence, but I would be grateful to receive details of any corrections required to this work, whether they are path extensions, path closures, or entirely new routes. Any new contributors will be acknowledged in future editions, assuming that the book does well enough to warrant them. Please remember my stipulation above, that new routes must be at least 2 miles long in order to avoid turning this publication into a catalogue of trackbed fragments.

LIST OF ABBREVIATIONS

Users

C = Cyclists
CIP = Cyclists (in places)
H = Horse riders
HIP = Horse riders (in places)
W = Walkers

Suitability for Prams, Pushchairs and Wheelchairs

NF = Route not yet fully open
NI = Route not inspected
NO = Route not yet open
UT = Usable throughout
UP = Usable in places
UX = Mostly unusable

Type of Path

DC = Disused canal (used as diversion)
DR = Disused railway
DT = Disused tramway
TP = Trackside path alongside operational railway

Distances

All distances are in miles.

Railway Companies

This gazetteer does not identify what railway company built or operated which route, but occasionally abbreviations of company names appear in the text for an entry.

B&MR = Brecon & Merthyr Railway
BR = British Railways, latterly British Rail
CR = Caledonian Railway
DLR = Docklands Light Railway
DNSR = Didcot, Newbury & Southampton Railway
GCR = Great Central Railway
GER = Great Eastern Railway
GNR = Great Northern Railway
GNSR = Great North of Scotland Railway
G&SWR = Glasgow & South Western Railway
GWR = Great Western Railway
HR = Highland Railway
L&YR = Lancashire & Yorkshire Railway
LBSCR = London, Brighton & South Coast Railway
LMSR = London, Midland & Scottish Railway
LNWR = London & North Western Railway
LSWR = London & South Western Railway
M&GNR = Midland & Great Northern Railway
M&SWJR = Midland & South Western Junction Railway

MR = Midland Railway
NBR = North British Railway
NER = North Eastern Railway
NSR = North Staffordshire Railway
PTR = Port Talbot Railway
R&SBR = Rhondda & Swansea Bay Railway
S&DR = Somerset & Dorset Railway
SR = Southern Railway
SVR = Severn Valley Railway
SWMR = South Wales Mineral Railway

General

LDP = Long Distance Path
NCB = National Coal Board
NCN = National Cycle Network, usually followed by route number, e.g. NCN24
NT = National Trust
OS = Ordnance Survey
OSi = Ordnance Survey Ireland
RR = Railway Ramblers
RUPP = Road Used as a Public Path

ENGLAND AND OFFSHORE ISLANDS

Introduction

England started to reuse its lost railways constructively from 1972, when both the Downs Link in West Sussex and the Wirral Way in Cheshire were created. Given that the London, Midland & Scottish Railway had donated the trackbed of the Leek & Manifold Railway to the nation after its closure in 1934, prompting contemporary suggestions that this would be a good use for other closed railways (not an uncommon phenomenon in the 1930s), the wonder is that it took so long for the movement to get started. The big catalyst for what happened in the 1970s was the publication in 1963 of the so-called Beeching Report, innocuously entitled 'The Re-Shaping of British Railways'. It might as well have been entitled 'The Mutilation and Sabotage of British Railways', for that is what it amounted to and that is what successive governments did – and, by the way, that is why the nation is having to rebuild some of these lost lines almost fifty years later. However, this is not the place to discuss the work of the report's main author, Dr Richard Beeching, for there are railway historians who regard him as the saviour of the railways in these islands. Their argument goes along the lines of, 'if we hadn't had Beeching, we would have had something much worse' (if you want an example, investigate the history of the anti-rail Ulster Transport Authority in Northern Ireland). What cannot be denied is that Dr Beeching suddenly increased the nation's stock of disused railways by thousands of miles – and here are what countless local authorities, community groups, cycling charities and suchlike have done with them ...

Avon

Axbridge–Yatton: CIP, HIP, W, UP, DR, 8m, ST 423549–ST 425660. This scenic trail is a pioneering community-based railway path, saved after closure as a working railway by the Cheddar Valley Railway Walk Society, now the Strawberry Line Society. A long diversion was reduced significantly in 2007 when the trail was moved on to the trackbed north of Sandford & Banwell station; a diversion around an electricity substation remains, but that too should disappear in a few years' time when the nuclear power station at Hinckley Point C is commissioned and the substation becomes redundant. Sandford

AVON

& Banwell station was restored and reopened as a railway museum in 2010. At Axbridge, the trail connects with a separate railway path from Cheddar (see entry under Somerset); while at Yatton the trail ends at the station on the still operational Bristol–Taunton line. Current proposals envisage this route becoming part of a trans-Somerset railway path network called the Strawberry Line after the area's famous fruit, which is making a revival; if successful, it will run from Clevedon in the west to Cranmore (near Shepton Mallet) in the east.

Bath–Bristol: C, W, UT, DR, 13m, ST 722652–ST 601731. This is the pioneering cycle trail whose success in the 1970s led to the formation of Sustrans and ultimately the National Cycle Network. To cut a long story short, a group of Bristol cycling enthusiasts, frustrated by the failure of local authorities to take the needs of cyclists seriously, acquired part of the MR's Bath–Bristol line and converted it into a cycle trail themselves. It did not take long for the new route to be generating 1 million journeys per year, split more or less equally between cyclists and walkers. This level of use has continued to grow for many years and is now well over 2 million journeys per annum. The old railway formation is joined in Brassmills Lane on the west side of Bath; the link to Brassmills Lane from Bath city centre is via the upgraded River Avon towpath. The Bristol ring road (the A4174) has claimed a short section of the trackbed to the south-east of Mangotsfield station but a new section of path, on a new alignment, has been constructed to take its place: if you think

that the curves and gradients in this area are a bit extreme for trains, this is why – trains never ran here.

Bath (East Twerton)–Midsomer Norton: C, W, UP, DR, 12½m, ST 735648–ST 665538. This route, based on the famous Somerset & Dorset Railway, has come from nowhere to become one of the most impressive railway paths in the UK. It starts in Bath on the Old Bristol Road and includes a cornucopia of civil engineering. Apart from the railway's surviving bridges and viaducts (all brought up to standard for their new use as part of NCN244 and NCN24), two new bridges have been installed to replace those removed during the 1960s and 1970s, while both Devonshire and Combe Down Tunnels have been opened up, the former quite literally having been dug out from its tomb in a corner of a suburban park. That this has happened is thanks to the vision and hard work of the local volunteers who set up the 'Two Tunnels' project over a decade ago, and campaigned tirelessly to turn their vision of a railway path on the S&DR into a reality. Please note the following:

- Between Midford and Wellow (ST 761607–ST 746584), the trail has permissive access only and is closed for a few days each year during the pheasant-shooting season, usually only for a day at a time. There is a riding school at the Wellow end and often sheep grazing in adjoining fields, so **dogs are not allowed on this section at all**; please respect the landowner's wishes.
- Between Wellow and Shoscombe (ST 746584–ST 713559), parts of the railway have been absorbed back into fields, so please follow the NCN24 waymarking, which connects the two trackbed-based parts of the route. If you stop at the bridge parapets at ST 735576 just out of Wellow and look north and south, you will see how completely the railway has been erased from the landscape. If you are on foot, you can start

0   kilometres   50
0   miles   30

following the old line again from Stony Littleton (ST 725566), where footpaths run parallel to the old track (use the local OS Explorer map); cyclists have to wait until they reach Shoscombe (about a mile further on) before getting 'back on track'.

- West of Radstock, be sure to turn left at Welton Hollow (ST 679549) just after the Five Arches Viaduct, otherwise you will stay on the ex-GWR line to Pensford and Bristol, and end up in Thicket Mead.

Coalpit Heath–Keynsham: W, UP, DR, 8m, ST 675806–ST 662699. This route is known as 'The Dramway' – the Avon & Gloucestershire Railway, a nineteenth-century horse-drawn line that once carried coal from Coalpit Heath down to the River Avon, just north of Keynsham. It is one of the very last horse-drawn railways to be built in this country, since its promoters had the misfortune to construct and open it just before the steam locomotive boom. It is laid out now as an official path and is very easy to follow with parts following the Bath–Bristol railway path (see above), or running parallel to it. Near Mangotsfield, the Bristol ring road (the A4174) seems to have nudged a few sections of the route slightly to the east, but there is still much to enjoy along the way, especially various tramway bridges, a short tunnel, and the stone sleeper sets which the observant will find in places such as Siston Common.

Hallatrow–Limpley Stoke: This is not a railway path in any conventional sense, but a fascinating day's walking can be had with an OS Explorer map making one's way along the Cam Valley using parts of the old railway, the towpath of the former Somersetshire Coal Canal, and the public footpath that follows the Cam Brook; the experience provides a fascinating insight into the industry that once thronged this now quiet rural backwater. Access to the trackbed is currently as follows:

- **Hallatrow–Goosard Bridge, near Paulton:** W, UX, DR, 1m, ST 639573–ST 654577. This permissive footpath along the old railway is a considerable improvement upon the public right of way (the Limestone Link), which runs just to the north.
- **East of Goosard Bridge–Radford:** W, UX, DR/DC, 1½m, ST 657577–ST 673578. There is some permissive access to the trackbed on this section, with the Limestone Link using the last ¼m up to the public highway at Radford. In late 2011, a traveller encampment on the trackbed (where one might otherwise have walked) made the parallel canal towpath an appealing option; the empty canal bed is intact throughout, while at the western end both Timsbury and Paulton Basins remain in water. The footpath from ST 660577 northwards to Timsbury Bottom and Timsbury is a former tramway, while the public footpath that starts at ST 659576 and heads south towards Paulton is believed to follow the course of that village's connecting tramway.
- **Combe Hay–near South Stoke:** W, UX, DR, ½m, ST 738602–ST 746604. A short footpath based on the old railway, although really this is canal country. Just to the north are some of the twenty-two conventional locks in the Combe Hay flight, which replaced three revolutionary caisson locks.
- **Monkton Combe–Dundas Aqueduct:** C, W, UP, DR, ½m, ST 776621–ST 782621. This part of NCN24 is actually the access road to the private Monkton Combe School and was the part of the line featured in *The Titfield Thunderbolt*, the famous Ealing Studios comedy. At the eastern end, just beyond the viaduct which carries the A36 above the old railway, a new connecting path has been constructed, which runs north (below the only part of the Somersetshire Coal Canal still in water) to join the towpath of the Kennet & Avon Canal at Dundas Aqueduct, which continues north to Bath and south to Devizes.

Mangotsfield–near Pucklechurch: C, W, UT, DR, 2m, ST 660754–ST 685775. Connects at Mangotsfield with the Bath–Bristol railway path. At the Pucklechurch end, just south of the M4, there is a connection with the Dramway path which continues on to Coalpit Heath, but currently one cannot go much further on the trackbed of the old MR. However, South Gloucestershire Council wants to extend the trail to Yate by continuing under the M4 and following the old railway corridor north. Following trackbed clearance by volunteers and the installation of a sealed surface, the section up to the M4 Bridge was officially opened in July 2012 but there, for the time being, the trail stops.

Radstock–Great Elm (near Frome): C, W, UT, DR, 5½m, ST 691544–ST 751498. Part of Colliers Way (NCN24), based on the former GWR line from Frome to Bristol via Radstock and Hallatrow. Mostly in Somerset, q.v.

Radstock–Welton–Thicket Mead: C, W, UT, DR, 2m, ST 688550–ST 657548. The Midsomer Norton Greenway; another part of the old GWR line from Frome to Bristol. Five Arches Bridge (west of Radstock) is the most notable engineering feature.

Bedfordshire

Bedford–Sandy: C, W, NI, DR, 8m, TL 058491–TL 166504. The Bedford to Sandy Country Way forms part of both NCN51 and NCN12. A few local diversions are required, but the majority of this old railway (once part of a long cross-country route from Oxford to Cambridge) has now been converted into a good quality cycle trail. Proposals to reopen the old 'Varsity Line' from Oxford to Cambridge mean that this trail may have a fairly short life: the Oxford–Bedford section is expected to reopen in 2019, with the Bedford–Sandy section following maybe by 2024. Whether the reopening will continue on to Cambridge remains to be seen.

Bromham (near Oakley Junction)–Turvey: W, NI, DR, 3m, TL 007524–SP 961522. The Stevington Country Walk, once part of the MR's Bedford to Northampton line. Note that a diversion off the trackbed is required west of SP 982522: at this point, walk south to Tythe Farm (SP 981518) and there turn west on to a bridleway which leads back to the trackbed by an overbridge. The station site at Turvey, at the west end of the trail, was proposed for redevelopment in 2007, but the Grade II-listed station building will be retained.

Dunstable–Stanbridgeford: C, W, NI, DR, 2m, TL 004227–SP 970230. Part of NCN6, a Sustrans cycle trail which reuses part of the former LNWR line from Dunstable to Leighton Buzzard. Between Stanbridgeford and the outskirts of Leighton Buzzard (c. 2 miles), the A505 has been relocated on to the trackbed, which effectively rules out any westward extension of the cycle trail.

Near Luton–East Hyde–Wheathampstead: C, W, NI, DR, 4¾m, TL 106203–TL 127172–TL 162144. This is part of the Upper Lea Valley Greenway, which can be accessed off a roundabout on Parkway Road near Luton Airport station. En route the still extant Luton Hoo station is passed at TL 120180. The route was extended from East Hyde to Harpenden and Wheathampstead in August 2009. In railway terms, this trail is a continuation of the Ayot Greenway (see Welwyn Garden City to Wheathampstead under Hertfordshire), i.e. the former GNR line from Hatfield to Welwyn, Harpenden, Luton and Dunstable. The westernmost part of this line, from Luton to Dunstable, was kept open for many years to serve an oil terminal and cement works at Dunstable, but has now become a guided busway like the old line from Cambridge to St Ives in Cambridgeshire, q.v. In Dunstable between TL 027218 and TL 044222 (1¼m), a public footpath – part of the Icknield Way Path – runs along the southern perimeter of the old GNR line.

Berkshire

Parts of Newbury–Lambourne: W, UX, DR, *c.* 3m. A waymarked footpath (the Lambourne Valley Way, 12 miles long) links together several sections of this ex-GWR branch line. Grid references are not provided since only short sections of the line are used. The best approach is to follow the Lambourne Valley Way, but approach it as more a rural than a railway walk.

Buckinghamshire

Quainton Road–Westcott: W, UX, DT, 2m, SP 737189–SP 720168. This is part of the historic Brill Tramway, which closed in 1935. Signed as the Brill Tramway Walk, the path starts alongside the minor road on the south-west side of Quainton Road station, which now serves as the Buckinghamshire Railway Centre. (The start of the tramway ran alongside the road here.) There is a very good account of the tramway course as it survives today at http://underground-history.co.uk/brill.php.

Princes Risborough–Thame: C, W, UT, DR, 7½m, SP 786036–SP 697054. This route was purchased by Railway Ramblers and constructed by Sustrans; the Thame end is just in Oxfordshire.

Wolverton–Newport Pagnell: C, W, UT, DR, 4m, SP 824408–SP 871435. Swan's Way, which reuses the former LNWR Wolverton to Newport Pagnell branch. The trackbed was tarmacked in the 1980s and now forms part of the cycle trail network within the town of Milton Keynes. The branch was intended to reach Olney on the MR Bedford to Northampton line (see entry for Bromham under Bedfordshire) but never made it, presumably due to problems in raising the necessary capital.

Cambridgeshire

Other than the routes listed below, publicly accessible trackbeds in Cambridgeshire are usually mere fragments, since the flat fenland landscape made it very easy to absorb old railways back into surrounding fields.

Chesterton (Cambridge)–St Ives: C, H, W, NO, DR, 14m, TL 468612–TL 318710. This old GER line has become a guided busway, so its appearance here may seem odd but Cambridgeshire County Council intended from the start that 'Pedestrians, cyclists and horse riders [would] also benefit from a brand new bridleway running all the way from Cambridge Science Park to St Ives …' The conversion of the old railway started in 2007 but there have been problems ever since, many caused by the consequences of laying over 100,000 tonnes of concrete busway on a fen; the escalating costs, now at *c.* £80 million are a consequence. Nonetheless, cyclists, horse riders and walkers now have a dedicated bridleway, part of NCN51, which will take them from Milton Street, Chesterton, to Harrison Way, St Ives. It is probably the most expensive facility of its kind in the UK and proves the engineer's old maxim: 'Stick with the technology you know'.

Chatteris–Somersham: C, H, W, NI, DR, 6½m, TL 386856–TL 367777. A public bridleway dedicated over part of the former GNR and GER joint line between March and St Ives. In Chatteris, the bridleway starts at the south-western edge of the town, where the A141 (which occupies the trackbed from Wimblington to Chatteris) turns south-west. The bridleway dedication stops at Somersham Fore Fen, but a path (believed to be permissive) continues on to the B1050 at TL 367777, which is the site of Somersham's former station. In 2007, only a single concrete level crossing gatepost remained at the station site, which was due for redevelopment, but the timber station building was dismantled and re-erected at Fawley (near Henley) in Oxfordshire, where it now forms the centrepiece of Sir William McAlpine's private railway. Sir William is a well-known railway enthusiast and hosts three or four open days at Fawley every year, so one can still – occasionally – board a train from Somersham station, albeit over 100 miles from its original location!

Wisbech–Tydd: W, NI, riverside path, 4½m, TF 458106–TF 465177. Despite being shown as a railway path in Smith and Turner's *Railway Atlas: Then and Now*, this is actually part of the Nene Way, which runs on the west bank of the River Nene. For all that, it is an excellent way to trace the remains of the southern end of the M&GNR's line from Wisbech to Sutton Bridge, which runs parallel, just a few feet to the west. Ends on the Lincolnshire border.

Cheshire

Chester–Hawarden Bridge–Connah's Quay: This path has now been extended back to Mickle Trafford. See entry under Mickle Trafford.

Congleton–Biddulph: C, H, W, UP, DR, 5m, SJ 865633–SJ 878568. A former NSR line which for over a century carried coal from the Potteries to Congleton, now revived as the Biddulph Valley Way and part of NCN55; it continues into Staffordshire (q.v. for continuation to Chell Heath and Milton).

Cuddington–Winsford & Over: W, NI, DR, 6m, SJ 590711–SJ 653678. The Whitegate Way, a lost Cheshire line that carried much salt traffic. Access at the Cuddington end is from SJ 582707 on the lane between Stonyford and Crabtree Green. At the Winsford end, trail users can follow another spur of old trackbed southwards from SJ 650677 to the car park at SJ 651667 on the northern edge of Winsford village.

Ettiley Heath (near Sandbach)–Hassall Green–Lawton Heath End (near Alsager): C, HIP, W, NI, DR, 4½m, SJ 741604–SJ 775582–SJ 794566. The NSR's former line from Sandbach to Lawton Junction is now a permissive bridleway between Ettiley Heath (to the south of Sandbach) and Lawton Heath End (to the north of Alsager), although a diversion via the Trent & Mersey Canal is required between Malkin's Bank and Hassall Green, where the trackbed has been lost to the greens of the local golf club. The route is now part of NCN5; from west to east, it comprises the Wheelock Rail Trail, the canal towpath and the Salt Line.

Hooton–West Kirby: C, H, W, UT, DR, 12m, SJ 349783–SJ 215869. The Wirral Way, one of the first railway paths in the UK and now part of NCN56. Includes the restored Hadlow Road station, which was the only station to survive the line's closure in 1962. The trail starts immediately outside the still open Hooton station and ends within a stone's throw of West Kirby station.

Latchford–Heatley–Oldfield Brow: C, W, UT, DR, 8m, SJ 639871–SJ 703882–SJ 751889. Part of the Trans Pennine Trail (NCN62). The majority of the trail is in Greater Manchester, with only the Latchford end reaching into Cheshire.

Macclesfield–Marple: C, H, W, UT, DR, 10m, SJ 918743–SJ 950888. The Middlewood Way was opened on 30 May 1985 by Dr David Bellamy and is now part of NCN55. The trail starts alongside the A523, which occupies the trackbed for the first mile to Tytherington, and ends at the still open Rose Hill Marple railway station. Along the way, there is an impressive viaduct at Bollington.

Mickle Trafford–Chester–Hawarden Bridge–Connah's Quay: C, W, NI, DR, 10m, SJ 448691–SJ 420679–SJ 311695–SJ 300698. A railway path opened in the late 1990s, which links the western half of the old Mickle Trafford line (Mouldsworth to Hawarden Bridge) with the Connah's Quay Dock branch. The extension from Mickle Trafford to Newton (east of Chester) was opened in October 2009, with access in Mickle Trafford from Station Lane. The trail finishes in Clwyd.

Cleveland

Redmarshall Junction (near Thorpe Thewles)–Oxbridge (Stockton on Tees): W, NI, DR, 2½m, NZ 406225–NZ 425187. Part of NCN1, and once part of the NER link line from Thorpe Thewles to Thornaby. This route and the next entry are actually parts of the same line; they are separated because a 1-mile section of trackbed in Thorpe Thewles is privately owned and no longer possesses the means whereby the railway crossed it. To be specific, this section used to include the twenty-arch Thorpe Thewles Viaduct. Cleveland County Council had intended to retain the viaduct as part of the Castle Eden Walkway, but concerns arose about maintenance costs and public safety. Accordingly, the decision was taken to demolish the structure and in 1979 11-year-old Helen Wilson and 20-year-old Laura Grainger blasted it to oblivion, having won a competition in the local newspaper to press the plunger that ignited 1,000lb of gelignite packed into 2,800 holes drilled into the brickwork.

Slapewath–Boosbeck: C, H, W, NI, DR, 1½m, NZ 641158–NZ 659171. Part of the former NER line from Nunthorpe to Saltburn, which in May 2008 had its status as a bridleway confirmed by Hilary Benn, Minister of State for the Environment.

Slapewath–Guisborough–Morton Carr: C, H, W, NI, DR, 5¼m, NZ 633158–NZ 618154–NZ 558147. This route reuses more of the former NER branch line from Nunthorpe to Saltburn and includes both the Guisborough Branch Walkway Nature Reserve (main access at NZ 585152 in Pinchinthorpe) and a section of NCN168. At Hutton Gate, a section of trackbed has been built over, necessitating a diversion via Hutton Village Road and the bridleway past Home Farm. The western end of the trail is about 1½ miles from Nunthorpe via public footpaths.

Thorpe Thewles–Station Town (near Wingate): W, NI, DR, 9½m, NZ 403238–NZ 409360. The Castle Eden Walkway, part of NCN1; ends in County Durham.

Cornwall

Bodmin–Wadebridge–Padstow: C, HIP, W, UT, DR, 12½m, SX 061674–SW 990723–SW 920751. Cornwall County Council's scenic Camel Trail now rivals the Bath–Bristol path in terms of its number of users. The John Betjeman Centre, passed at Wadebridge, is the town's old station. Near Bodmin, the trail runs past Boscarne Junction station on the preserved Bodmin & Wenford Railway.

Dunmere Junction–Wenfordbridge: C, H, W, UP, DR, 6½m, SX 045674–SX 085751. This is a branch off the Camel Trail, which leaves the main route at

Dunmere Junction (just over a mile west of Bodmin). In 2006, the trail was extended from Poley's Bridge to Wenfordbridge, which was the 1836 terminus of the line; from there, a cable-worked incline led to De Lank Quarries, nearly a mile to the east.

Hayle Station–Hayle Harbour–Ventonleague: C, W, UP, DR, 1¾m, SW 559373–SW 554379–SW 575383. On 23 August 2014, a scheme to convert the disused Hayle Harbour branch line into a walkway and cycle trail received its official opening. Although the Hayle Harbour branch is only ½m long, it connects on the north side of Copperhouse Pool with part of the Hayle Railway's former trackbed, which can be walked eastwards from SW 552381 to SW 575383, including a little diversion down Guildford Road (you'll need the local OS Explorer Map). Between Redruth and Gwinear Road, the Hayle Railway became part of the GWR's main line to Penzance.

Luxulyan (Treffry Viaduct)–Ponts Mill–Par: W, UP, DT, 3m, SX 056572–SX 073562–SX 075535. This route is part of Treffry's Tramway: it starts about ¾m south-east of Luxulyan station (on the still operational branch line to Newquay) at an out-of-the-way spot, which requires good map reading skills. It is worth finding, for the trail gives the lie to the notion that tramways are dull and bereft of engineering features: it strikes off across the listed 650ft long Treffry Viaduct which crosses the Luxulyan Valley on ten arches of 40ft span at a maximum height of 89ft. The viaduct is also an aqueduct, for it once carried a water supply to turn thirteen water wheels in the valley, including one of 34ft diameter, which powered Carmears Incline (further south) where loads were hauled up the incline against gravity. English China Clay (now Imerys) made a gift of the Luxulyan Valley to Cornwall County Council (now Cornwall Council) in 1992, and the site was given World Heritage status in 2006 due to its historical importance to Cornish mining. It is worth getting hold of a local guide to the valley because there is both an upper and a lower tramway between the Treffry Viaduct and Ponts Mill which permit a round trip of 3m from either end; a useful interactive map will be found at www.luxulyanvalley.co.uk. South of the car park at Ponts Mill, the tramway can be followed to Par Green (the A3082) in Par. This section can get very muddy in winter, but sections of narrow gauge track and stone sleeper sets will be found in situ along the way; it finishes alongside an extant length of the Par Canal.

Mineral Tramways Network: The Mineral Tramways Project has established a large network of mainly off-road walking and cycling routes, which broadly link the north and south coasts of the Duchy. Most of the work is now complete, although extensions were still being added in 2013; the waymarking is excellent, and uses engraved granite stones for each route. A large proportion of the trails are based on old mineral tramways. There's a tremendous brochure on the Cornish Mining website (www.cornish-mining. org.uk), which superimposes the trails on to OS Landranger mapping. The principal trails with a railway or tramway content are listed below.

- **The Coast to Coast Trail,** Portreath–Devoran: C, H, W, UT, DT, 11m, SW 657454–SW 807390. This is the principal trail in the Tramways Network, based on the main line of the Redruth & Chacewater Railway, and featured in an episode of the BBC's *Railway Walks* series in autumn 2008. It starts in Portreath along Sunnyvale Road, which will be found adjacent to the Portreath Hotel in The Square.
- **The Great Flat Lode Trail,** a circular route around Carn Brea Hill: C, H, W, NI, DT, 7½m, easiest access from car park at SW 682394. Utilises parts of the Basset Mine Tramway but is otherwise predominantly of non-railway origin; the route is steep in places but is packed with industrial archaeology.

- **The Portreath Branchline Trail,** Pool–Portreath: C, H, W, NI, DT, 2¾m, SW 665420–SW 656454. Links together extant parts of the former Portreath Railway trackbed and the historically important Portreath Incline. At the Pool end, a waymarked path leads back to Brea to join the Great Flat Lode Trail.

- **The Redruth & Chacewater Railway Trail,** Twelveheads–Carharrack–Lanner–Redruth: C, H, W, NI, DT, 5m, SW 759422–SW 736418–SW 729412–SW 711406–SW 697402. Branching off the Coast to Coast Trail at Twelveheads, this path follows the route of the original R&CR as closely as possible, although some material deviations are necessary to bypass sections in private ownership. On the western edge of Carharrack, the railway's old coal yard can still be seen, and shortly beyond that there is a length of relaid track in the woods alongside Pennance Road. Connects at the western end with the Great Flat Lode Trail.

- **The Tresavean Trail,** Lanner–Tresavean: C, H, W, NI, DT, 1m, SW 707405–SW 719394. Uses part of the Tresavean branch of the Hayle Railway and connects with the R&CR Trail (see above). This route may be short, but the views from it across the valley towards Lanner are stunning, especially on a sunny afternoon. Ends at the site of the important Tresavean Copper Mine. At the western end, note the old railway station, which never handled a passenger, only freight.

St Austell–Pentewan: C, W, UT, DT, 3¼m, SX 013516–SX 018472. This route – now the Pentewan Valley Trail and part of NCN3 – started life as the Pentewan Railway, a horse-drawn tramway built to carry china clay from St Austell to the harbour at Pentewan. The line was rebuilt for locomotive working in 1874, when the gauge was reduced from 4ft 6in to 2ft 6in.

Truro–Newham: C, W, NI, DR, 2m, SW 812446–SW 831435. The abandoned part of the West Cornwall Railway's original line to Truro, now incorporated into NCN3 and reused as a cycle trail around the city.

Cumbria

Alston–Haltwhistle: CIP, W, UP, DR, 12m, NY 717467–NY 710632. A highly scenic rural branch line and one of the last passenger railways in England to close (in May 1976); includes ten viaducts of various shapes and sizes, including the lofty and elegant Lambley Viaduct. For further details, see entry under Northumberland, in which county most of the route is situated.

Broughton-in-Furness–Park Head: C, W, UT, DR, 1¼m, SD 213875–SD 228890. Part of the Furness Railway's scenic branch line from Foxfield to Coniston, opened for walkers and cyclists in c. 2005. See also entry for Torver–Coniston, below.

Carlisle (near Bog Junction)–Willowholme Junction: C, W, UT, DR, ½m, NY 399553–NY 395560. This railway path, only a stone's throw from Carlisle Citadel station, may be short but it is certainly interesting. It is most of the Carlisle Goods Avoiding Line and now forms part of the Caldew Riverside Trail and NCN7. At one time, the line included three river crossings, one of which, Dentonholme South Viaduct, now forms part of the trail. The line closed in 1984 as the result of an accident when a freightliner train from Warrington divided, the signalman routing the rear half over the goods line where it destroyed part of the first (i.e. southernmost) viaduct over the River Caldew. Railtrack considered reinstating the line in 1999 in order to cope with a major increase in coal traffic through Carlisle and in April 2007 Network Rail was reported to be toying with the same idea.

Hincaster–Arnside: C, W, UP, NF, 6m, see text for GRs. The Hincaster Trailway Group (see www. hincastertrailway.co.uk) is a local community project set up in 2008 to convert the Furness Railway's disused branch line from Hincaster to Arnside into a multi-use trail. This is a work in progress, which is not yet open throughout, but several sections can be walked already, including Hincaster (SD 512847–SD 513839, ½m), Heversham (SD 506834–SD 502832, ¼m), Milnthorpe Bridge (SD 489813–SD 483812, ½m), Sandside (SD 478807–SD 473803, ½m) and Sandside–Arnside (SD 473802–SD 461788, 1¼m). The latter starts from Arnside station car park and is an attractive section of the old line that runs along the south bank of the Kent Estuary.

Keswick–Threlkeld: W, UP, DR, 4½m, NY 271237–NY 328249. One of the best short railway walks in the country, featuring magnificent scenery and lots of engineering features, especially bowstring bridges. Starts from the former Keswick railway station and now forms part of NCN71. On the west side of the station, a further section of this line is open between NY 263243 and NY 253243 (c. ¾ mile). In December 2015, floodwater from Storm Desmond swept away a bowstring girder bridge near Threlkeld; within weeks of the damage, Sustrans was working on a diversion but it is to be hoped that the bridge can be replaced, as happened at Workington (see entry for Westfield–Siddick).

Lambley–Tindale: W, NI, DR, 3½m, NY 662586–NY 621591. Part of Lord Carlisle's Railway. Planned eventually to go all the way through to Brampton Junction (8m) on the still open Newcastle–Carlisle railway line. For full details, see entry under Northumberland.

Lowca (near Parton)–Distington–Westfield (near Harrington): C, W, NI, DR, 4m, NX 986216–NY 009241–NX 999268. Part of NCN72, comprising parts of the Whitehaven, Cleator & Egremont and Cleator & Workington Junction Railways, which met at Distington.

Mirehouse East (near Whitehaven)–Rowrah: C, H, W, UT, DR, 7m, NX 982153–NY 054184. The first disused railway purchased by Railway Ramblers; once part of the Whitehaven, Cleator & Egremont Railway's network, but now a popular railway path from Whitehaven to the Fells. The route includes no less than thirty-two bridges, which have been preserved to ensure 'grade separation' of vulnerable path users from the traffic on local roads. The route connects at Cleator Moor with a separate trail to Egremont, parts of which are also built on the trackbed of the old WC&ER.

North Side (near Workington)–Broughton Moor: C, W, NI, DR, 3½m, NY 003297–NY 044314. Part of NCN71, based on an old Cleator & Workington Junction line which BR kept open until 1992 for the now decommissioned Royal Navy Armaments Depot at Broughton Moor. Connects at North Side with the Westfield–Siddick route (see below).

Newbiggin-on-Lune–Smardale: W, NI, DR, 3¼m, NY 703054–NY 739082. Part of the former NER's trans-Pennine Stainmore line which ran from Darlington to Tebay, this is now the Smardale Gill National Nature Reserve which includes the impressive Smardale Gill Viaduct. Note that bicycles are strictly forbidden on the reserve. There is a sizeable car park at the Smardale end.

Stenkrith (near Kirkby Stephen)–Hartley: W, NI, DR, 1m, NY 773074–NY 784084. Another part of the former Stainmore line from Darlington to Tebay, this short permissive footpath includes two notable viaducts restored by the Northern Viaducts Trust –

Podgill and Merrygill (actually at Hartley) – which repay a visit. In 2010, the NVT opened a small car park at Stenkrith (at NY 773074) on the west side of the B6259. RR member Phil Earnshaw advises that, beyond Hartley, the trackbed can be walked on a permissive basis for another 1¼m to Rookby Scarth (NY 799101), although the two sections are separated by a few hundred yards at Hartley, where access to the Rookby Scarth walk is further down the lane.

Torver–Coniston: C, W, UT, DR, 2½m, SD 284941–SD 300972. RR member David Pedley has supplied the following directions:

> Starting from Torver, a new section of path leaves the A5084 about 30yds north of the village centre and passes behind the former station (now holiday cottages). It uses the trackbed almost exclusively and, after ¾m, passes under a minor road (connecting the A593 with the A5084) by a railway underbridge. Soon after this, it makes an end-on connection with the pre-existing National Park path, which immediately leaves the railway track to run alongside the A593, mainly in sight of the trackbed. It rejoins the old railway just before the Caravan Club site at Park Coppice, and about ½m later rejoins the A593 where an underbridge is filled in. Turn right towards Coniston, and about 100yds along the road turn left up a track. The line can then be followed to the site of Coniston station (now a housing estate) and goods yard (now an industrial estate). The centre of Coniston is just down the hill.

Westfield (near Harrington)–Siddick: C, W, NI, DR, 2½m, NX 997271–NY 000313. A further part of NCN72, which connects at Westfield with the route from Lowca (see above). The highlight is the new bowstring Navvies Bridge over the River Derwent north of Workington town centre, which replaces a previous bridge washed away in the floods of autumn 2009. At the Siddick end, this trail joins a traffic-free path to St Helens (NY 011326), which runs alongside the A596; it's a big improvement on much road-based provision in the UK because it is separate from the highway.

Derbyshire

Derbyshire is one of the great railway walking counties, along with Devon and Durham. As a bonus, many of the trails listed below pass through stunning countryside.

Ashbourne–Parsley Hay: C, W, UT, DR, 13m, SK 182460–SK 147637. The Tissington Trail, part of NCN66, which starts at the site of the former Ashbourne station and includes the now illuminated Ashbourne Tunnel. Connects at Parsley Hay with the High Peak Trail; see entry below for Cromford–Dowlow.

Bakewell–Blackwell Mill (near Buxton): W, UP, DR, 10½m, SK 230679–SK 112726. The Monsal Trail, a highly scenic route through the Peak District, and now an easy walk or cycle ride because four long-closed tunnels were finally opened in April 2011. The twin viaducts at Miller's Dale once carried four tracks into the station and are a powerful testament to the scale of railway closures in the 1960s. It is instructive to note that Dr Beeching earmarked this route for development, not closure; and that says something about the railway-destroying mentality, which he helped to unleash. There are long-established and well-developed plans (part of the 'Pedal Peak Project') to extend this trail southwards to Matlock, and in 2016 contractors for Derbyshire CC were constructing part of the extension between Rowsley and Darley Dale. A further extension is planned to Buxton to link up with an extended High Peak Trail coming up from Parsley Hay, with connections from Ashbourne and Cromford; see entries for these places above and below.

Bamford–Ladybower Reservoir: C, W, UT, DR, 1¾m, SK 202830–SK 198855. The Thornhill Trail, based on part of the former dam construction railway; the trail goes as far as the western end of Ladybower Reservoir, but the railway continued to Howden Dam.

Beighton–Killamarsh–Staveley (Inkersall Green)–Arkwright Town: C, W, NI, DR, 9½m, SK 446836–SK 449824–SK 425723–SK 426705. Part of the Trans Pennine Trail based on a section of the GCR. Starts in South Yorkshire, q.v.

The station at Millers Dale used to be an important junction where passengers travelling between London St Pancras and Manchester Central could change trains for a local service to Buxton. Today, it is a fraction of its former size, but the buildings on the up platform survive as an office used by rangers of the Peak District National Park. (Ali Ridgway)

Blackwell–Huthwaite: see entries for the Pleasley Trails under Nottinghamshire.

Breadsall (near Derby)–Morley (Lime Lane): C, W, NF, DR, 2½m, SK 363385–SK 398400. Using contractors, Sustrans and Derbyshire County Council aspire to convert the former GNR line from Egginton Junction to Nottingham into the 13-mile Great Northern Greenway between Breadsall (SK 363385) and Ilkeston (SK 453417). At the moment, the section listed here is all that is open, but it is already part of NCN672 and includes the cleared and restored platform at Breadsall station (SK 369394). In the current economic climate, it remains to be seen how much more progress will be made, but there is hope. For example, on the same line beyond Ilkeston (and after decades of neglect), the Grade II*-listed Bennerley Viaduct is being restored by Railway Paths and its partners.

Burbage Tunnel (North Portal)–Fernilee: W, UP, DR, 3m, SK 031741–SK 015777. The top section of the Cromford & High Peak Railway is a footpath, which crosses open moorland. Bunsal Incline has been converted into a minor road and, at the bottom, the railway can be followed along Fernilee Reservoir on a hard core path. There are car parks at the top of the incline and Fernilee. See also entry for Cromford below.

Creswell–Clowne: W, NI, DR, DR, 2¼m, SK 522729–SK 493756. Part of the old GCR line from Langwith Junction to Woodhouse, near Sheffield. The western end has been developed as Clowne Linear Park, which can be reached from Rectory Road. Also at Clowne, Derbyshire CC acquired the former MR line to Seymour Junction on the edge of Staveley for £1 from Network Rail; this too should become a greenway in due course.

DERBYSHIRE

Cromford–Dowlow: C, W, UP, DR, 17m, SK 314560–SK 110673. About two-thirds of the former Cromford & High Peak Railway, now the High Peak Trail, which starts at High Peak Junction; this was not a railway-to-railway junction, but a canal-to-railway junction. The route connects at Parsley Hay with the Tissington Trail to Ashbourne (see above). This is an extremely early railway, which was built on canal principles with a series of level sections connected by inclined planes. The engine house at Middleton Top has been preserved and is steamed occasionally, although it no longer has to haul wagons up and down Middleton Incline. North of Dowlow, between Hindlow and Laidmanlow, further sections of trackbed have been absorbed into the public right of way network and can be walked with the aid of an Explorer map. A northern extension to this trail is part of the Pedal Peak Project which, when complete, will enable trail users to reach Buxton where connection will be made with a similarly extended Monsal Trail (see entry for Bakewell above).

Egginton–Mickleover: C, W, DR, 5m, SK 260297–SK 309359. Part of the Mickleover Trail, which in turn is part of NCN54; reuses the whole of BR's former Mickleover test track. The route continues from Mickleover into Derby, but this final section does not use any more of the old railway formation.

Hadfield–Woodhead: C, W, NI, DR, 7m, SK 024960–SK 113999. The Longdendale Trail, part of the Trans Pennine Trail, which starts outside Hadfield station and follows the course of the old 1,500V electrified Woodhead route, once part of the GCR network and a much lamented railway closure. Ends at the western portals of the Woodhead Tunnels.

Hayfield–New Mills: W, NI, DR, 2½m, SK 036869–SK 001855. The Sett Valley Trail.

Ilkeston–Stanton by Dale: W, NI, DR, 2m, SK 454413–SK 475393. Part of NCN67 and the Nutbrook Way, an easy 10m off-road route from Shipley Park, Heanor, to Long Eaton, which uses the towpath of the Erewash Canal as well as this section of the former MR line from Stanton & Shipley Branch Junction to Mapperley and Nutbrook collieries.

Stockley–Bolsover: C, W, UT, DR, 1½m, SK 463676–SK 462704. This trail starts just east of Stockley Farm alongside the Stockley Brook before joining part of the former MR line from Pleasley to Staveley Town. At Bolsover, the tracks remain in place but disused following the loss of traffic from the town's Coalite Fuels and Chemical Plant. Bolsover DC's local plan says that no planning permission will be granted which prejudices the line's reopening to passenger services, but also acknowledges the potential of

Not all of the remains on old railways are the obvious ones such as stations, signal boxes, bridges, tunnels and viaducts. Here on the Sett Valley Trail (the former GCR and MR joint line from Hayfield to New Mills), the frame of a cabinet for a lineside telephone survives (note the rusty padlock at the top right hand corner), along with its accompanying public notice. This probably instructed users to ring the signalman before crossing the line. (Mark Jones)

disused railways for 'informal leisure purposes' – a statement which leaves the way open for a future extension.

Swarkestone (near Derby)–Worthington: C, W, NI, DR, 4m, SK 385283–SK 408211. The Cloud Trail, once part of the MR's former line through Worthington and Melbourne. The Worthington end is in Leicestershire.

Tibshelf–Grassmoor: W, NI, DR, 4¼m, SK 439608–SK 410670. Part of the Five Pits Trail and NCN67 in places. Based on a GCR network which once served the five main collieries of Grassmoor, Williamthorpe, Holmewood, Pilsley and Tibshelf. The trail follows the approximate course of the railway but diverts from it in places due to the extensive landscaping, which has taken place here (and which won a Countryside Award back in 1970). There is a connecting spur from Heath Junction, north of Pilsley, to Holmewood (SK 428648–SK 434660, ¾m).

Ticknall–near Heath End: C, ·W, NI, DT, 2½m, SK 355237–SK 359208. In March 2014, the National Trust completed work on the final stage of its Derbyshire 'Tramway Project' to create a footpath and cycleway between Calke and the Staunton Harold Estate. The tramway in question is the Ticknall Tramway, which was a 12½-mile network of tramways built to connect the brickyards, lime quarries and lime yards of Ticknall with the Ashby-de-la-Zouch Canal. Built between 1802 and 1804, the tramway finally closed in 1915, although the last train ran in May 1913. To conserve the underlying archaeology, a membrane was laid over the tramway remains and the new path laid on top.

Devon

Devon County Council's achievements in reusing old railways are amongst the best in the UK. There hardly remains a line in the county where nothing has been reclaimed, and even a mile of the Bideford, Westward Ho! & Appledore Railway (closed in 1917) is in use again as part of the South West Coast Path; this runs along Cornborough Cliff between SS 413282 and SS 420290 approximately. Additionally, there is a plethora of old tramways on and around Dartmoor, not all of which are listed here. Any reader interested in exploring these should obtain a copy of Eric Hemery's *Walking the Dartmoor Railroads* (2nd ed., Peninsula Press, 1991).

Torrington is on the longest railway-based section of the Tarka Trail; it used to be an end-on junction where the LSWR met the North Devon & Cornwall Junction Light Railway, which took a circuitous route through the folds of the north Devon countryside to Halwill Junction. In the 1970s, the author used to travel through here on china clay trains travelling between Barnstaple and Meeth. (Author)

Barnstaple–Bideford–Torrington–Meeth: C, W, UT, DR, 21m, SS 553326–SS 546078. This is a substantial section of Devon CC's popular Tarka Trail, which reuses over half of the old SR line from Barnstaple to Halwill Junction. Until 1982, the section from Barnstaple to Meeth conveyed china clay traffic from Meeth Clay Works, which has now been extended across the old line, thereby necessitating a diversion via woods to the west. Now part of NCN27 and NCN3.

Barnstaple–Braunton: C, W, UT, DR, 6¼m, SS 557331–SS 487371. Another section of the Tarka Trail, this time sharing the trackbed with NCN27 and the South West Coast Path. The route starts at the former Barnstaple Town station and passes both Chivenor and Braunton station sites en route. Originally part of the Ilfracombe branch, Devon CC is working to reuse more of this line by negotiating access to the trackbed where possible between Braunton and Willingcott, but this will take time to achieve.

Bittaford–Red Lake: W, UX, DT, 8½m, SX 658572–SX 646668. This is the whole of the 3ft gauge Red Lake Railway, which was built to serve a remote community at Red Lake, where employment was available at the now water-filled china clay quarries. The line conveyed passengers and general freight, but never china clay, which was pumped out by pipeline. For much of the route, the trackbed is shared with the Two Moors Way. At Red Lake, there are two options: either return the way you came, or rejoin the Two Moors Way and continue north-east to Scorriton (6 miles) where there is a pub, i.e. civilisation! Be warned that this is a very remote railway path: the views are stunning in good weather, but the walk can be very lonely and cold when Dartmoor is shrouded in mist.

Bovey Tracey–near Knowle: C, W, UT, DR, 1½m, SX 811784–SX 795799. This is the start of Devon CC's intended Wray Valley Way, which will reuse much of the former GWR Moretonhampstead branch. The trail can be picked up in Bovey's Station Road (SX 814782), where it heads north across Marsh Mill Park; nearby, the town's charming little station has been restored as a local heritage centre, which features a good collection of railway memorabilia. A further section of this line has been converted at the Moretonhampstead end (SX 753856–SX 766852), which includes a fine new bridge over the A382. The Bovey end of the route is close to the Haytor Granite Tramway (see Ullacombe–Haytor Vale–Holwell Tor below).

Budleigh Salterton–Littleham–Exmouth: C, W, UT, DR, 3m, SY 053830–SY 023814–SY 005815. This is part of the former LSWR line from Tipton St John to Exmouth, now part of NCN2. The trackbed is not followed through Littleham due to redevelopment, but the trail rejoins it at SY 017815 and then continues to Phear Park in Exmouth, not far from the town's still operational railway station.

Clearbrook–Yelverton: C, W, NI, DT, 2m, SX 519651–SX 520677. Part of the Plymouth & Dartmoor Railway, which was actually a tramway opened in 1823 to connect Princetown with Crabtree Wharf in Plymouth. Plenty of stone sleeper sets remain along the route. Connects at Clearbrook with the route to Marsh Mills, Plymouth, and at Yelverton with the route to Tavistock (see below) – all part of Drake's Trail.

Devon Great Consols Mineral Railway: C, W, UP, DR, c. 3m, access from SX 440724 (see text). The ever-enterprising Devon CC has opened most of the Devon Great Consols Mineral Railway as a network of multi use trails. Access is from SX 440724 on the

For many years, the southern approach to Moretonhampstead on the A382 passed through a gap where a railway bridge had been. Now, thanks to the good offices of Devon County Council, the bridge is back and carrying walkers and cyclists on a part of the as yet unfinished Wray Valley Trail, which will eventually link Moretonhampstead with Bovey Tracey. (Author)

A390 Tavistock–Gunnislake road, which leads to a pay-and-display car park at Bedford Sawmills. The trails collectively explore the whole area occupied by the railway and associated mines – and there were a lot of them, for in the 1840s this was one of the most productive copper-producing locations in the world. The whole area is a world heritage site, and there's enough industrial archaeology in here to sustain interest for a day. The trails extend down to Morwellham Quay on the River Tamar and provide an opportunity to visit the southern portal of the Tavistock Canal Tunnel and the mine railway that runs below Sheepridge Wood. For further details, visit tamarvalley.org.uk.

East Bowerland (near Meldon)–Thorndon Cross–Venndown Gate: C, H, W, DR, 3m, SX 544931–SX 533941–SX 505942. This route was opened by Devon CC in April 2009 thanks to local landowners. This is part of a larger project, whose long-term aim is redevelop the former railway line from Meldon Junction to Bude (via Halwill Junction). A further section between Halwill Junction and Cookworthy Forest Centre is also open (see below under Halwill Junction).

Exmouth–Topsham: W, C, UT, TP, 5m, SY 000815–SX 972879. This part of the Exe Valley Way and NCN2 runs alongside the southern half of the still operational branch line from Exeter to Exmouth. The five stations along the route with a half-hourly service (M-F) make this ideal for one-way trips, i.e. walk/cycle out and catch the train back. The route includes a number of long boardwalks and offers some fine views across the Exe Estuary. North of Topsham, the Exe Valley Way continues up to Exeter and then back down the other side of the estuary as far as Dawlish – not a railway path as such, but often alongside the railway, and with similar easy gradients.

Feniton–Woodford Barton: W, DR, NX, 1½m, SY 098990–SY 102970. This short trail starts beyond the first overbridge south of Feniton station, which

DEVON

is still rail-served by the Salisbury–Exeter line. In its railway days, the trail was the start of the branch from Sidmouth Junction (Feniton's earlier railway name) to Tipton St John, which was the junction for Sidmouth or Exmouth via Budleigh Salterton. While the northern end of this branch has been unlucky in terms of reuse, the section between Budleigh Salterton and Exmouth has fared much better; see entry above. The line south of Woodford Barton is privately owned, but the Otter Valley is well served by public footpaths, which makes it easy to 'shadow' the railway to Budleigh Salterton. Stations survive at Ottery St Mary (the local youth club) and Tipton St John (a private residence).

Halwill Junction–Cookworthy Forest Centre: C, W, NI, DR, 2½m, SS 443004–SS 417018 with link via public bridleway to forest centre at SS 414014. One of the new Ruby Trails in West Devon, which, when complete, will provide a route for walkers and cyclists from Hatherleigh and Holsworthy to Bude. Access at Halwill Junction is from Beeching Close. Note that Halwill Junction is the railway-inspired name of this village, which should not be confused with nearby Halwill; four railways used to converge here.

Hollacombe–Holsworthy–near Derriton: C, W, UP, DR, 3m, SS 379031–SS 329035. Another part of the Ruby Way project. Currently, the route uses public roads to get through Holsworthy, which can be very busy; the problem is a lack of funding to restore Coles Mill Viaduct on the preferred railway route. On the west side of Holsworthy, the trail can be picked up again off Bodmin Street, where it leads straight on to the restored Derriton Viaduct. Further west, the trail turns left (south) off the trackbed to reach Derriton Road, a quiet lane that leads to the village of Pyworthy.

Loddiswell–Topsham Bridge: W, NI, DR, 3½m, SX 731483–SX 732510. Part of the former GWR branch from South Brent to Kingsbridge. This public footpath starts on the east side of Loddiswell – half of the route is on the old railway with convenient detours that skirt around privately owned sections.

Nodden Gate (near Bridestowe)–Rattlebrook Peat Works (near Great Links Tor): W, UX, DT, 3¾m, SX 531863–SX 559871. Save this walk over the 1879 Rattlebrook Peat Railway for a clear day, for the views are tremendous and include Lake Viaduct on the Granite Way to the north-west. The trams reversed at SX 546887 before the final ascent to the old peat workings at the top, which include the remains of the former peat drying sheds. In practice, this is a 7½m trail because one must walk both ways.

Okehampton–Lydford: C, W, UP, mainly DR, 10m, SX 591944–SX 516852. This is Devon CC's superb new railway path, the Granite Way (part of NCN27). It starts at the restored Okehampton station and follows the mothballed freight line as far as Meldon Quarry, where the rails now stop. It then crosses the towering Meldon Viaduct and stone-built Lake Viaduct on the empty trackbed, which it follows to the northern edge of Lydford; if you are not following NCN27, you can follow local footpaths beneath the hidden giant of Lydford Viaduct. A further section of this old line has been used through Tavistock (see below).

Oreston (Hooe Lake)–Laira Bridge–St Jude's (Plymouth): C, W, UT, DR, 2m, SX 501531–SX 502542–SX 497548. This Plymouth City Council trail begins from The Old Wharf (a road) on the north side of Hooe Lake; the piers of the bridge that carried the old line to its terminus at Turnchapel will be found about 400yds to the west. It then weaves through Oreston to come out at a pair of roundabouts on the west side of Pomphlett. Here, follow the cycle trail alongside the A379 as far as

Right: This view along the trackbed of the 1823 Plymouth & Dartmoor Railway, between Clearbrook and Yelverton, shows to good effect the stone sleeper blocks, which were used to mount the rails. Transverse sleepers of the type we are accustomed to nowadays could not be used because they would trip the horses, which provided the motive power on this line. (Author)

Far right: As remarked elsewhere in this book, the National Cycle Network accommodates a huge amount of public sculpture, including these distinctive cast iron mileposts, which were installed as a Millennium Project funded by the Royal Bank of Scotland. This one is near Plym Bridge on NCN27, but there are 999 more out there on the network. (Author)

the southern end of The Ride (SX 502542) where the railway path resumes on the opposite side of the road just east of the restored Laira Bridge, whence it continues alongside the moribund Cattewater branch to come out near the site of Lucas Terrace Halt, just east of the LSWR's old Plymouth Friary terminus. An extension to the route east of Laira Bridge is planned, and in 2016 Plymouth CC secured the funding to build it.

Plymouth (Marsh Mills)–Clearbrook: C, W, UT, mainly DR, 9m, SX 521567–SX 524656. Part of Drake's Trail and NCN27, both based on the former GWR line from Plymouth to Tavistock and Launceston. See also the entries for Clearbrook–Yelverton and Yelverton–

Whitchurch. Note the tunnel and four viaducts en route, one with peregrine-spotting opportunities.

Princetown–Dousland: C, W, UX, DR, 8m, SX 588734–SX 542679. Most of the GWR's Princetown branch. As with the Red Lake Railway (see entry above for Bittaford), the views are tremendous on a good day, but this walk can be rather alarming when a Dartmoor mist sets in; there are no landmarks along the way and it can be very disorienting to see only 20ft ahead. In 2015, the county council replaced the long-lost railway bridge over the B3212 at Peek Hill (SX 549696). As the trail nears Dousland, there are marvellous views over Burrator Reservoir.

Tavistock: C, W, UT, DR, 1½m, SX 492757–SX 471739. Two further linked parts of the former LSWR main line through Tavistock which run from a point just north of Mount Kelly School to a residential road just before the missing bridge over the A390. Wallabrook Viaduct crosses a deep valley before the trail skirts around Mount Kelly's playing fields and passes Tavistock North station. The route is heavily engineered with many bridges, cuttings and embankments, and includes a further superb viaduct over the town. To the south of Tavistock, Devon CC has reused the former GWR trackbed to provide a traffic-free route into Plymouth; see entries for Yelverton–Whitchurch, Clearbrook–Yelverton and Plymouth (Marsh Mills)–Clearbrook. (Follow the NCN27 and Drake's Trail signs from The Wharf in Tavistock.)

Tipton St John–Bowd (near Sidmouth): C, H, W, UX, DR, 1½m, SY 092912–SY 107901. The start of the former LSWR branch line to Sidmouth, now part of NCN248; the climb out of Tipton indicates what a slog this must have been for a heavily loaded holiday train. This permissive route exists by courtesy of Clinton Devon Estates.

Tiverton–Copplestone: CIP, W, UP, DR, 2m, SS 963128–SS 987123. This route used to continue through Tiverton to the site of West Exe Halt until the GWR's bridge over the River Exe (just west of Tiverton station site) was adapted to accommodate a busy new road. Nowadays, although part of NCN3, this section of old railway is of mainly local significance. At Copplestone, the towpath of the Grand Western Canal is only a few hundred yards to the south, and this can be followed back to Tiverton to provide an attractive circular walk of 4m.

Ullacombe–Haytor Vale–Holwell Tor: W, UX, DT, 2m, SX 782777–SX 750778. This trail, once part of the Haytor Granite Tramway, is unique in that, west of Haytor Vale, it retains in situ the granite tramway tracks laid there in the eighteenth century; these are a scheduled ancient monument. There is a network of about 2 miles of track around Haytor, including pointwork. The tramway forms part of the Templer Way, a Devon CC route which continues another 12 miles from Ullacombe to Shaldon following further parts of the tramway, the Stover Canal and finally the path along the south bank of the River Teign from near Newton Abbott Racecourse to the sea at Shaldon. The riverside part of this route should be tackled at low tide.

Willingcott–Ilfracombe: C, W, NI, DR, 3m, SS 485431–SS 514463. This is the north end of the Ilfracombe branch, which Devon CC hopes in time to connect, via the old trackbed, with the southern section from Barnstaple to Braunton (see above). Just north of Willingcott, the trail passes Mortehoe and Woolacombe station inconveniently situated 2 miles from both villages; it is now a private residence. Slade Reservoirs and twin tunnels (one open) are notable features as the trail nears the lofty former station site above Ilfracombe.

Yelverton–Horrabridge–Whitchurch (Tavistock): C, W, UT, mainly DR, 4m, SX 521679–SX 488725. Another section of Drake's Trail. Although Horrabridge is where this railway path starts, the village is not a practical place to join it, far less to park a car. Therefore, pick up Drake's Trail (part of NCN27) from the west side of the roundabout at Yelverton and enjoy some fine views over Dartmoor before dropping into the Walkham Valley to join the old trackbed at Old Station Road (SX 510695). Once on the trackbed, the trail crosses Magpie Viaduct and the new £2.1 million Gem Bridge (which, despite its modest name, is another viaduct) before plunging into Grenofen Tunnel. Between Whitchurch and Tavistock, the old trackbed has been built over extensively but the NCN27 signs will guide you into the town centre, including a stretch alongside the attractive Tavistock Canal.

Dorset

Dorset was a late starter in terms of reusing its disused railways, which has had the unfortunate effect of making some of the projects in the county rather more difficult than they would have been thirty or more years ago. The most notable project is the North Dorset Trailway, which aims to create a long-distance cycle trail along the course of the former Somerset & Dorset Railway from Stalbridge to Wimborne, where it will connect with the existing Castleman Trailway to Poole. Over one half of this has been achieved

already, but progress is slow since virtually all of the trackbed has been purchased by private landowners, making patient negotiation the order of the day.

Abbotsbury–Portesham: W, UX, DR, 1m, SY 580852–SY 598854. Part of the former GWR Abbotsbury branch, closed in 1952, which has been lucky enough to survive as a public footpath. Included for the sake of the local scenery.

Broadstone–Fleet's Corner (Poole): C, W, UT, DR, 2m, SZ 003958–SZ 008931. This path can be found most easily at the roundabout in the centre of Broadstone. It shares the route of Castleman's Trailway (see entry for Oakley–Upton Heath) as far as approximately SZ 000950, where a cycle trail (part of NCN25) starts on the east side of Broadstone

The delightful little station at West Bay, the westernmost point on the former branch line from Maiden Newton, is a lucky survivor. The building was still occupied in the late 1970s, reputedly by the last stationmaster, and this may explain its survival. Nowadays, it is a popular tea room, while the former trackbed accommodates a cycle trail to the south end of Bridport, which comes out near the Crown Inn and Palmers Brewery. (Author)

Way, this road having been built on the course of the former LSWR line from Broadstone to Poole. The cycle trail continues alongside Broadstone Way all the way to Poole railway station, although it departs from the trackbed just south of Fleet's Corner, after passing beneath the A35 and A3049.

Bridport Branch: In 1994, West Dorset District Council produced a feasibility study into the recreational potential of the former Bridport to Maiden Newton railway. Nothing came of this, but in 2008 a Sustrans team led by Peter Henshaw revived the project and, in 2015 Dorset CC appointed a project officer. A series of public consultations demonstrated widespread support for a 'trailway' along the line and in January 2010 an inaugural walk took place along the trackbed from Toller to Powerstock Common. Currently, much of the trackbed can be walked on a permissive basis, but the problem is finding – and joining together – these sections without an expert local guide. The best advice is to wait until the railway path is complete and signs have been installed. Some sections must be avoided in order not to jeopardise ongoing negotiations with landowners; one such lies between the bridge over the River Hooke (east of Toller Porcorum) and Tollerford. Despite these caveats, the following parts of the line, listed from west to east, are open to the public. Detailed directions are supplied because this is one of the most scenic disused railways in the south of England and represents railway rambling at its best.

- **West Bay–Bridport (South):** C, W, UP, DR, ¾m, SY 465903–SY 466915. Includes the restored West Bay station, where two track panels have been installed at the platform, although the restored coaches (supplied by the Swanage Railway) were removed some years ago. The trail ends at the site of the infilled Wanderwell Bridge, near the Crown Inn.

- **Bridport (South)–Bridport Station:** CIP, W, UT, DR, 1½m, SY 466915–SY 474934. This, unfortunately, is a roadside section. From opposite the Crown Inn, the A35 (Sea Road South, with a cycle trail alongside) occupies the line to the site of Bridport's East Street station (SY 471928), where there is a roundabout; after this, the A3066 (Sea Road North, with a wide pavement) continues along the trackbed to the site of Bridport station, now marked by a large Co-op supermarket.

- **Bridport Station–Bradpole Level Crossing:** C, W, UT, DR, ½m, SY 474934–SY 480939. Almost hidden away behind Bridport's Co-op is this new multi-use trail, which uses a further section of the trackbed. At Bradpole level crossing (SY 480940), local joiners John Gale and Bernie Joy have fabricated a new level crossing gate as a reminder of the railway's existence. The rails remain here, presumably since it was too much trouble for the demolition gang to rip them out of the tarmac. East of the level crossing, a small grassed area occupies the old line, followed by allotments, after which the trackbed towards Loders has been ploughed out, and the land restored to what the railway company's surveyor would have seen in the early 1850s.

- **Loders–Powerstock:** W, UX, DR, 2m, SY 497941–SY 522954. This is a permissive route, which starts from the road-over-rail bridge on New Street Lane in Loders (**not** the lane to Uploders – there are two such bridges in close proximity) and ends opposite Powerstock station adjoining the abutment of a demolished bridge. The east abutment of the bridge was thought to be collapsing, though it turned out that the fault was only with the facing wall – but the railway engineers removed it anyway. Powerstock station is immediately opposite but privately owned, so please respect the owners' privacy.

- **Powerstock–Powerstock Common:** W, UX, DR, 2m, SY 522954–SY 545974. The next section of the branch starts a little to the east of Powerstock station so, if you have walked from Loders, turn right at the lane and then left on to an unsigned track (SY 523953) to rejoin the trackbed just north of the station. The trackbed is then clear to Powerstock Common although, shortly before the rail-over-road bridge at SY 547974, a thicket across the line indicates the end of the permissive section. Turn right here and then, after about 100yds, left to reach the small car park at SY 547974, just off Barrowland Lane (the route up to Eggardon Hill). This section includes Powerstock Common Nature Reserve, which is managed by Dorset Wildlife Trust, as well as the infamous Witherstone bank which often caused heavily loaded trains to stall.
- **Powerstock Common–Toller Porcorum:** W, UX, DR, 1m, SY 545975–SY 557979. On reaching Barrowland Lane from Powerstock, turn right (south) and proceed for 100yds to a public footpath on the left at SY 548973, which is easily missed when the leaves are out. Take this footpath, which parallels the old railway, and proceed for 500yds to the hedge on the far side of the fifth field. Turn left here and walk down the slope, alongside the hedge, to a gate that gives access to the trackbed, which from here on is a permissive path. Nearing Toller, leave the trackbed via a kissing gate on the left hand side, and then continue in the same general direction, keeping the railway about 50yds to your right. Ahead, you will see the tower of the parish church: aim for it, crossing a stile en route, and you will come out in the car park by the village hall – right behind the church. The current lack of signage here is a problem, but should be remedied in time.
- **Toller Porcorum–River Hooke Bridge:** W, UX, DR, ½m, SY 563979–SY 571978. A little to the east of the Old Swan Inn on Lower Road, a track between cottages leads back on to the old line for another permissive section – but it ends just after the bridge over the River Hooke, by which time conditions underfoot are getting soggy. Treat this as the effective end of the walk and do not attempt to force your way through towards Maiden Newton. The platform of Toller station is located at SY 562979 on a public footpath, which starts behind the village telephone box.
- **River Hooke Bridge–Tollerford:** SY 571978–SY 593980. No public access. This section is privately owned and may never become part of the railway path. Intruding here will make the work of the negotiators more difficult and could make the landowner refuse to support the railway path project. Therefore please – here as elsewhere – do not even think about trespassing.
- **Tollerford–Maiden Newton:** W, UT, DR, ½m, SY 593980–SY 599979. This short cycle trail skirts around the village of Maiden Newton, and ends in the Bridport bay platform at the village station on the still open Weymouth–Bristol line. The trail was resurfaced in June 2010. Maiden Newton station is the easiest place to find the start.

Crow–Ringwood–West Moors: C, H, W, UP, DR, 5½m, SU 168037–SU 152048–SU 079029. See notes under entry for Oakley–Upton Heath. The first 2½ miles between Crow and the A31 west of Ringwood are in Hampshire, q.v.

East Weare–Easton: W, UX, DR, 2m, SY 704725–SY 691718. Most of the Easton branch is used as a footpath, although it is not shown as a right of way on OS maps. It is best accessed from the village of Grove, whence public footpaths can be used to access the old line as it skirts the east side of the island. The trackbed is clear from just south of the naval installation at Castletown and provides a superb coastal walk until it turns inland just north of Church Ope Cove. It can then be followed with a few minor diversions as far as the site of Easton station at SY 691718.

Oakley (near Wimborne)–Upton Heath–Hamworthy: C, W, UP, DR, 6m, SZ 018985–SY 991943–SY 987925.Both this and the Crow–Ringwood–West Moors route (see above) are part of the former LSWR main line from Brockenhurst to Hamworthy Junction via Ringwood. Following the creation of the Castleman Trailway by Dorset County Council they were joined together using public footpaths in 1993. This section includes Merley Tunnel.

North Dorset Trailway: Dorset County, East Dorset District and North Dorset District Council are running a bold project to convert the long-closed Somerset & Dorset Railway into a shared use path running from Stalbridge to Broadstone and Poole. Completion is currently expected in about 2020. All of the following sections (listed from north to south) are now open.

- **Stalbridge:** C, W, UT, DR, ½m, ST 740180–ST 744176. Accessible from the site of the town's old station, but currently a cul-de-sac with no exit at the southern end.
- **Sturminster Newton–Blandford Forum:** C, H, W, UT, DR, 8½m, ST 787142–ST 887066. Starts from the south of the main car park in Sturminster Newton (which used to overlook the town's station) and ends at the site of Blandford station, where the rails from a few sidings survive in the tarmac, together with a road-over-rail bridge (complete with steam deflectors). The creation of this route is a testament to the hard work of Dorset Countryside and the co-operation of local landowners; it is substantially faithful to the old railway and includes replacement river bridges at both Fiddleford (opened in October 2006

at a cost of £200,000) and Hodmoor, west of Stourpaine (opened in October 2010 at a cost of over £300,000). Along the way, one passes the superbly restored Shillingstone station, home to the Shillingstone Railway Project which aims to restore the station and its environs to how they were in the 1950s and 1960s; passengers waiting for a train here enjoyed some of the finest rural views available from any station in the UK. Also at Shillingstone is a small car park for trail users at ST 823120.

- **Lower Blandford St Mary–Charlton Marshall–Spetisbury:** C, W, UT, DR, 3¼m, ST 888050–ST 897041–ST 918018. Includes the remains of the stations at both Charlton Marshall and Spetisbury, where the steps down to road level are particularly noteworthy. At the north end, the trail currently starts/stops on another bridleway west of Lower Blandford St Mary, requiring trail users to walk or cycle a short distance alongside the A350 in order to reach Blandford Forum. A cross-town route was waymarked across Blandford in the winter of 2012–13, but it does not use the trackbed because that was overhead on a long, and long-demolished, viaduct.
- **Corfe Mullen:** C, W, UX, DR, 1m, ST 969985–ST 985986. This section of the old line can be accessed at the site of a former level crossing over the A31. It continues through Corfe Mullen Junction, where the lines to Wimborne and Broadstone diverged, the Trailway following the old line to Wimborne, which was closed in 1933. It is intended that the Trailway will include a spur to Wimborne, and the section east of Corfe Mullen Junction will form part of it. However, be warned that in January 2013 the surface here was very difficult due to severe churning by horses.
- **Broadstone–Fleet's Corner (Poole):** See separate entry above (under Broadstone). This part of the route was built by the LSWR rather than the

S&DR, but the latter's trains used this link on their way to Bournemouth West.

Purbeck Mineral Tramways: The Isle of Purbeck is fortunate in having a number of old china clay tramways which can now be walked with official blessing or, in some cases, were absorbed into the local rights of way network long ago. The main sections that are open for public access are listed below, although other short lengths exist for those with endless patience and good map-reading skills.

- **Bushey–Newton Heath:** C, H, W, NI, DT, 2m, SY 977835–SZ 008849. Part of Fayle's Tramway.
- **Norden Heath–Middlebere Farm (start of access road):** W, UP, DT, 2m, SY 951835–SY 963853. Part of the Middlebere Plateway.
- **Ridge–Stoborough Heath:** W, UP, DT, 1m, SY 937862–SY 936845. Part of Pike Brothers' Railway.
- **Swanage, Mowlem Theatre–Pier:** W, UT, ½m, SZ 031788–SZ 035787. Part of the 2ft 6in gauge Swanage Pier Tramway. The amusement arcade passed en route is the tramway's former fish store, which was built c. 1855. About 100yds of track (including some pointwork) survives in the surface of the promenade, while the local council has installed coloured bricks to mark out the rest of the route.

Weymouth–near Fortuneswell: W, UT, DR, 3½m, SY 675793–SY 673747. This route, opened in 2000, starts from near the site of the long demolished Melcombe Regis station, but access from the nearby Weymouth railway station is a bit tricky due to the busy roads in the area. South of Westham, the trail includes a new bridge over Newstead Road (SY 674789), opened in 2012, before continuing through Rodwell Tunnel to end officially just before Ferry Bridge. However, by taking a detour around the site of the demolished Backwater Viaduct, walkers can follow the trackbed across the eastern end of Chesil Beach as far as an oil depot to the north of Fortuneswell. In addition to this standard gauge line, many tramways on the Isle of Portland have been absorbed into the local footpath network. This network can be accessed from SY 685743, where the incline of the old Merchants Railway is now a very steep public footpath up on to the island's heights. Along the way, the old stone sets that supported the rails can be seen. On a fine day, the views from up here are tremendous.

Durham

For many years, Durham County Council routinely demolished rail-over-road bridges on the disused railways it purchased in order to reduce the long-term maintenance costs of its railway paths. However, it retained (and continues to maintain) a considerable number of viaducts on these routes. Apart from the major trails listed below, the eastern part of the county contains many shorter railway paths, most of which are fragments of the county's once extensive colliery network. Overall, Durham runs Devon a close second in terms of all that it has achieved with its abandoned railways. The hubs of its railway path network are Broompark (near Durham City), Consett and South Hetton.

Belmont (near Durham)–Pittington–Hetton-le-Hole: C, W, NI, DR, 3½m, NZ 314432–NZ 323448–NZ 353471. Part of the former Murton–Sherburn line; ends in Tyne & Wear.

Bishop Auckland–Spennymoor: W, NI, DR, 4½m, NZ 222291–NZ 245337. The Auckland Walk, part of the former line from West Cornforth (Auckland Line Junction) to Bishop Auckland.

Blackhill (Consett)–Swalwell: W, UP, DR, 10½m, NZ 099514–NZ 200621. Once the direct line from Consett to Newcastle; includes four major viaducts. Now part of NCN14, but known as the Derwent Walk after the nearby River Derwent. There is a 1-mile link path from NZ 099514 southwards to NZ 099493, where a connection is made with the Lanchester Valley Railway Path, the Waskerley Way and the Consett & Sunderland Railway Path. This is a notable location amongst railway paths, for no less than four separate railway-based routes meet here.

Broompark (near Durham)–Consett: W, UP, DR, 9m, NZ 254417–NZ 099493. The Lanchester Valley Railway Path, a further part of NCN14. West of Hurbuck, there is a diversion off the trackbed where *c.* 1m of the old line is now privately owned. East of Hurbuck, there is a very steep-sided embankment which crosses the valley of the Smallhope Burn – the timber-built Hurbuck Viaduct lies buried beneath this structure.

Broompark (near Durham)–Crook: W, UP, DR, 11m, NZ 254417–NZ 163361. The Deerness Valley Railway Path, a former colliery line – although modern landscaping has left little sign of its industrial past.

Broompark (near Durham)–Bishop Auckland: W, UP, DR, 9½m, NZ 254417–NZ 207300. The Brandon–Bishop Auckland Walk is a long-established railway path, which once again continues over Newton Cap Viaduct to High Bondgate on the edge of Bishop Auckland, thanks to a new trail installed alongside the A689. (Trail users were not catered for in 1995 when the road was first moved on to the viaduct.) There's a car park for the trail at the north end of the viaduct, at NZ 205307. There are great views *from* the viaduct, but if you want a great view *of* it then it's best to enter Bishop Auckland via the parallel Wearside Way.

Consett–Weatherhill–Crawleyside (near Stanhope): W, UP, DR, 13m, NZ 099493–NY 999424–NY 993405. The Waskerley Way, now part of NCN7, is an old railway with a lot of history. The trail takes its name from the village of Waskerley, which is just over halfway along, an old railway community that now has a hint of the deserted village about it. The highlights of the walk are near the two end points – Howns Gill Viaduct, just west of Consett, and Weatherhill Incline, just after the junction with the Rookhope branch (see

This relic on the Waskerley Way reveals what happened to parts of the 1834 Stanhope & Tyne Railway: they ended up in the hands of the famous Stockton & Darlington company, whose initials are inscribed on this boundary marker. Railway companies installed these markers for obvious reasons, but the designs varied immensely. A few survive, usually lost in ground cover; not so here on the exposed Durham moors. (Phil Earnshaw)

below). Although the official trail ends just above Weatherhill Incline (at NY 999424), walkers will have no difficulty in continuing on to Crawleyside, since a public footpath runs alongside the trackbed for the drop down into the Wear Valley. Crawleyside is less than a mile north of Stanhope.

Consett–Chester-le-Street–Washington: C, W, UT, DR, 18m, NZ 099493–NZ 273535–NZ 313550. The Consett & Sunderland Railway Path, a high-quality cycle trail built by Sustrans and featuring some unusual sculptures along the way, including the Beamish Shorthorns by Sally Matthews, a collection of cattle figures made from old JCB parts. Sustrans and Railway Paths are carrying out a three-year programme of maintenance to the line's structures, which will finish in 2018. This route is so long (it actually ends in Tyne & Wear) because it survived as an operational railway serving the steelworks in Consett; when these closed and the line was abandoned, it was converted into a railway path almost immediately. At Washington, the trail continues to Roker (in Sunderland), but this section is not railway based. (There is a railway path from Washington to Sunderland, but it is on the south side of the River Wear.)

Darlington (A66)–Dinsdale: C, W, NI, DR, 2m, NZ 327153–NZ 352137. This trail used to start at Darlington (New Road) but in *c.* 2007 the 2½-mile section from central Darlington to the A66 was converted into a new link road, the B6279. The trail now starts on the east side of the roundabout at NZ 327153.

Haswell–Hart: See entry for South Hetton.

Middleton-in-Teesdale–Lartington, near Barnard Castle: W, NI, DR, 6m, NY 952245–NZ 021177. This is most of the Middleton-in-Teesdale branch, which – except for a short diversion around the privately owned Romaldkirk station – is walkable from the B6277 (east of Middleton-in-Teesdale station, now part of a holiday park) to Lartington, which had a station on the connecting Stainmore route to Tebay. Includes Mickleton Viaduct. RR member Phil Earnshaw advises: 'Sadly the east end of the branch approaching Tees Valley Junction is no longer passable due to [vegetation] growth but the adjacent Stainmore route has been opened as a short permissive footpath and this substitutes for the branch formation at this point.' There are also bridleways north and south of the Stainmore line, which lead down to the River Tees, where Barnard Castle can be reached via Deepdale Aqueduct.

Seaham–South Hetton: C, W, UT, DR, 4m, NZ 429488–NZ 384453. The former South Hetton Colliery

'Terra Novalis' by Tony Cragg can be found on the Leadgate to Annfield Plain section of NCN7, where it also forms part of the C2C and Three Rivers routes. When installed, this sculpture raised eyebrows due to its high cost, but then it was made from stainless steel. It comprises two pieces, a theodolite and an engineer's level, reproduced at twenty times their actual size. The piece symbolises the economic regeneration of the Consett area, which suffered terribly when the town's steelworks closed in 1980. (Phil Cheatle/Sustrans)

branch, now converted into a cycle trail (part of NCN1). Includes Hesledon Bank and Stony Cut Bank.

Shildon Station–West Auckland–Etherley: Much remains of the Stockton & Darlington Railway's branch from Shildon to Etherley, where Witton Park Colliery near modern Phoenix Row (NZ 167292) was the source of traffic. It is sad to report that this historic line features on the English Heritage At Risk Register, with its condition described as 'Generally unsatisfactory with major localised problems'. The branch included two substantial inclines at Brusselton and Etherley, which enabled trains to negotiate the valley of the River Gaunless; Bankfoot Farm along the way indicates where Brusselton Incline ended. The sections of trackbed listed below are now trails or public footpaths, and, with the aid of the local OS Explorer map, it is easy to join them together via other public footpaths or minor roads; the end-to-end distance, including the necessary diversions, is about 5½m.

- **Shildon Station–A6072–Haggs Lane:** W, NI, DR, 2m, NZ 236257–NZ 219255–NZ 206258. Includes Brusselton Incline. From Shildon station, head west and pick up the trail which runs between the parallel Station Street (north side) and Railway Terrace (south side); these roads were once either side of the railway, which is why the trail runs down the middle. Keep on a westerly bearing to the A6072, by which time the old railway appears as a public footpath on the OS map.
- **West Auckland (Burnshouse Lane)–Oakley Green:** W, NI, DR, ¾m, NZ 197260–NZ 187264.
- **West Auckland (Greenfields Road)–Phoenix Row:** W, NI, DR, 1¼m, NZ 176278–NZ 167292. Includes Etherley Incline.

South Hetton–Haswell–Hart: W, UP, DR, 10m, NZ 384453–NZ 484363. The Haswell to Hart Countryside Walk. The trail is part of NCN1 as far as NZ 408380, which is the site of Wellfield Junction. At this point, walkers and cyclists bound for Hart should bear left (east) and follow NCN14.

Station Town (near Wingate)–Thorpe Thewles: W, NI, DR, 9½m, NZ 409360–NZ 403238. The Castle Eden Walkway, part of NCN1; ends in Cleveland. By continuing south on NCN1, this line can be rejoined at Redmarshall Junction and then followed as far as Oxbridge in Stockton-on-Tees; see entry under Cleveland.

Weatherhill–Rookhope: W, NI, DR, 6m, NZ 003432–NY 939429. The start of this branch line is a very remote spot, about ¾ of a mile north of the old Weatherhill Engine House. The trail, part of NCN7, is the trackbed of the former Weatherhill & Rookhope Railway, which reaches a height of 1,670ft above sea level, thus making it the highest railway (or

A charming view of Mickleton Viaduct on the former NER branch line from Barnard Castle to Middleton-in-Teesdale; it offers fine views of the tree-lined banks of the River Lune, more than 100ft below. The line closed on 30 November 1964, but the viaduct was given listed building status on 12 January 1967 – an unusually prompt move by the standards applied to many other historic railway structures. (Mark Jones)

rather ex-railway) in the British Isles. Connects at Weatherhill with the Waskerley Way (see entry above for Consett–Weatherhill–Crawleyside).

Wellfield Junction (near Wingate)–Trimdon Colliery: C, W, NI, DR, 2m, NZ 408380–NZ 389362. Starts at Wellfield Junction from the South Hetton–Haswell–Hart trail, and connects at Station Town (via a short walk across the village) with the Castle Eden Walkway to Thorpe Thewles.

West Auckland–Ramshaw: W, NI, DR, 2½m, NZ 182265–NZ 150258. Part of the former Stainmore route from Darlington to Tebay, converted into a trail in late 2005. Just before Ramshaw, the trail switches on to the trackbed of the old branch line to Butterknowle Colliery. Between Ramshaw and Low Lands, a public footpath runs alongside the next mile of the Butterknowle line (NZ150258–NZ 135251). Further sections of the Stainmore line have been reused

in Cumbria (see entries for Newbiggin-on-Lune–Smardale and Stenkrith–Hartley).

Essex

Braintree–Start Hill (near Bishops Stortford): CIP, HIP, W, UP, DR, 15m, TL 760227–TL 519213. Essex County Council's popular Flitch Way, which includes restored stations at Rayne, Takeley and since 2011 Bannister Green Halt. Currently, cyclists and horse riders have been granted local access only and may not use the whole length of the trail, although parts of it are now incorporated into NCN16.

Witham–Maldon East & Heybridge: C, W, NI, DR, 5m, TL 826150–TL 847080. Most of this branch has been converted into a cycle path called the Blackwater Rail Trail. The most convenient place to join the path at Heybridge is the access point near the entrance to Elms Farm Park, off Heybridge Approach (the B1018). Note that the section between Oliver's Farm and Wickham Bishops is still privately owned: this part of the route includes two timber viaducts (designated ancient monuments) that were restored by Essex County Council in 1995. The official route between Oliver's Farm and Wickham Bishops follows the B1018 and public footpaths. The station building at Maldon East & Heybridge survives, with its impressive listed Jacobean-style nine-arch arcaded frontage; in August 2004 it was in use as offices.

Wivenhoe–Brightlingsea: W, NI, DR, 5m, TM 053208–TM 083166. This route starts about 1½m south-east of Wivenhoe station. The old trackbed can be reached near Alresford Grange by following a convenient footpath along the edge of the River Colne. The line is bisected by Alresford Creek thanks to a missing bridge, but there is a ford just under ½ mile upstream accessible by footpaths on both sides.

This photograph of a muddy creek at low tide repays further study, for above the mud stand two piers from the GER swing bridge, which once carried branch line trains from Wivenhoe to Brightlingsea on the Colne Estuary. Fortunately, there is a ford east of here, but one does need to plan a walk along the branch to coincide with low tide. (Derek Wilkin)

Gloucestershire

Cheltenham–Marle Hill: C, W, UT, DR, 2m, SO 933221–SO 945238. This trail is the southernmost end of the former GWR line from Cheltenham to Stratford-on-Avon via Honeybourne; it starts near Cheltenham Spa railway station and ends at the Prince of Wales Stadium, Tommy Taylors Lane. Cheltenham Racecourse station on the Gloucestershire Warwickshire Railway lies about ¾ mile to the north, but local roads must be used to make the connection. A further section of this line has been opened at the Stratford-Upon-Avon end (see entry under Warwickshire).

Cricklade–South Cerney: W, NI, DR, 3½m, SU 091939–SU 048979. Part of the Midland & South Western Junction Railway; the first mile is in Wiltshire. Includes four distinctive brick-built viaducts of nine or ten arches each that carry local roads over the old railway.

Dudbridge–Stroud: C, W, UT, DR, 1m, SO 837045–SO 846049. See notes under entry for Stonehouse–Nailsworth.

Forest of Dean: Due to its industrial past, the Forest of Dean is a labyrinth of former industrial tramways and railways. The main railway paths (all but the first built by the Severn & Wye Railway) are listed below, but there are many former tramways in the area. If you wish to trace these, use the local Explorer map in conjunction with a detailed historical map; there are some good materials at www.deanweb.info/history2.html.

- **Cinderford–near Churchway Mine:** C, W, NI, DR, 2m, SO 650127–SO 642153. Part of the GWR's line from Bullo Pill to Drybrook Halt, diverging north-west at Bilson Junction on to the short spur to Churchway.

- **Drybrook Road (Cinderford)–Upper Lydbrook:** C, W, UX, DR, 3¼m, SO 632144–SO 604157. Since it was opened, this route has involved a difficult crossing of the A4136 at Mierystock, but in 2008 four retired Forest of Dean miners excavated Mierystock Tunnel so that it could be used as an underpass to eliminate this hazard. Disappointingly, the tunnel has still not been incorporated into the trail, although Sustrans has made encouraging noises. At Upper Lydbrook, it is easy to continue on to Lower Lydbrook via minor roads and the public footpath that runs alongside the old railway from SO 601161 to SO 597168.

- **Drybrook Road (Cinderford)–Moseley Green:** C, W, UX, DR, 4½m, SO 632144–SO 633093. The old 'mineral loop', which served collieries rather than passengers.

- **Drybrook Road (Cinderford)–Parkend:** C, W, UX, DR, 4½m, SO 632144–SO 612080. Part of the main passenger line through the Forest, now part of NCN42. Trains on the preserved Dean Forest Railway operate from the restored Parkend station, to the south-east of the village.

Parkend–Coleford: C, W, NI, DR, 3¼m, SO 611079–SO 577104. An extension of the earlier short Milkwall–Coleford trail, which now connects with the rest of the Forest's railway path network at Parkend.

Stonehouse–Nailsworth: C, W, UT, DR, 6m, SO 806048–ST 850999. The MR's Nailsworth branch, now part of NCN45 but once a bold incursion into traditional GWR territory. There was a 'branch off the branch' at Dudbridge, which took MR trains into their own terminus at Stroud. The link between the two trackbeds no longer exists, but a mile of the Dudbridge–Stroud branch has also been converted for use by walkers and cyclists (see above).

GLOUCESTERSHIRE

Tetbury–near Ilsom: C, W, NI, DR, ¾m, ST 893930–ST 903939. A linear walk and cycle trail constructed in 2005 on part of the former Tetbury to Kemble branch, starting at the long-abandoned goods shed in Tetbury, now restored as an arts centre. At the north end, the trail meets a three-way junction of local footpaths near the source of the River Avon. Interest remains in reusing the trackbed right through to Kemble: Sustrans held a public consultation in May 2007 and in August 2012 the *Wilts and Gloucestershire Standard* reported that Tetbury Rail Lands Trust had been meeting with local landowners to secure access to the Trouble House pub on Tetbury Common.

Woodbridge (near Withington)–Chedworth: W, NI, DR, 1½m, SP 037147–SP 054128. Another part of the Midland & South Western Junction Railway, which runs as far south as the northern portal of Chedworth Tunnel. The access point at the Chedworth end is at SP 052133, a few yards by public footpath from Chedworth Roman villa, which is one of the National Trust's top ten sites and well worth a visit.

Wye Valley Walk: This is a long-distance footpath from Rhayader to Chepstow, which in the vicinity of Monmouth utilises the following sections of disused railway:

- **Near Lydbrook Junction–Symonds Yat Tunnel:** W, NI, DR, 1½m, SO 583167–SO 566158.
- **The Slaughter–near Far Hearkening Rock:** W, NI, DR, 1½m, SO 553143–SO 539154.
- **Redbrook–Whitebrook:** see entry under Gwent (Wales).

The Wye Valley Walk joins the disused GWR line from Ross-on-Wye to Monmouth at grid reference SO 583167, near Great Collins Grove. By using the long-distance footpath and local rights of way, it is possible to walk in a westerly direction on or next to the line all the way from Great Collins Grove to the outskirts of Monmouth (SO 517132), giving a continuous walk of 7 miles. A diversion is necessary over Symonds Yat Tunnel but there is a convenient footpath. The section from Redbrook to Whitebrook, also part of the Wye Valley Walk, uses part of the ex-GWR Monmouth–Chepstow line.

Greater Manchester

Adlington–Red Rock: C, H, W, NI, DR, 2m, SD 600126–SD 584099. Part of NCN55. At the southern end, passes under an aqueduct on the Leeds & Liverpool Canal.

Bolton–Bury: C, W, NO, DR, 5m, SD 725082–SD 797104. This as yet unopened trail, set to become part of NCN80, will use the old L&YR line between Bolton and Bury. It will include one large and one gigantic viaduct (Burnden and Darcy Lever respectively), which are owned by Railway Paths and have been restored by Sustrans. At the Bury end, it will link up with the ½m Daisyfield Greenway, an existing trackbed-based section of NCN6, to end about ½ mile from Bury's railway and tram stations. Due to the amount of development in this area, there will be some on-road links to join the various railway parts together.

Chorlton-cum-Hardy–Fairfield: C, W, NI, DR, 6m, SJ 824936–SJ 897965. Ten years after the first proposals were published for the Fallowfield Loop Line, the route was opened in 2006 along the whole of this former LNWR line, passing through Manchester's southern suburbs of Fallowfield and Levenshulme. The route is now part of NCN6 with various links including a path along the infilled Stockport Canal at Debdale.

Eccles–Roe Green–Bolton: C, W, NI, DR, 6½m, SJ 764996–SD 749017–SD 713080. Part of NCN55. Most of the LNWR line from Eccles to Bolton (Great Moor Street), with minor diversions around the M61 and some subsequent developments. Connects at Roe Green with the former LNWR line to Pennington via Tyldesley. The section from Roe Green to Ellenbrook (1m, SD 749017–SD 727018) was wet underfoot in July 2016, but things improve at Ellenbrook where one can now continue to Tyldesley and Leigh on a path alongside the new Leigh–Manchester guided busway (3¾m, SD 727018–SD 665004).

Greenmount–Bury: C, W, NI, DR, 2¼m, SD 778143–SD 802116. Part of Kirklees Trail and NCN6, this

Above: Darcy Lever Viaduct near Bolton is set to become part of a new railway path from Bolton to Bury. It comprises eight lattice girder spans on stone piers and stands up to 80ft above the River Tonge. As can be seen, Sustrans has already prepared the deck for the path. (Author)

Left: Darcy Lever's setting has shades of the fictional Coronation Street, with the railway viaduct towering above houses and the street-corner pub. It was classified as non-operational in 1983, despite the last train having crossed in 1970, and received its Grade II-listed building status in 2002. (Author)

route stopped for many years at Woolfold (SD 788123) about a mile west of Bury. However, all that came to an end when the new Woolfold Viaduct was opened in 2012 at a cost of £654,291, and another ¾ mile of trackbed converted to take the trail on to the east bank of the River Irwell, a short distance north of Bury railway station.

Latchford–Heatley–Oldfield Brow: C, W, UT, DR, 8m, SJ 639871–SJ 703882–SJ 751889. Part of the Trans Pennine Trail (NCN62). Starts near Warrington but is mostly in Greater Manchester. The station house at Dunham Massey (once the stop for the National Trust's Dunham Massey Hall) survives en route as a private residence.

Macclesfield–Marple: C, H, W, UX, DR, 10m, SJ 918743–SJ 950888. The Middlewood Way. Only the northern (i.e. Marple) end of this route is in Greater Manchester. For further details, see entry under Cheshire.

Oldham–Grotton & Springhead: W, NI, DR, 2m, SD 937049–SD 961044. A cycle trail along part of the Oldham–Greenfield line managed by Oldham Council.

Oldham–Park Bridge–Ashton-Under-Lyne: C, W, UT, DR, 3½m, SD 928044–SD 939022–SJ 938999. Much of the former Oldham, Ashton & Guide Bridge Joint Railway from Oldham to Ashton-Under-Lyne; the trail, part of NCN626, ends just north of Ashton station. Hopes of a new viaduct over the River Medlock at Park Bridge were dashed in February 2010 when Oldham Council announced that it could no longer afford it, despite financial assistance from Sustrans' Connect2 project, but the council opened the link into Oldham without it. Park Bridge is a bit tricky to negotiate, so follow the signs for NCN626.

Radcliffe–near Clifton Junction: C, W, UT, DR, 2½m, SD 782069–SD 791037. This section of the L&YR's former line from Bury to Clifton Junction is now the Outwood Trail and part of NCN6. It includes the impressive Outwood Viaduct at SD 781067, while just beyond its end the Grade II-listed Clifton Viaduct at SD 792035 can be viewed by continuing on to the footpath along the north bank of the River Irwell.

Reddish Vale–Portwood (near Stockport): C, W, NI, DR, 1½m, SJ 906930–SJ 901912. A short section of the Trans Pennine Trail utilises part of the link line from Brinnington to Tiviot Dale. At Brinnington Junction (SJ 906917), a short connecting path on the former line to Romiley incorporates Brinnington No. 2 tunnel.

Rossendale Tramways: There are many disused tramways on the hills to the south of the Rossendale Valley, described at www.valleyofstone.org.uk/journey/heritagesites/. Although the quarries which supported them failed between the two world wars, a lot of the trackbeds and inclines remain as rights of way which provide excellent upland walking; many of the 'Valley of Stone' heritage walks use these former industrial lines as links between the old quarries. The following is the longest extant route, but collectively there are c. 20m of trackbed walking on these hills:

- **Cloughfold–Cragg Quarry–Ding Quarry (near Rooley Moor):** W, NI, DT, 4m, SD 822224–SD 828199–SD 850188. The Cloughfold to Ding Quarry Tramway, which at SD 818218 (the site of Cloughfold Scrubbing Mill) includes branches to Brow Edge Quarry (SD 815213) and Hurdles Quarry (SD 823217).

Uppermill–Delph: C, W, NI, DR, 1¼m, SD 994062–SD 987075. Included due to its proximity to the Tame Valley Way (see below), this Oldham Council route is formed from the former Delph branch. It starts on the west side of Uppermill, about a ¼ of a mile from the northern end of the Tame Valley Way. All of Oldham's railway paths are shown clearly in a brochure that can be downloaded from www.oldham.gov.uk/cycle-routes-in-oldham.pdf.

Uppermill–Stalybridge: The Tame Valley Way, another Oldham Council route, has reused most of the LNWR line from Diggle to Stalybridge via Micklehurst:

- **Uppermill–Micklehurst:** C, W, NI, DR, 4m, SE 000065–SD 977020.
- **Millbrook–Stalybridge:** C, W, UP, DR, 1¼m, SJ 975999–SJ 968986. A permissive section of railway path, which runs parallel to the restored Huddersfield Narrow Canal.

Wallbank, near Whitworth–Rochdale: C, W, UT, DR, 2¾m, SD 883175–SD 899144. The largest part to date of the projected trail along the L&YR's heavily engineered line from Rawtenstall to Rochdale via Bacup. Includes a large viaduct over Healey Dell Nature Reserve at SD 880160. In 2015, John Grimshaw & Associates were complementing the local council's efforts by determining how best to resolve the various barriers which currently splinter the rest of the line into little-used fragments; John Grimshaw is a former CEO of Sustrans, who now specialises in developing 'long sought routes which have proved intractable in the past'.

Whelley (near Wigan)–Tyldesley: C, W, UT, DR, 8m, SD 594068–SD 685018. Part of NCN55, this trail links together various old lines, all of LNWR origin, between Rose Bridge Junction (Tyldesley) and just north of Whelley Goods. Includes a ½m connecting spur from Hindley Green to Bickershaw (SD 622029–SD 625020).

Guernsey

No railway paths of any significance, although a few short sections of old railway have been converted into roads.

Hampshire

In addition to the routes listed below, there is a well-supported local scheme to reuse part of the Mid Hants Railway west of Itchen Abbas under the title 'The Watercress Way' (see thewatercressway.org.uk). Currently a section of *c.* 1m can be walked from Itchen Abbas station site (now a small housing estate) to Bridgetts Lane at Martyr Worthy (SU 537332–SU 516332). Further west, the Worthys Conservation Volunteers have been looking after part of the former DNSR around Worthy Down Halt for a decade, where just over 1m of trackbed can be walked from near Springvale to South Wonston (SU 481338–SU 478356). Since the MHR and the DNSR met at Winchester Junction (SU 483333), the plan is to link the two trackbeds together to form a new rail trail from Itchen Abbas to Sutton Scotney (7m).

Brockenhurst (Cater's Cottage)–near Burley (Burbush Hill): W, UP, DR, 7m, SU 286004–SU 202017. A superbly scenic walk across the New Forest, including two reinstated bridges at Long Slade Bottom (a reflection on the popularity of the route) and Holmsley station, now a popular tea room. The mile of trackbed to the east of Holmsley station has been converted into a road, which is usually busy. NCN2 provides a diversion to the south, although it bypasses Holmsley station, so those with good map-reading skills are advised to use the paths through Wilverley Inclosure to the north of the line.

Chawton (near Alton)–Farringdon: W, UX, DR, 1½m, SU 705373–SU 702354. This is the northern part

The so-called 'old road' through the New Forest was the Southampton & Dorchester Railway's main line from Southampton to Dorchester via Ringwood, Wimborne and Hamworthy Junction. It featured a large number of these cottages, built to accommodate the staff who manned the often-remote level crossings on the line. This example is at Cater's Cottage, just west of Brockenhurst. (Author)

A32 at SU 689305, and there is another permissive path notice at the southern end of this section, just before the trackbed crosses the final field towards the viaduct site. However, it is not clear where this second permissive footpath starts, so confirmation and grid references would be welcomed. As usual, please do not trespass on any former railway land if you are unsure of your right to be there.

Crow–Ringwood–West Moors: C, HIP, W, UP, DR, 5½m, SU 168037–SU 152048–SU 079029. The section of line from Crow to the A31 west of Ringwood is a fairly recent opening (c. 2005). The extensive Ringwood station site was redeveloped in the 1980s for new housing and warehouses, with the trackbed used to accommodate a new road called Castleman Way. West of the station, the major bridges over the River Avon have all survived intact and may now be used by walkers and cyclists. Continues into Dorset, q.v., where it becomes part of the Castleman Trailway.

Fort Brockhurst–Gosport–Alverstoke: C, W, UT, DR, 3½m, SU 591021–SU 613002–SZ 605983. Part of the old Fareham–Gosport railway. William Tite's colonnaded Gosport station remains at SU 614002, recently restored after decades of neglect when only its listed building status saved it from demolition. A £4.5 million scheme to restore it as housing, offices and a community centre was finally completed in early 2011.

Havant–Hayling Island: C, W, UT, DR, 6m, SU 717066–SZ 709997. This is the Hayling Billy Trail, which starts on the south-east side of Havant station; it is based on the Hayling Island branch which made a profit throughout its existence but, infamously, was closed because the authorities in 1963 were not prepared to spend money on repairing the wooden superstructure of the viaduct over Langstone

of the Meon Valley line (see entry below for West Meon), the section here having been dedicated as a public footpath. Access is from the A32 but if driving it is more sensible to park in Chawton village and walk from there as a convenient footpath leads from the village and comes out on the A32 directly opposite the start of this path at SU 705373. From the south side of Farringdon, the line continues largely intact to East Tisted, where the station survives in private ownership. There is a permissive footpath along the trackbed somewhere between Farringdon and East Tisted, but it is unclear precisely where it starts; it appears to be where a footpath crosses the line at SU 705330 – the only permissive path signs are south of that point. South of East Tisted, the line continues, largely intact again, to near the site of the long-demolished viaduct over the

Harbour. The missing viaduct necessitates a short detour via the nearby road bridge, but the trail is continuous and joins the two halves of the railway path together (Havant–Langstone and Langstone–Hayling). NCN2 uses this trail between Havant and Portsmouth, the latter being reached via a ferry between Ferry Point (Hayling) and Eastney Beach (Portsmouth). The ferry, which ceased operating in March 2015, resumed in August 2016 under new management.

Hockley–Winchester: CIP, W, DR, 1¼m, SU 475265–SU 486286. This route was opened in April 2013. It may be short, but the southern end includes the LSWR's thirty-three-arch Hockley Viaduct, which was built to extricate the DNSR from its terminus in Winchester's backstreets. The trail threads together extant parts of the old railway using the towpath of the Itchen Navigation where necessary. When core samples were taken from the viaduct, it was found to be constructed from concrete faced with stone, making it possibly the UK's first concrete railway viaduct.

The closure of the Hayling Island branch would have caused national outrage had it occurred in 2013 instead of 1963. This scenic branch line never lost money but was closed because the authorities at the time were not prepared to pay for repairs to the viaduct over Langstone Harbour, the remains of which can be seen here. This is the view at low tide; at high tide the foundations for the wooden superstructure are completely submerged. (Author)

Litchfield–Burghclere: W, UX, DR, 3m, SU 463551–SU 466604. Part of the Didcot, Newbury & Southampton Railway. Irritatingly, there is no direct access to the route from the village of Litchfield, so it is best to walk out and back from Burghclere, which is where the railway built a station called Highclere. It had already used the name Burghclere for its station at Lower Burghclere. Confused? Passengers must have been too!

Mottisfont–Fullerton: C, H, W, UX, DR, 9m, SU 332264–SU 379395. The railway-based part of the Test Valley Way long-distance path, formerly part of the LSWR's Romsey–Andover branch. This line started life as the Andover Canal, and parts of the old canal bed can still be seen alongside the route, especially around Stockbridge. Some miles north of Fullerton, between Upper Clatford and Andover, a public footpath of about 1m follows a further section of this line between SU 355439 and SU 361451 (on Anton Mill Road, near the site of Andover Town station), with a tarmac path continuing to SU 363452, by a large roundabout on the A3057 just west of the town centre. From this roundabout northward, the A3057 has been upgraded into a dual carriageway, Western Avenue, built on the trackbed towards Andover Junction station (now plain Andover) on the still operational Waterloo–Salisbury line. For walkers, the adjacent Junction Road offers a much quieter link to the station, and has the benefit of a pavement on both sides. In the vicinity of Anton Mill Road, you would not realise that the path was an old railway unless you were a railway rambler or student of old maps.

South Charford–Breamore–Burgate Cross: W, NI, DR, 2m, SU 166193–SU 159174–SU 154163. This is a new permissive path that was opened in stages by Hampshire CC along part of the former LSWR line from Salisbury (Alderbury Junction) to West Moors. The section from South Charford to Breamore was opened in 2010 with financial help from the New Forest National Park Authority, which paid for a new bridge, and local voluntary conservation groups, which cleared the trackbed. Breamore station survives at SU 160176 with the former stationmaster's house opposite; until about 2008, the widow of the last stationmaster still lived there.

West Meon–Knowle Junction: H, W, UX, DR, 11m, SU 644240–SU 556100 (at the West Meon end, the easiest access is from the old station approach road at SU 642237). This is the southern part of the former Meon Valley Railway, now the Meon Valley Trail. In 2014–15, Hampshire CC and the South Downs National Park finally cut back some of the lineside growth that had turned the route into a green tunnel with minimal views, and installed a new surface to remedy the often wet and muddy conditions underfoot. The intention was to increase use but instead generated vociferous complaints from locals who claimed that the new surface was too rough and abrasive, yet the trail was underused and needed improvement. Recent feedback suggests that the new surface is 'mellowing', as might be expected after a couple of leaf-fall seasons.

Whitehill–Liss: C, W, UX, DR, 6m, SU 792339–SU 777278. This route is part of the former Longmoor Military Railway. Individuals and small groups (of five or fewer) are permitted to use it on a permissive basis, but access may be restricted when military manoeuvres are taking place. (Fortunately, this happens rarely, and then only at times of national or international emergency.) Groups of more than five used to require a permit from the Defence Land Agent at Aldershot but given current fears about terrorism assume that such groups are either banned or require special consent. These restrictions do not apply to the section south of Liss Forest (SU 781293), which is owned and maintained by East Hampshire District Council.

Whitehill–Holm Hills–Longmoor: C, W, UX, DR, 4½m, SU 792339–SU 821327–SU 797313. This is a further section of the Longmoor Military Railway, which together with the interconnecting part of the Whitehill–Liss route, forms a complete circuit of about 7 miles. A further ½ mile of the LMR may be walked from the site of Bordon station to Bordon Camp (SU 785366–SU 788361), while the section from Bordon Camp to Whitehill (long used as a tank run) is set to become the new alignment of the A325, including a cycle trail. The army's presence in the area is being reduced, and the new road is intended to improve Bordon town centre.

Hereford & Worcester

Dowles (near Bewdley) to Park House (near Wyre Forest): C, W, UT, DR, 2m, SO 772763–SO 740760. Part of NCN45 based on the easternmost section of the former GWR branch line from Bewdley to Tenbury Wells. Wyre Forest was the first stop on the line, its very name suggesting remoteness; the station, which is now privately owned, lies some ½m beyond the end of the trail.

Hereford (Bartonsham)–Rotherwas: C, W, NI, DR, ¾m, SO 524389–SO 534380. This short trail, the start of the former GWR line to Ross-on-Wye, gets an entry here because Herefordshire CC hopes to extend it 2m along the trackbed to Holme Lacy. In the meantime, access to the trail from the Hereford side of the River Wye is from Green Street which

The NBR branch line from Spean Bridge to Fort Augustus closed to passengers in December 1933, but a section can be walked between North Laggan and Aberchalder. The viaduct seen here is near Aberchalder and crosses the Calder Burn just before it flows into Loch Oich. (Author)

Aberlour Tunnel is situated on The Speyside Way, which reuses much of the GNSR's former line from Keith to Boat of Garten – a railway that once served an uncommon number of distilleries. The one at Aberlour is still going strong. (Phil Earnshaw)

The viaduct over Platts Lodge Lake, near Accrington station, lost its superstructure many years ago, but the ingenious designers of the Woodnock Greenway used the surviving piers to form a causeway across the lake for walkers and cyclists. (Richard Lewis)

The Italianate station at Alton, Staffordshire, has been attributed in the past to Augustus Pugin (the Gothic revival architect associated with many Roman Catholic churches), but is now believed to have been the work of H.A. Hunt, the North Staffordshire Railway's architect who designed other stations on the company's scenic Churnet Valley line. It seems astonishing that the line serving Alton Towers theme park should have been closed. (Mark Jones)

Right: The SR's halt at Ashley Heath was opened in 1927 on the so-called 'old road' from Southampton to Dorchester via Ringwood and Wimborne Minster. Much of this bygone line now accommodates the Castleman Trailway, named after Charles Castleman – the Wimborne solicitor who promoted the railway in the nineteenth century. (Author)

Below: The railway path from Dolgellau to Barmouth is a memorable estuarial walk or cycle ride, like that from Wadebridge to Padstow in Cornwall. The crowning glory comes at the western end where it crosses the Grade II*-listed Barmouth Viaduct – one of the longest timber railway viaducts still in regular use in the British Isles. (Bob Morgan)

Bideford Signal Box on the former LSWR line from Barnstaple Junction to Torrington, now part of the popular Tarka Trail, is a reconstruction, but reinforces the railway atmosphere of this former West Country holiday line. (Author)

Black Dog Halt has the sort of name that Michael Flanders and Donald Swann should have included in their evocative song, 'The Slow Train'. What could be more appropriate than a black Bernese mountain dog, Patsy, waiting at Black Dog Halt? But the train will never come. (Mark Jones)

Breamore station was situated on the scenic LSWR line from Salisbury to West Moors, whence trains continued to Wimborne, Poole and Bournemouth West. It is now a holiday cottage, and the adjoining trackbed Hampshire's newest railway path. (Alan Clarke)

This charming station is Cambus O'May on the GNSR's branch line from Aberdeen to Ballater; its Swiss appearance is due partly to the large eaves, which were intended to deflect snow away from the building. Queen Victoria and Prince Albert used this line regularly on their way to and from Balmoral, which is just 9 miles beyond the line's terminus. (Phil Earnshaw)

Cefn Coed Viaduct once carried trains from Brecon to Merthyr Tydfil but is now part of the popular Taff Trail, which uses old railways, tramways and canals to provide a largely off-road walking and cycling route from Brecon to Cardiff Bay. (Phil Earnshaw)

The tiny village of Clydach was served by a station on the LNWR's Heads of the Valleys Line, which linked Abergavenny with Merthyr Tydfil. This was one of the most heavily engineered railways in Wales because it ran east–west across the north–south grain of the land. Clydach station and its grass-covered platform can be seen on the extreme left, while the prominent structure in the foreground is Clydach Viaduct, crossing a steep-sided coomb. (Phil Earnshaw)

Opposite: The SVR's old station at Coalport now accommodates 'Coalport Station Holidays', where paying guests can take a short break or longer holiday in a BR Mark 1 carriage, now luxuriously refitted. It's like staying in a 1950s camping coach but without the noise of passing trains, and with decidedly more comfort. (Author)

Left: This is Craig Aderyn on the former GWR line from Bala Junction to Trawsfynydd and Blaenau Ffestiniog. A common misconception is that railway paths are necessarily boring and flat but, as Ira Gershwin said, 'It ain't necessarily so'. (Phil Earnshaw)

Below: Cromdale station was situated on the GNSR's line from Boat of Garten to Craigellachie, but was closed in 1965 as part of the Beeching cuts. It is now on the Speyside Way long-distance path. (Maurice Blencowe)

Right: The little station at Cymmer in the Afan Valley north-east of Port Talbot has served for many years as the village pub, aptly named 'The Refreshment Rooms'. Not only is it in a very scenic location, but it is also situated on a sizeable railway path network. (Phil Earnshaw)

Below: Donyatt Halt was opened in 1928 south of Ilminster on the GWR's branch line from Taunton to Chard; the southernmost section between Ilminster and Chard is now part of NCN33. In the late twentieth century, the little halt was almost buried in vegetation, but the local community rescued it to create the attractive feature seen here. (Jenny Vinter)

Above: Earlsheaton Tunnel is now an important link on a short but heavily engineered route from Savile Town, Dewsbury, to Ossett. Here it is being prepared for its new role after years of dereliction; at this stage, the contractors were working on the parapet above the portal. (Graeme Bickerdike)

Right: This path through Edderacres Plantation, south-west of Peterlee, was once part of an extensive network of NER lines between the East Coast Main Line and the Durham coast, the scene here being part of a route that once linked Stockton and Sunderland via Wingate. With just a few diversions, one can still make the same journey, but on a bicycle following NCN1. (Robert Greenall)

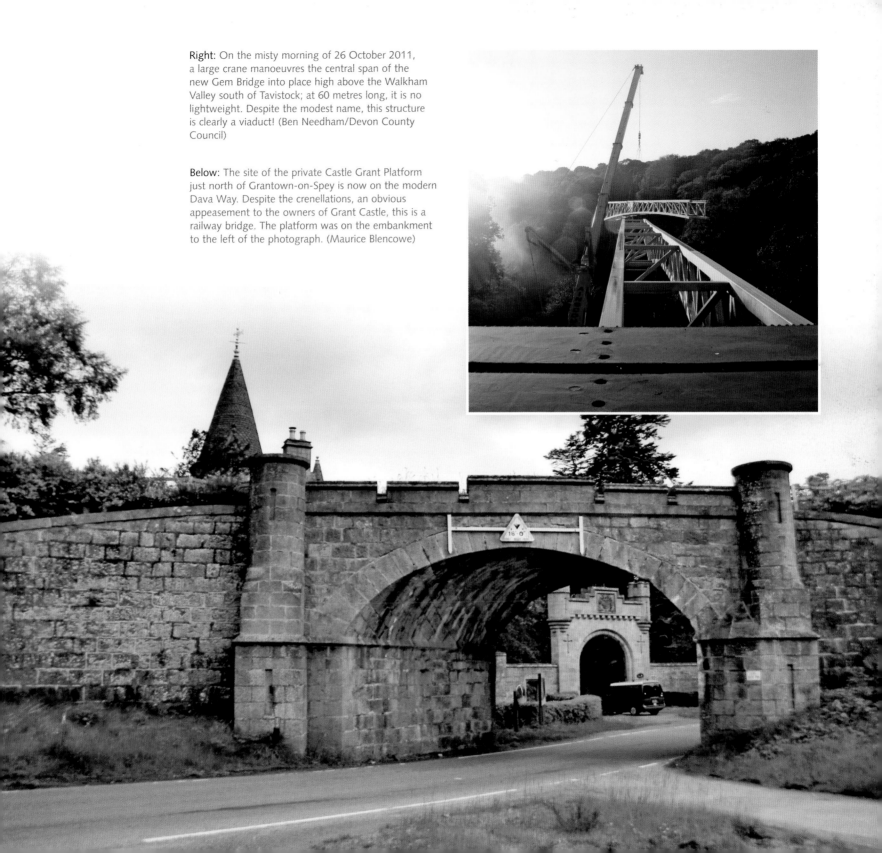

Right: On the misty morning of 26 October 2011, a large crane manoeuvres the central span of the new Gem Bridge into place high above the Walkham Valley south of Tavistock; at 60 metres long, it is no lightweight. Despite the modest name, this structure is clearly a viaduct! (Ben Needham/Devon County Council)

Below: The site of the private Castle Grant Platform just north of Grantown-on-Spey is now on the modern Dava Way. Despite the crenellations, an obvious appeasement to the owners of Grant Castle, this is a railway bridge. The platform was on the embankment to the left of the photograph. (Maurice Blencowe)

Left: The Axholme Joint Railway in Lincolnshire was a combined enterprise of the Lancashire & Yorkshire and North Eastern Railways; that it lost its passenger service in 1933 gives some indication of the light returns from ticket sales, although it did better from agricultural traffic. This attractive brick-built underbridge is just north of Haxey at grid reference SE 771018. (Jonathan Dawson)

Below: Hornsea station was unusual in that it had a turntable at its seaward end, recalled by the decorative paving in the foreground of this photograph. The sign 'SOUTHPORT 215 MILES' is a reminder that this is one end of the extensive Trans Pennine Trail, a coast-to-coast network of trails based largely on old railways. (Phil Earnshaw)

SOUTHPORT 215 MILES

The Test Way, a long-distance path from Eling in Hampshire to Inkpen Beacon in Berkshire, uses 9 miles of the LSWR's old Test Valley line between Mottisfont and Fullerton. This is the view from the trail at Horsebridge, looking north towards the privately preserved station; the trail takes a diversion to the left. (Alan Clarke)

The telltale rails in the tarmac reveal that this site near Ironbridge, on the former Severn Valley line from Bewdley to Shrewsbury, used to be a level crossing. The bridge in the near distance reinforces the railway atmosphere. (Mark Jones)

Most railway paths utilise empty trackbeds. An exception to the rule is Colliers Way between Radstock and Great Elm in Somerset, where in 2016 the rails still remained in place, accommodating near Kilmersdon this now skeletal brake van which was being engulfed by vegetation. (Author)

Above: The National Cycle Network is now home to the largest display of public sculpture in the country, and some of the artworks are gigantic in scale. This is 'King Coal' by David Kemp, a 30ft-high head in masonry and steel at Pelton Fell on NCN7 near Chester-le-Street, County Durham. (Steve Morgan/Sustrans)

Left: The eastern elevation of Lavant station, looking north towards Midhurst, shows the modern railway path running past on the right. The grandeur of this rural station reveals why the LBSCR found itself short of money after completing this line. (Author)

Left: Leaderfoot Viaduct was opened in 1865 to link Reston on the East Coast Main Line with St Boswells on the Waverley route. Last used by a train in 1965, the viaduct fell into disrepair until restored in the early 1990s. It now has Scottish Grade A listing and accommodates a permissive footpath, waymarked in 2010, from a car park on the A68 north of St Boswells. (Phil Earnshaw)

Below: Sally Matthews has developed a specialism in sculpting farm livestock from scrap metal, as illustrated here by her 'Lincolnshire Reds' at Washingborough on the Water Rail Way between Lincoln and Boston, part of NCN1. Another example of Sally's work is the popular 'Beamish Shorthorns' near Beamish in County Durham, which were made from JCB parts that started life in the nearby Consett steelworks. (David Martin/ Sustrans)

Left: Llanerchayron Halt, the penultimate stop on the Aberayron branch, had its name anglicised by the railway, just like the line's seaside terminus; the modern OS ends these names correctly in '-aeron'. The pagoda-style hut was a feature of many out-of-the way GWR branch lines; a few examples survive to this day, e.g. on the scenic Cornish branch between Liskeard and Looe. (Grahame Cox)

Above: Remote Linley station in Shropshire is situated on the former Severn Valley Railway between Bridgnorth and Coalport. Like neighbouring Coalport station, it is now involved in local tourism, being owned by the Apley Estate from whom it can be rented as a holiday cottage. (Author)

ends at SO 515392, from where a new trail leads on to a new suspension bridge, the central feature of Sustrans' £3.9 million scheme to improve cycling infrastructure in the city.

Hereford (Newton Farm)–Hereford (Wide Marsh): C, W, UT, DR, 2m, SO 498375–SO 506406. This is most of the line from Barr's Court Junction to Red Hill Junction, which was basically a north–south link that ran across Hereford just west of the A49. Now part of NCN46, the trail includes a substantial bridge over the River Wye at SO 502393.

Stourport-on-Severn–near Hartlebury: C, W, UR, DR, 1¼m, SO 817718–SO 837720. Part of the Stourport branch of the Severn Valley Railway, which was converted into a rail trail following its last turn of duty serving Stourport Power Station; now part of the Leapgate Country Park and NCN45. Includes a viaduct over the River Stour at SO 823720.

Hertfordshire

Harpenden–Hemel Hempstead: C, W, NI, DR, 6m, TL 134152–TL 059074. The so-called Nickey Line, part of NCN57. The railway was renowned for its steep gradients, which reached 1 in 39, but is still easy-going for walkers and cyclists. See also entry under Bedfordshire for Luton–East Hyde–Wheathampstead, which also serves Harpenden; the two trails are at opposite ends of Ox Lane.

St Albans–Hatfield: C, W, UP, DR, 6½m, TL 149061–TL 232092. The popular Alban Way, now part of NCN61. Some good artefacts survive in St Albans, including a viaduct over the River Ver, an impressive tunnel beneath the Midland Main Line, and London Road station, which is now used as offices.

Watford–Rickmansworth: C, W, UP, DR, 3¼m, TQ 106952–TQ 062941. The former LNWR Rickmansworth branch can now be walked from Watford West Junction on the western edge of Watford through to the site of the old terminus in Rickmansworth. The route is now known as the Ebury Way and forms part of NCN6.

Welwyn Garden City–Hertford: W, NI, DR, 6½m, TL 255125–TL 317119. The Cole Greenway, named after the intermediate station at Cole Green. On-road links at Welwyn provide a signed connection to the Ayot Greenway (see next entry). At the Hertford end, the trackbed can be reached via the RUPP, which starts at TL 321121.

This unprepossessing and easily missed structure is Salvation Army Halt on the GNR's branch line from St Albans to Hatfield; it can be found at grid reference TL 163071. The sleeper-built platform was originally used by staff at a local orchid nursery, but in later years staff at the Salvation Army's Campfield Road printing works used it; hence the name. (Neil Hebborn)

Welwyn Garden City–Wheathampstead: W, NI, DR, 3½m, TL 237135–TL 186144. The Ayot Greenway named after the intermediate station at Ayot, which is just over a mile from George Bernard Shaw's former home at Ayot St Lawrence. The trail was upgraded in early 2007 to cope with the high level of use it now receives, which is not surprising since it now forms part of NCN57. In summer 2010, volunteers located and restored the platform of Wheathampstead station in time for the 150th anniversary of its opening.

Wheathampstead–East Hyde–Near Luton: C, W, NI, DR, 4¾m, TL 162144–TL 127172–TL 106203. Part of the Upper Lea Valley Greenway, which was extended from Wheathampstead to East Hyde in August 2009. Continues into Bedfordshire, q.v.

Humberside

Beverley–Market Weighton: W, UX, DR, 11m, SE 877420–TA 037409. The Hudson Way, named after the nineteenth-century 'railway king' George Hudson, who kept 'everything but his accounts' and ended his life in public disgrace and humiliation – proof, were it needed, that huge financial scandals are not a modern phenomenon.

Bubwith–near Shiptonthorpe (A164): W, UX, DR, 9½m, SE 708355–SE 840405. Part of the old NER line from Selby to Market Weighton, now known as the Bubwith Rail Trail – a real rural backwater, and quite delightful. At Bubwith, the best access is from SE 714357. The end of the trail near Shiptonthorpe is very remote, although Market Weighton is only about 2 miles east as the crow flies.

Hull–Hornsea: C, W, UP, DR, 15m, TA 106297–TA 208477. The Hornsea Rail Trail, which is also the easternmost section of the Trans Pennine Trail (NCN65). When leaving Hull, take care at Wilmington (TA 107305) to follow NCN65 to the north east, and not NCN1 to the north. Once beyond Sutton on the Hill, this is another extremely rural route. Hornsea is delightful, with its sea front recalling the genteel days of Victorian and Edwardian seaside holidays. The LNER poster that declared that 'Skegness is so bracing' might have said the same of the whole east coast.

Hull (Marfleet)–Keyingham–near Patrington: W, NI, DR, 11m, TA 123297–TA 300234. This is most of the former branch line from Hull to Withernsea, although it should be noted that the last 4 miles between Patrington and Withernsea are privately owned and therefore not part of the trail.

Stamford Bridge–Gate Hemsley: C, W, UT, DR, ½m, SE 712552–SE 705556. The shortness of this route, part of NCN66, should preclude it from this gazetteer. However, it is notable since it includes Stamford Bridge Viaduct, which was restored in 2005, having narrowly escaped demolition in 1991. The structure comprises fifteen brick-built arches and a central cast-iron span. The eastern part of this line, between Market Weighton and Beverley, has been in use as the Hudson Way for many years. The Gate Hemsley end of the route is in North Yorkshire; the village is reached via a trail alongside the A166.

Isle of Man

The Isle of Man is a remarkable place for the railway rambler, since most of the abandoned trackbeds on the island are now public rights of way. However, bear in mind that a few sections are still privately owned and therefore not open to the public; please do not trespass.

Douglas–Peel: W, NI, DR, 10m, SC 366764–SC 240838. Now known as 'The Heritage Trail', this walk follows the Isle of Man Railway's first line, which was built across the island from coast to coast; the modern trail starts from the Quarterbridge in Douglas. While generally faithful to the course of the old line, the walk deviates slightly at its two ends due to redevelopments in Douglas and Peel.

St John's–Foxdale: W, NI, DR, 2m, SC 278813–SC 280780. This walk follows the course of the former Foxdale Railway, which was opened in 1886 to carry lead from mines around Foxdale, although it was later used to serve a military camp at Foxdale between 1940 and 1943. The route is not physically connected to the other two railway paths at St John's (see above and below), although it was when the railways were operational. Nowadays, one must head south from St John's and pick up the trackbed just off the lane to Slieuwhallian.

St John's–Sulby (near Ramsey): W, NI, DR, 16m, SC 271820–SC 389948. This route reuses most of the Manx Northern Railway, which used to link St John's (near Peel) with Ramsey in the north-east of the island. Those wishing to walk from Peel can reach St John's via 'The Heritage Trail' (see above), but must turn sharply north-west at the junction where the lines to Peel and Ramsey diverged (SC 271820). East of Sulby, most of the trackbed to Ramsey survives, but in private ownership. There are no public footpaths from Sulby to Ramsey, only the busy A3, so the safest option is to catch the number 5 bus from the shelter in Sulby village (hourly Monday–Saturday and every two hours on Sunday).

Isle of Wight

The Isle of Wight is a rambler's paradise. Apart from a large network of well-maintained public footpaths and bridleways, the local authority has also salvaged at least something of every closed line on the island,

although some of the publicly accessible fragments are too short to warrant an entry here. However, do be aware that parts of the old railway network remain privately owned, particularly on the lines between Yarmouth and Newport, and Merstone and Ventnor West. Please take care not to trespass.

Brading–Bembridge: C, W, UP, DR, 3½m (including diversions), SZ 611871–SZ 621883 and SZ 631885–SZ 640884. Most of the short branch line to Bembridge. Start at Brading station (now restored and painted in SR livery thanks to Brading Town Council), proceed north up Station Road and then take the first footpath on the right. This leads over the operational line to Ryde and on to the start of the branch just north of the station. After a narrow and enclosed section, most of the trackbed forms a wide path with fine views over the flood plain of the east River Yar. The section through St Helens is privately owned necessitating a hilly detour via Carpenters Road, Upper Green Road and Station Road, but this regains the trackbed just west of the privately owned St Helens station. (Please do not trespass on this property.) The line then survives

Kirk Michael station on the Isle of Man Railway's branch line from St John's to Ramsey saw its line close completely in 1965, reopen in 1967, close to passengers in 1968 and finally close completely again when oil trains ceased in 1969. The station was of a common design on the IMR's network, so other examples can be found readily on the island's modern railway paths. Many are now private homes, but Kirk Michael became the local fire station; the fire tender is housed in the nearby goods shed. (Neil Hebborn)

This is Yarmouth station on the Isle of Wight. If you think it looks rather large, you're right. The new owners have more than doubled its size with the original part extending from the tricycle to the first gable. The building now houses the 'Off the Rails' restaurant, which possibly offers the best views of any eating house on the island. The signal box is a replica, intended for 'twitchers' to use as a bird hide. (Brian Loughlin)

as a footpath through the RSPB's Brading Marshes Nature Reserve and can be followed for all but the last 200yds into Bembridge, where the station was situated opposite the Pilot Boat public house.

Freshwater–Yarmouth: W, UP, DR, 2½m, SZ 345870– SZ 364896. An attractive railway path alongside the west River Yar, which continues east past Yarmouth station as far as the B3401 at Thorley Bridge. Yarmouth station has been extended to form the 'Off the Rails' restaurant; the adjoining signal box is a replica, used as a bird hide. For 'completists', a further ½ mile of the Freshwater, Yarmouth & Newport Railway east of Watchingwell Halt (SZ 449884) has been dedicated as a public footpath.

Newport–Sandown: C, W, UP, DR, 8m (including diversion), SZ 504881–SZ 593849. From a railway point of view, this path starts at Shide on the southern edge of Newport; if starting in Newport, head south via Furrlongs (off South Street) and follow the signs for NCN23. The trail uses the old line as far as the site of Blackwater station, where it follows a diversion via the Stenbury Trail to a point just south of Merstone Manor, where it rejoins the trackbed to Merstone station. The next section, between Merstone and Horringford, includes a cutting and bridge, which were re-excavated in 2002, having been infilled after closure. From Horringford to Sandown, the trackbed has been in use as a railway walk for many years. If you are making for Sandown railway station, follow Perowne Way southwards from the end of the trail.

Newport–Cowes: C, W, UT, DR, 4½m, SZ 500901– SZ 498947. The popular Newport to Cowes Cycleway, now part of NCN23, which includes Mill Pond Bridge, actually a low viaduct over a tributary of the River Medina.

Newport–Wootton Bridge: C, W, UP, DR, 3m (including diversion), SZ 503895–SZ 509905 and SZ 516914–SZ 536913. The section between SZ 509905 and SZ 516914 is privately owned and requires a diversion of just under a mile alongside the adjacent A3054 Newport–Ryde road. There is a pavement throughout.

Shanklin–Wroxall: W, UX, DR, 2½m, SZ 580819–SZ 551799. Part of the old main line to Ventnor. At Wroxall, the energetic can follow quiet lanes and footpaths south of the village over Wroxall Down and on to the site of Ventnor High Level station, noting the ventilation shafts of the closed railway tunnel at SZ 559789 and SZ 560787. The tunnel is now used by the local water company and carries Ventnor's water supply.

Ventnor–near St Lawrence: W, UP, DR, 1m, SZ 555773–SZ 540769. The only walkable part of the branch line to Ventnor West. Starts as a road (Castle Close) where the privately owned Ventnor West station can still be seen on the south side. Castle Close occupies the trackbed for approximately ½ mile to SZ 545771 where a footpath leads on to the trackbed, which soon becomes a high, tree-lined embankment. This section was dedicated as a public footpath in *c.* 2001. Local footpaths and residential roads can then be used to 'shadow' the old railway as far as St Lawrence station, which also survives in private ownership.

Jersey

St Helier–La Corbiere: W, UT, DR, 7½ miles, 648486–555481. This route represents virtually all of the Jersey Railway, opened in 1870 and closed in 1936. The trackbed now forms the promenade from St Helier (where the magnificent terminus station still stands) to St Aubin (3½ miles), where the line turns west and runs inland via St Brelade before dropping down to the western coast at its terminus. The section from St Aubin to La Corbiere (4 miles) is known as 'La Corbiere Walk'; the end of the line at La Corbiere is a lonely spot, with little more in the vicinity than the old station, a few cottages and a lighthouse. Apart from the terminus at St Helier, stations survive at Millbrook, St Aubin and La Corbiere, the latter having been extended during 2008. The minor stations were all demolished after the States of Jersey acquired the trackbed, although keen-eyed walkers can still spot the remains of a platform here and there. The tunnel at St Aubin is closed to the public, but a short and convenient detour is provided.

Kent

Canterbury–Whitstable: C, W, NI, partly DR, 5m, TR 145588–TR 115665. The so-called 'Crab and Winkle Line' has seen revival as a cycle trail in recent years, but currently only a small proportion of it uses the old trackbed – which is hardly surprising given that the line closed to passengers in 1931 and to freight in 1952. Despite this, the trail is supported by a very keen local group, the Crab and Winkle Line Trust, which aims to reclaim as much of the trackbed as possible in order to provide a traffic-free path between Canterbury and the north Kent coast. In recent years, the trust – with support from Sustrans' Connect2 programme – obtained consent for two replacement bridges and an entirely new one to go in at the Whitstable end; the original planning consent lapsed, but was renewed in 2015 with the Planning Committee of Canterbury City Council commending the quality of the trust's planning documents. The city council has published a superb leaflet for the trail on its website, and, given the level of commitment to this project locally, it is possible that more of this historic railway will become accessible in the future.

Elham–Lyminge–Peene: W, NI, DR, 5m, TR 181444–TR 163411–TR 185378. This section of the Elham Valley Railway from Canterbury to Folkestone is part of the Elham Valley Way. For many years, the only section of walkable trackbed ran from Elham to Lyminge, but from *c*. 2014 an extension was opened through to Peene, just short of the former Cheriton Junction (which has now been obliterated by the Channel Tunnel Terminal). Rather than being a continuous trackbed walk, this trail threads together the extant sections but, given that the line closed in the 1940s, Kent County Council has done well to reclaim any of it at all.

Lancashire

Ainsdale–Maghull: C, W, NI, DR, 6m, SD 322094–SD 365017. Part of the Halewood to Southport section of the Trans Pennine Trail (NCN62), which starts and ends in Merseyside (q.v.) and provides a nearly continuous railway path of about 25 miles. The only significant non-railway section follows the towpath of the Leeds & Liverpool Canal, which is interesting in its own right.

Foulridge–Thornton-in-Craven: W, UX, DR, 5m, SD 888426–SD 910482. Part of the former L&YR line from Skipton to Colne. See entry under Yorkshire, West.

Hyndburn Greenway: This is an 8-mile cycle trail, largely traffic free, which links Accrington town centre with Blackburn, Rishton and Baxenden, with a spur to Great Harwood. It is part of NCN6 and includes the following sections of reclaimed railway:

• **Accrington–Baxenden:** C, W, NI, DR, 2½m, SD 758283–SD 775259. Rather confusingly, this section is known as the Woodnook Greenway, despite being part of the Hyndburn Greenway. It features a striking causeway across Platts Lodge Lake, starting near Accrington station, which has been constructed between the piers of the former railway viaduct.

• **Great Harwood–near Rishton:** C, W, NI, DR, 1m, SD 739321–SD 727311. A short section of the old L&YR line from Blackburn to Rose Grove (see entry for Rose Grove below).

Lancaster–Caton Green: W, UP, DR, 6m, SD 472620–SD 546653. Part of the former MR line from Lancaster Green Ayre to Wennington, now known as the Lune Valley Ramble. Starts from near Lancaster Castle and begins with a steep descent down the former MR link line that once connected Lancaster's Castle and Green Ayre stations. Includes two fine viaducts over the River Lune at Crook o'Lune.

Lancaster–Glasson: C, H, W, UP, DR, 5½m, SD 459605–SD 446561. The old Glasson Dock

There isn't much left to show of the MR's Lancaster Green Ayre station, which closed to passengers in 1966 and was demolished in 1976 when freight traffic ceased. The area is now a public green space by the River Lune; the ex-railway crane provides a reference to the past – even though it is not authentic but an import from Hornby goods shed, which was further east along the line to Wennington. (Richard Lewis)

branch, now part of NCN6 and the Lancashire Coastal Way. The best place to join the trail is at SD 461620 alongside the River Lune, since the trackbed has been redeveloped within Lancaster. The old railway is joined just to the south-west of Abraham Heights.

Lancaster–Morecambe: C, W, UT, DR, 3½m, SD 471625–SD 432641. While this route is now a popular and well-used cycle trail, it was once an electrified railway – one of relatively few electric lines in England to have been closed. The trail ends alongside the still open Morecambe station.

Preston–Bamber Bridge: C, W, UT, DR, 2¼m, SD 537288–SD 555261. Part of the East Lancashire Railway's former line into Preston, later absorbed by the L&YR and now part of NCN55. Lancashire CC has made some big improvements to this trail in recent years, including extending it over Avenham Viaduct to near the station, and using the north and south chords of a disused railway triangle to take the route under the West Coast Main Line into Lower Penwortham at SD 532278 (add 1m if you take this diversion). The trail will be extended again, right up to Preston station, now that agreement has been reached to replace a life-expired bailey bridge installed in the 1950s by the Royal Engineers on top of an original 1848 overbridge as a 'temporary' measure. Just a short distance to the east of Avenham Viaduct, the course of the Walton Summit Plateway can be followed from SD 542285 to SD 551269 (1¼m); this was built to connect the two separate sections of the Lancaster Canal south of Preston. The old railway and plateway can be combined to make an excellent circular walk of about 4m.

Ribbleton–M6 Footbridge–Grimsargh: C, W, UT (but currently not open right into Grimsargh), DR, 2¼m, SD 553306–SD 571324–SD 583340. This is part of the former Preston to Longridge line, which was run jointly by the L&YR and LNWR. Lancashire CC began by establishing a cycle trail from Ribbleton (starting near the West View Leisure Centre) to a footbridge over the M6 and then obtained planning permission to extend along the trackbed to Grimsargh; at the end of August 2010, this extension stopped about ¼ mile short of the B6243 Bridge to the south of Grimsargh. The Ribbleton end of the route has the potential to be a pleasant walk or ride through the Preston suburbs, but is blighted by rubbish. When the extension to Grimsargh is complete, it will connect with a short but well-used public footpath, which follows the old trackbed through the village (SD 583340–SD 585345).

Rose Grove–Simonstone (near Padiham): C, W, UT, DR, 2¼m, SD 808320–SD 780335. The Padiham Greenway. In recent years, Sustrans and other agencies have been converting parts of the former L&YR's line from Rose Grove to Blackburn into a cycle trail. Further west, the trackbed accommodates a permissive trail from the south end of Martholme Viaduct, intact but securely locked, to Mill Lane in Great Harwood (SD 751338–SD 749329), and a cycle trail from Hameldon View, Great Harwood, to the towpath of the Leeds & Liverpool Canal, just east of Rishton (SD 739321–SD 727311).

Stubbins–Waterfoot (near Haslingden): CIP, W, UP, DR, 3m, SD 790187–SD 780225. This old line, parts of which now belong to NCN6, is a work in progress. Currently, the north and south ends are on the former railway, and in 2015 a further section at the south was moved on to the trackbed when Lumb Viaduct (SD 790198) was rehabilitated thanks to a scheme involving Railway Paths, Sustrans and the local authorities. Work on this viaduct included installing new parapets using stone from the same quarry as had supplied the originals in the nineteenth century. (After the railway closed, the parapets were

Railway Paths restored three structures on the Padiham Greenway just before it reaches Padiham Memorial Park: a bridge over Park Road (behind the photographer), this three-arch viaduct, and the accompanying pedestrian footbridge over the River Calder. The latter now leads up to the trail. (Author)

dismantled and heaped up on the deck, but some of the stones were 'lost'.)

Leicestershire

Braunstone Gate (Leicester)–Aylestone–Glen Parva: C, W, UT, DR, 3½m, SK 580041–SP 560989. The Great Central Way. Unfortunately, the imposing Braunstone Gate Bridge which marked the start of the route and crossed the Old River Soar, Western Boulevard and Braunstone Gate was demolished in November 2009 – partly due to its state of repair, and partly because De Montfort University wanted to build a new swimming pool nearby.

Coalville (LNWR)–Loughborough. The following sections of this former LNWR branch line have been converted into local cycle trails, although they do not appear to be part of an overall scheme to reuse the branch:

- **New Swannington–Whitwick:** C, W, UT, DR, ¾m, SK 428152–SK 435162.
- **Thringstone–Grace Dieu Priory:** C, W, UT, DR, ¾m, SK 431172–SK 435182.
- **Snell's Nook–Loughborough:** C, W, UT, DR, 1¾m, SK 499185–SK 520198.

Moira–Measham: C, W, NI, DR, 3m, SK 304162–SK 331119. Part of NCN63 and the Ivanhoe Way, this trail is part of the former LNWR and MR joint line from Moira West Junction to Shackerstone (now the northern terminus of the Battlefield Line) and Nuneaton. A further section of this route is open at the southern end (see entry for Nuneaton–Higham on the Hill under Warwickshire).

Muston (near Bottesford)–Harston (near Denton): C, W, UT, DR, 4¾m, SK 831371–SK 848324. The freight-only Denton branch, which operated from 1883 to 1974, was built by the GNR to convey ironstone from local quarries in the Belvoir area; the vast majority of the branch now forms part of NCN15. There is a short diversion off the trackbed at Woolsthorpe Bridge, which is interesting in its own right since it follows the towpath of the Grantham Canal.

Northampton (King's Heath)–Market Harborough: C, W, UT, DR, 15½m, SP 742631–SP 737869. The Brampton Valley Way, now part of NCN6. Less than a mile of this route is in Leicestershire, the rest being in Northamptonshire, q.v.

Ratby–Glenfield: C, W, UT, DR, 1½m, SK 520054–SK 542065. A very historic section of NCN63, which was formerly part of the early Leicester & Swannington Railway. The L&SR was opened in

1832 to transport coal from pits in the west of the county to the burgeoning city of Leicester. The promoters saw its purpose entirely in terms of freight, so passenger services were an afterthought – so much so that tickets were initially sold from local pubs. At the Glenfield end of the route, a walk of c. 1½ miles eastwards along the A50 (map advisable, although the signs for NCN63 are helpful) enables a further part of this historic railway to be followed:

- **Glenfield (east)–Leicester West Bridge:** C, W, UT, DR, 1m, SK 569056–SK 579045. This section of the L&SR, a further part of NCN63, provides an attractive entrance into Leicester. The site of the former Leicester West Bridge station includes a track panel and short section of platform to underline its railway significance.

Swarkestone (near Derby)–Worthington: C, W, NI, DR, 4m, SK 385283–SK 408211. The Cloud Trail, once part of the MR's former line through Worthington and Melbourne; another railway path which ends in Leicestershire but starts elsewhere, this time Derbyshire.

Lincolnshire

Bratoft–Burgh-le-Marsh: W, DR, NI, 1m, believed to be TF 466651–TF 475663. This short section of the GNR Firsby to Louth line is now owned by the National Trust and carries a sign which reads: 'Visitors are welcome to walk this section of the railway line now owned by the National Trust'. The Trust's web page for Gunby Hall and Gardens confirms this and extols the summertime display of wildflowers on the trackbed, but neither provides grid references nor marks the extent of the trail on its map.

Horncastle–Woodhall Spa: W, UP, mainly DR, 6½m, TF 256680–TF 217647. The Spa Trail, now part of the Viking Way. The start points are TF 258694 in Horncastle and TF 194631 in Woodhall Spa, with a canal towpath and public rights of way being used to bypass the privately owned sections of the line. In 2009–10, Lincolnshire CC invested £226,000 in improving the trail surface and providing car parks at each end.

Isle of Axholme Light Railway: Parts of this north Lincolnshire byway have survived to become short rail trails, and the Haxey Parish Plan of 2010 included an aspiration to establish a trackbed-based cycle trail from Haxey to Epworth; North Lincolnshire Council appears sympathetic. The sections currently open are listed below, from south to north; the gap between Low Burnham and Epworth is only a mile.

- **Haxey–Low Burnham:** CIP, HIP, W, UP, DR, 1½m, SK 773997–SE 772025. Starts as a bridleway off Haxey High Street but becomes a permissive path after The Nooking is crossed.
- **Epworth–Belton:** CIP, HIP, W, NI, DR, 1½m, SE 776044–SE 787073. Part of the Peatlands Way.

Langrick–Anton's Gowt–Boston: C, W, DR, UT, 4¼m, TF 265475–TF 300475–TF 324445. Part of the former GNR line from Lincoln to Boston, now incorporated into NCN1. For further details, see next entry.

Lincoln–Bardney–Kirkstead Bridge: C, W, UT, DR, 17m, SK 983708–TF 112691–TF 177621. This trail forms part of NCN1 between Hull and Harwich and is known as the 'Water Rail Way' due to the proximity of the River Witham, local canals and drainage channels. The restored Bardney Lock Viaduct is a notable feature near the middle of the trail. A link from Kirkstead Bridge to Langrick is waymarked via local lanes, so it is easy to bypass the 13 miles of old trackbed that were not available for inclusion in the

Here's something you don't see very often on an old railway nowadays – the remains of a signal. This example is situated near Utterby Halt on the former GNR line from Louth to Grimsby. The Beeching Report, which led to the demise of many of the lines listed in this gazetteer, was published in 1963, so the few signals that were left behind after demolition have had a very long time to decay. Few now survive. (Phil Earnshaw)

but there are signs along the route to say that it is open to walkers on a permissive basis. Sooner or later, the railway will want it back, but in the meantime this is a railway walk au naturel – it has not been improved in any way and is a good representation of what an old railway looks like when left to moulder for forty years. There are lots of railway relics along the way, such as signal posts and slowly rotting level crossing gates, but the downside is the vegetation, which during the summer gets very dense in the central section around Fotherby.

Skellingthorpe (near Lincoln)–Harby–High Marnham: C, W, NI, DR, 9m, SK 943721–SK 881715–SK 797712. Part of the former GCR line from Lincoln to Clipstone Junction, including the massive Fledborough Viaduct. Most of the trail is in Nottinghamshire, q.v.

Torksey–Cottam: W, NI, DR, 1¼m, SK 838791–SK 818798. A chance to visit the huge Torksey Viaduct, which offers the only intermediate crossing of the River Trent between Gainsborough and Dunham-on-Trent. Most of the trail is in Nottinghamshire, q.v.

London

Given the huge demands on land in London, it is remarkable that any old railways survive there at all. However, it must be emphasised that (with the exception of Custom House to Beckton), none of the following routes are continuous, although detours are never particularly long due to the abundance of roads and paths in the capital.

Lincoln–Boston leg of this impressively long cycle trail. A few hundred yards south of Kirkstead Bridge is the site of Woodhall Junction, which marked the start of the Horncastle branch (see above). Much of this is open to the public, except for the section between the junction and Woodhall Spa. According to locals, BR sold this off – and the southward extension of the main line to Dogdyke and beyond – because it did not form part of the river flood defences.

Louth–Utterby: W, UX, DR, 4m, believed to be TF 332881–TF 315937. This part of the old GNR line from Grimsby to Louth is owned by the Lincolnshire Wolds Railway based at Ludborough, to the north,

Crystal Palace High Level–Nunhead: W, UX, DR, 3½m (including diversions), TQ 343723–TQ 348737, TQ 346731–TQ 348737 (Horniman's section) and TQ 351742–TQ 355745. The Crystal Palace High Level branch is the most fragmentary of London's railway walks, so an A–Z Guide and OS Explorer Map will be useful to anyone trying to trace its remains. The main walkable sections, from south to north, are a nature reserve accessible from Sydenham Hill (actually the name of a road); a well-kept section, which belongs to the Horniman Museum (No. 100 London Road, Forest Hill, SE23 3PQ), accessible only from the museum and a stretch through Brenchley Gardens. The branch has been included because the extant sections (excluding Horniman's) are now linked together as part of the 'Green Chain Walk'. However, there is much else that the explorer of old railways can find, including the portals of both intermediate tunnels as well as cuttings, embankments and the old station house at Sydenham.

Custom House–Beckton: C, W, UT, DR, 1m, TQ 410809–TQ 431815. Part of the former GER branch from Custom House to Beckton, which was not reused as part of the Docklands Light Railway. Starts just east of Custom House station and then follows a ruler straight course to the A117 opposite the DLR station at Beckton.

Finsbury Park–Highgate–Alexandra Palace: CIP, W, UP, mainly DR, 4m, TQ 313873–TQ 287880 and TQ 284891–TQ 292899. This trail starts near Finsbury Park station and can be followed with ease to Highgate Tunnels, where it links into a backstreet near Highgate underground station. North-west of Highgate, London Underground has reclaimed part of the trackbed for a new depot for rolling stock on the Northern Line. (It is surprising to see rows of electric trains parked in a cutting where railway ramblers used to walk freely in the early days of the club.) However, the path around the western edge of Highgate Park offers a convenient detour, which remains close to the old line until it can be rejoined at Cranley Gardens. From Cranley Gardens, the trackbed is a cycle trail, which passes over St James's Viaduct before reaching Muswell Hill Primary School, formerly the site of Muswell Hill station. The path then reaches the grounds of Alexandra Palace, where the trackbed is privately owned and inaccessible. However, footpaths allow the line to be traced from nearby, while a detour via adjacent Dukes Avenue leads to Alexandra Palace station, which has now been fully restored as a community centre.

Mill Hill East–Edgware: W, UX, DR, 3½m (including diversions), TQ 237914–TQ 224911 and then only fragments. This route makes another unconventional railway walk, but enough survives to repay investigation. From a point just beyond the Northern Line terminus at Mill Hill East, the trackbed is a cycle trail which can be followed to near where the M1 crosses the old line. Here, an abandoned road occupies the trackbed, this being the original feeder road from the A1 to the M1; the M1 ended here before it was extended south to Staples Corner. After passing under the motorway, the line has to be paralleled using local roads (an A–Z Guide is useful), but then things improve at the west end of Lyndhurst Park, which starts immediately west of Mill Hill Broadway station. Here, the old trackbed has been converted into a nature reserve, which runs behind Hale Drive and is managed by London Wildlife Trust, whose officers will open the reserve on application from organised groups. At the end of the nature reserve, a further very short section of the trackbed can be walked, but this stops abruptly in front of Edgware Depot. Local roads and paths must then be used to reach Edgware station.

Lundy

The island of Lundy is situated 7 miles north of Hartland Point in Devon. While its railway remains are less than the 2-mile threshold required for inclusion in this gazetteer, this entry was considered worthwhile because it is unusual that the island should have had any kind of rail transport at all.

William Hudson Heaven purchased Lundy in 1834 and, in 1863, opened granite quarries on the east side of the island, together with a pair of horse-drawn tramways that conveyed the stone to the top of an incline, whence it was lowered to a landing stage at sea level and transferred on to ships. The enterprise was not a success and closed in 1868, but the route of the tramway can be followed to this day. At the island's north lighthouse, there is an even more obscure tramway: it is very short, but the rails and sleepers are still in place over a century after they were last used.

Lundy is owned by the National Trust and managed by the Landmark Trust. It is accessible throughout the year, but day trips – from Ilfracombe or Bideford, depending on the tides – are easiest during the warmer months. Further details are available from the island's website, www.lundyisland.co.uk.

Merseyside

Hooton–West Kirby: H, W, UX, DR, 12m, SJ 349783–SJ 215869. The Wirral Way, which (thanks to prompt local lobbying) was the first official railway path in the UK. For further details, see entry under Cheshire.

Southport–Halewood: C, W, NI, mainly DR, *c.* 25m, SD 321164–SJ 448856. The western end of the Trans Pennine Trail (NCN62), including 5 miles in Lancashire (between Ainsdale and Maghull) and a section along the towpath of the Leeds & Liverpool Canal. The Merseyside sections of the trail are as follows:

- **Southport–Maghull:** C, H, W, NI, DR, 11½m, SD 321164–SD 365017. This route now has a much-improved surface, churning by horses having been a problem in the past. The section between Southport and Ainsdale runs alongside a road built on the old railway, but this is left behind at Ainsdale.

- **Aintree–Halewood:** C, W, NI, DR, 8½m, SJ 373976–SJ 448856. The Liverpool Loop Line, which starts just south of the famous Aintree racecourse. The start of the trail at Aintree uses a short connecting line that heads almost due west, with the Liverpool Loop Line proper being joined at SJ 364973. There are two exits at Halewood, the other being at SJ 438853; this is because the loop line terminated at a railway triangle. The third chord is occupied by the still open Warrington to Liverpool line.

Norfolk

Aylsham–North Walsham: W, NI, DR, 5m, TG 207281–TG 279302. Part of The Weavers Way, a long-distance footpath of 56 miles linking Cromer with Great Yarmouth. It was formerly a section of the M&GNR branch line from Melton Constable to Great Yarmouth. See also entry for Bengate–Stalham (another section of the same line).

Aylsham–Reepham–Hellesdon–Norwich: C, H, W, UP, DR, 21m, TG 195264–TG 225093. Marriott's Way now extended into central Norwich as the Wensum Valley Walk and forming part of NCN1 between Reepham and Norwich. The route utilises part of the former GER line from Wroxham to County School, which passed under the M&GNR's line from Melton Constable to Norwich at Themelthorpe. British Rail linked these two lines together in 1960 via the new 'Themelthorpe Curve', which was constructed for the use of freight trains from Anglian Cement and Concrete Works at Lenwade. The closure of this line (i.e. Lenwade to Wroxham via Themelthorpe) in 1983 paved the way for the creation of this rail trail. In recent years, Norfolk CC has been improving the surface and in 2014 invested another £250,000 in this work, but there are still a few trouble spots in wet weather, e.g. at Themelthorpe.

Aylsham–Wroxham: C, W, NI, DR, 9m, TG 195265–TG 303187. The Bure Valley Footpath and Cycle Way, which runs alongside the narrow gauge Bure Valley Railway throughout its length. The BVR finishes at Hoveton, which is just north of Wroxham station on the still open line from Norwich to Cromer. The route started life as part of the GER line from Wroxham to County School.

Bengate (North Walsham)–Stalham: W, NI, DR, 4½m, TG 207281–TG 279302. A further section of The Weavers Way; see entry for Aylsham–North Walsham.

King's Lynn–near North Wootton: C, W, UT, DR, 1¾m, TF 628199–TF 633222. This part of NCN1 starts just outside the still operational railway station in King's Lynn and reuses the former GER Hunstanton branch as far as the A1078 on the very edge of North Lynn. Further north, between Dersingham and just south of Snettisham, another section of the same line now accommodates a 1m public footpath between TF 680308 and TF 681326.

Norwich, Old Lakenham–near Chapelfield Grove: C, W, DR, ¾m, TG 230060–TG 229077. This is a rare and unexpected urban survivor – part of the old GER line from Victoria Junction to Norwich Victoria, now known as the Lakenham Way following a £429,000 improvement scheme. It is claimed that Norwich Victoria received its regal suffix because it was built on the site of Norwich's Victoria Leisure Gardens.

Stow Bedon–Hockham Heath: W, NI, DR, 3m, TL 940966–TL 927925. Part of the former GER line from Thetford to Swaffham, now known as the Great Eastern Pingo Trail – an 8-mile circular route on the eastern edge of the Breckland area. Access is off the A1075 near Stow Bedon, with car parking in the old railway station yard (TL 940966). Around ¾ mile before the site of Wretham & Hockham station, the trail merges with the Peddars Way as it heads north-west along the course of an old Roman road.

Swalfield–Old Hall Street: W, NI, DR, 1½m, TG 285316–TG 298329. Part of the 20-mile long Paston Way, which links North Walsham with Cromer. Originally part of the Norfolk & Suffolk Joint Railway (a combined GER and M&GNR company), which once connected the same two towns.

Northamptonshire

Daventry–Middlemore: C, W, UT, DR, 1½m, SP 576630–SP 560648. Part of the LNWR line from

The gentle landscape of Norfolk did not demand great feats of engineering from those who laid out and built the railway lines now incorporated into Marriott's Way, but between Themelthorpe and Norwich the M&GNR engineers installed three of these highly distinctive 'A-frame' bridges over local rivers, which are believed to be unique in the country. (Ron Strutt)

Weedon to Marton Junction, near Warwick. Daventry DC has said that it might extend the trail further along the old railway line to the village of Braunston to allow access to the countryside, which would add another 1½m to the route.

Irthlingborough–Thrapston: C, W, UT, DR, 7m, SP 958705–SP 990786. This railway path was opened in 2005, reusing a section of the LNWR's old Nene Valley line as part of NCN71; Northamptonshire CC now promotes it as their Stanwick Lakes to Thrapston route. The project involved the restoration of several viaducts over the River Nene, financed by Rockingham Forest Trust, which owns the trackbed from SP 958705 to SP 981769 (Woodford Lock). The section from Woodford Lock to Thrapston is under the control of Northamptonshire CC's Rights of Way Department, which is responsible for the bridleway that uses the trackbed as far as SP 990778, where it joins the Nene Valley Way LDP. From here to SP 989785 (Kettering Road, Thrapston), users should follow the Nene Valley Way, which runs alongside the river to the east, thereby avoiding a section of trackbed that has been partially obliterated by the creation of an artificial lake. The trail includes three substantial viaducts over the River Nene.

Northampton (King's Heath)–Market Harborough: C, W, UT, DR, 15½m, SP 742631–SP 738869. The Brampton Valley Way, now part of NCN6, which includes two sizeable unlit tunnels (Kelmarsh and Oxendon – bring a torch) and runs alongside the Northampton & Lamport Railway at Pitsford & Brampton station. Used to start at Boughton, about 4 miles from Northampton town centre, but has now been extended south to the site of the junction where the lines from Northampton to Rugby and Market Harborough diverged (Rugby Line Junction). NCN6 is signed from Northampton railway station.

Rushden–Higham Ferrers: C, W, NI, DR, 1¼m, SP 946673–SP 962682. Part of the East Northamptonshire Way, which reuses a section of the short MR branch to Higham Ferrers. The preserved Rushden station at SP 957672 is a notable feature; it is now the home of the outstanding Rushden Historical Transport Society (see rhts.co.uk), which in April/May organises one of the biggest transport rallies in the area.

Northumberland

Brinkburn–Rothbury: W, UX, DR, 2m, NZ 088995–NU 067015. The north end of the NBR's Rothbury branch descending into the Coquet Valley from the site of the former station at Brinkburn.

Coldstream (Cornhill on Tweed): There is now a trio of short railway walks around this attractive Borders town, although all of the railway paths are on the south (i.e. English) side of the River Tweed in Northumberland. Note that Coldstream station was actually in Cornhill on Tweed – Victorian railway companies took many liberties with the names of their stations.

- **Coldstream–East Learmouth:** W, NI, DR, 1m, NT 863394–NT 865378. See under Coldstream–West Learmouth below.
- **Coldstream–West Learmouth:** W, NI, DR, 1¾m, NT 863394–NT 846379. A public footpath runs from just south of the site of Coldstream station to Coldstream Junction, where the lines to St Boswells and Alnwick diverged. At the junction, the St Boswells line can be followed to West Learmouth, and the Alnwick line to East Learmouth. There are plenty of bridges on the West Learmouth arm, and quiet local lanes can be used to make a circuit of just less than 4m. The footpath to East Learmouth may actually end further south at NT 866372;

curiously, OS Landranger and Explorer maps show different lengths.

- **Twizel Stead–St Cuthbert's Chapel:** W, NI, DR, ½m, NT 877438–NT 873430. This short permissive path connects at both ends with the footpath along the south bank of the River Tweed. Its southern end includes the 390ft-long Twizell Viaduct over the River Twill, which has been renovated as the centrepiece of this project. The railway spelt the village's name as 'Twizell', but the rest of the world (including the Ordnance Survey) favours 'Twizel'.

Haltwhistle–Alston: CIP, W, UP, DR, 12m, NY 704638–NY 717467. The South Tyne Trail (part of NCN68), a scenic rural branch line which starts at Haltwhistle station and continues into Cumbria, q.v. Connects with Lord Carlisle's Railway (see entry below) at Lambley. Between Alston and Lintley, the trail runs alongside the narrow gauge South Tynedale Railway, which has ambitious long-term plans to extend northwards to Haltwhistle. The principal engineering feature en route is the towering Lambley Viaduct. In 2005 Railway Ramblers made a substantial contribution towards the restoration of Alston Arches Viaduct, just south of Haltwhistle station on the Newcastle–Carlisle line.

Kielder–Deadwater: C, W, NI, DR, 1½m, NY 623941–NY 603969. On the OS Explorer map, this route is labelled as 'Bundle and go to Kielder Stane Walk'; on the ground, it is called – more succinctly – 'Borderline', and has an attractive tiled logo at intervals to identify the route. The path is part of the former Border Counties Railway between Reedsmouth and Riccarton Junction (in Scotland). Just beyond Deadwater, the trackbed crosses the Scottish border and Rhys ab Elis's *Railway Rights of Way* claims that it can be walked to NY 556972, just west of Saughtree station – a further 2¼m. RR has not been able to verify this, but land access rights

are very different north of the border (see the notes on 'Trespass' in the section on Scotland). Only short and isolated sections of the BCR are accessible to the public. Two others are as follows:

- The privately owned Kielder Viaduct (NY 632924), which in 2011 was incorporated into the Lakeside Way, a 26-mile circuit of Kielder Reservoir, Europe's largest man-made lake; it can be accessed from the lane south of Butteryhaugh at NY 630927.
- A 1m section of trackbed at Falstone village, which runs west from NY 725875 to Kielder Dam, beyond which the railway is now submerged.

Lambley–Tindale: W, NI, DR, 3½m, NY 662586–NY 621591. Part of Lord Carlisle's Railway – a scenic former colliery line from Lambley to Brampton Junction, which straddles the border with Cumbria. The intended link from Tindale to Brampton Junction is not yet open, so walkers are advised to start from Lambley and divert on to local footpaths, bridleways and lanes until such time as access is negotiated all the way through. In February 2007, Sustrans reported that the extension from Tindale to Brampton was in the planning stages, and expressed the hope that the route would be open throughout 'within the next couple of years'; but unfortunately nothing has yet come of this.

Newburn (Newcastle)–Wylam Bridge: W, NI, DR, 4½m, NZ 163655–NZ 110642. This route should be a 'must' for all railway ramblers, since it passes the cottage where George Stephenson was born (NZ 127651); in the late nineteenth century, his entire family lived here in a single room. Now owned by the National Trust, the property appears to be open daily between 11 a.m. and 5 p.m., but check before making a visit – the opening used to be much more limited. There is a modest admission fee. The eastern part of the route is in Tyne & Wear.

Near Seaton Delaval Hall–Monkseaton Metro Station: W, C, HIP, NI, DR, 3m, NZ 317762–NZ 347721. Part of the NER's Monkseaton to Morpeth line. Continues into Tyne & Wear.

Wannie Circular Walk: W, NI, partly DR, 6½m, NZ 037865–NZ 034886 towards Morpeth and NZ 037865–NZ 011870 towards Reedsmouth. Named after the Wansbeck Valley Railway, this walk is based in the grounds of Wallington Hall (NZ 029842), a large National Trust estate near Scot's Gap, and covers sections of the branch lines to Rothbury and Reedsmouth Junction. Access is at Scot's Gap (NZ 037864), and there is a waymarked path at the end of each branch, which enables a circular walk to be completed, taking in all of the old railway remains.

Nottinghamshire

Bilsthorpe–Clipstone Forest: C, W, UT, DR, 2¾m, SK 648612–SK 608607. This trail along a former colliery railway, now part of NCN645, was opened in May 2013. The Bilsthorpe end is just ½m north of the Southwell Trail (see entry for Farnsfield–Bilsthorpe), while the Clipstone end links to cycle trails at Sherwood Pines Forest Park, which in turn link to Centre Parcs Sherwood Holiday Village.

Cottam–Torksey: W, NI, DR, 1¼m, SK 818798–SK 838791. This short walk includes Torksey Viaduct, which was built by the Manchester, Lincolnshire & Sheffield Railway (later part of the GCR) and earned its Grade II* listing as the first example of box girder construction; the engineer was John Fowler, who went on to co-engineer the Forth Railway Bridge. Torksey Viaduct comprises two 130ft spans over the River Trent, plus a 570ft approach viaduct of twenty spans on the eastern side. Its restoration and reuse were masterminded by Railway Paths who would like to open the structure to cyclists as well if the take-up by walkers proves the potential demand to grant-awarding bodies. If you are starting at the Cottam end, head east on the bridleway off Town Street to SK 829794; if you cannot go straight on here, turn left (north) to reach the Trent Valley Way and then turn right (south) to reach the western end of the viaduct.

Farnsfield–Bilsthorpe: W, NI, DR, 2m, SK 646572–SK 649601. An extension to the Southwell Trail (see below), which adds on the old line to Bilsthorpe Colliery.

Farnsfield–Southwell–Rolleston Junction: C, H, W, UX, DR, 7½m, SK 627574–SK 710541–SK 737525. The Southwell Trail, part of NCN645, which at the west end starts in a tricky location on the east side of the A614. For many years, one could travel no further east than Southwell, but in *c.* 2010 reports began to arrive that the trail had been extended to Rolleston Junction. This has now been corroborated in Nottinghamshire CC's leaflet 'Southwell Bramley Apple Heritage Walks', which states: 'Once a busy railway line, the old track bed [*sic*] between Farnsfield and Rolleston Junction now forms the Southwell Trail, the longest stretch of continuous lost railway … to be fully open to the public on foot, bicycle or horseback'. Southwell is where Mary Ann Brailsford achieved lasting fame by planting the pips from some apples that her mother was preparing; we now know this fruit as the Bramley apple.

Hempshill Vale–Kimberley: C, W, UT, DR, SK 526446–SK 502450, 1½m. This trail starts on Low Wood Road (the A6002) in Hempshill Vale and provides a traffic-free link to Kimberley School, including an underpass beneath the M1. It reuses part of the GNR's former line from Derby to Ilkeston and Nottingham, which between Derby and Ilkeston is being developed into the Great Northern Greenway (see entry for Breadsall–Morley under Derbyshire).

High Marnham–Harby–Skellingthorpe (near Lincoln): C, W, NI, 9m, SK 797712–SK 881715–SK 943721. Part of the former GCR line from Clipstone Junction to Lincoln, now part of NCN64. Continues into Lincolnshire. This route includes the gigantic Fledborough Viaduct, which is one of very few crossings of the River Trent for over 10 miles; 9 million bricks went into its fifty-nine arches, and there are also four central spans over the river.

Mansfield–Rainworth: CIP, W, NI, DR, 4m, SK 529601–SK 589589. The central part of this route is shown on the local OS Explorer map as a cycle trail (SK 545604–SK 587588, 2¾m) but rather more than this is accessible. The trail starts by the former junction off the Robin Hood line at SK 529601 and continues to Rainworth as far as the junction with the former line to Rufford Colliery at SK 586587. (A few hundred yards of the colliery branch can also be walked as far as the A617 dual carriageway at SK 589589, but the official status of this is not known.) A small viaduct remains near the start of the trail in Mansfield, which is an unusual survivor in this area. See also the entry for Rainworth–Blidworth (below), which uses part of another disused local colliery line.

Newark–Cotham: W, NI, DR, 6m, SK 804545–SK 799471. A railway path that starts from Newark Northgate station and reuses the first 6 miles of the former GNR line from Newark to Bottesford North Junction (between Grantham and Nottingham). Part of NCN64.

The Pleasley Trails: With the exception of Huthwaite–Blackwell, all of the trails listed below interconnect. There is a visitor centre and cycle hire facility at Fackley, near Teversal (NG17 3HJ). Both Nottinghamshire and Derbyshire county councils promote the Pleasley Trails, so presumably they are a joint venture. The routes are as follows:

- **Huthwaite–Blackwell:** C, W, UT, DR, 1¾m, SK 467583–SK 440577. Continues into Derbyshire.
- **Pleasley–Skegby–New Cross (Sutton-in-Ashfield):** C, W, UT, DR, 4m, SK 501644–SK 495610–SK 497591.
- **Pleasley–near Mansfield Woodhouse:** C, W, UT, DR, 1¼m, SK 511648–SK 527647. There is a link on to this trail from SK 506643 at Pleasley, off the A617 dual carriageway.
- **Pleasley–Teversal–Huthwaite–Blackwell:** C, W, UT, DR, 5½m, SK 494640–SK 479618–SK 460601–SK 427589. Continues into Derbyshire.
- **Pleasley–Rowthorne:** C, W, NI, DR, 1¼m, SK 492638–SK 476647.
- **Teversal–Skegby:** C, W, UT, DR, 1m, SK 478616–SK 495610.

Rainworth–Blidworth: C, W, NI, DR, 2m, SK 603596–SK 599573. A cycle trail on an old railway that skirts the eastern side of Rainworth; the line used to serve Blidworth Colliery.

Oxfordshire

Oxfordshire CC's record with abandoned railway infrastructure is poor, with Sustrans being responsible for all of the routes listed below. Elsewhere, only fragments of Oxfordshire's abandoned railway lines have been reused, an example being Kingham to Churchill Crossing (SP 261232–SP 271244, ¾m), which is a permissive route open to walkers only and is closed during the winter.

Abingdon–Radley: C, W, UT, DR, 1m, SU 508973–SU 522973. Part of the former branch line from Radley to Abingdon which now serves as part of NCN5 between Oxford and Abingdon. Developers nibbled away at the urban ends of the line, especially in Abingdon, leaving only the central section available for conversion.

Didcot–Upton: C, W, UT, DR, 2¼m, SU 532900– SU 513872. Part of the former Didcot, Newbury & Southampton Railway, starting from just south of Didcot. Sustrans negotiated with local landowners for seven years to get this path in place, and it is worth it. The southern end of the route is on a substantial embankment with excellent views of the surrounding countryside.

Princes Risborough–Thame: C, W, UT, DR, 7½m, SP 786036–SP 706053. The western end of this route is in Oxfordshire, but the majority of the path is in neighbouring Buckinghamshire (q.v.). Railway Ramblers provided Sustrans with the funds to acquire this trackbed.

Shropshire

Bridgnorth–Coalport: W, C, UP, DR, 5¼m, SO 722955– SJ 709010. In March 2011, Shropshire Council announced that the section of the former Severn Valley Railway between Bridgnorth and Coalport was to open the following month as an improved route for NCN45, thanks to successful negotiations with the Apley and Willey Estates, which own the trackbed and had agreed ten-year leases. Immediately beyond the Severn Valley Railway's Bridgnorth station, the line enters Bridgnorth Tunnel, after which housing development and the local golf course occupy the trackbed so walkers must make their way to Stanley Lane to gain access at SO 722955. Note that this trail is closed between November and January each year for the shooting season; there is nothing about this on the ground, but the restriction is mentioned on Sustrans' online mapping service.

Coalport–Ironbridge: W, UX, DR, 2½m, SJ 709010– SJ 661036. A short but interesting trail, where the sometimes uneven surface (especially in the Jackfield area) indicates the unstable geology in the Severn Valley. The easiest access at Coalport is at SJ 700020. The railway part of the trail ends immediately in front of the cooling towers of Ironbridge Power Station.

Coalport–Telford: C, W, UP, DR, 5m, SJ 701022– SJ 702081. The Silkin Way – a rail-to-trail conversion that has a rather sterile feel to it, and probably appeals more to cyclists than railway walkers and historians. This is best tackled from Coalport northwards, because so much landscaping and redevelopment has gone on near Telford town centre (e.g. in Town Park) that it is difficult to tell where the old railway actually went. If you have to start in Telford, look out for signs for NCN55, which uses the Silkin Way right through to Coalport.

Farley–Much Wenlock–Longville: C, H, W, NI, about two-thirds DR, 8m, SJ 632105–SO 549944. Part of the 100-mile Jack Mytton Way. Starts just south of Farley on the east side of the A4169 and continues to the B4371 about ½ mile north-east of Longville in the Dale. Although the trail uses most of the surviving

Many preserved railways rely on enamel signs like this to help create a period atmosphere; this example can be found at Linley station on the SVR between Bridgnorth and Coalport. Linley is a long way from Reigate, so the sign is probably an import. Bonny's was a family business with successively George, James and Alfred Bonny running it in the late nineteenth and early twentieth centuries. (Author)

Jackfield in the Severn Valley is perhaps best known for its tile makers, whose work can still be seen in many Church of England churches that were 'improved' by Victorian restorers. If the tiles went out by rail, it was not initially from Jackfield Sidings (seen here), which were opened only in 1934. The village's level crossing gates were reputed to be the widest in Britain. (Author)

The GWR's branch along Wenlock Edge must have been a beautiful line to travel, but the railway path, which uses part of it, is best walked in the winter months when one can see out through the trees. Fortunately, the Forestry Commission has carried out some felling, e.g. near Presthope, to create some viewpoints. A few GWR underbridges survive, such as this example near Easthope. (Author)

GWR trackbed through Much Wenlock, there is a 3-mile off-line diversion between the western edge of Much Wenlock and Presthope. Beyond Longville, the Jack Mytton Way leaves the old railway but continues along Wenlock Edge past Rushbury – a convenient and traffic-free way of exploring this scenic area.

Newport–Stafford: C, W, UT, DR, 10½m, SJ 759184–SJ 910233. Part of NCN55, originally known as the Stafford to Newport Greenway but now shown on the OS map as The Way for the Millennium. The vast majority of the route is in Staffordshire, q.v.

Rays Bridge (near Billingsley)–Netherton (near Highley): W, NI, DR, 1¾m, SO 715834–SO 734823. This is part of an industrial railway, which ran from Billingsley Colliery to a junction on the Severn Valley Railway about halfway between Arley and Highley stations. The trackbed runs along the south side of the Borle Brook and appears clearly on the

OS Explorer map for half of its distance as a public bridleway (the Jack Mytton Way), then a public footpath. The map also shows further evidence of the line on adjoining private land: at the north end, the incline from the mine (SO 716842–SO 716835), and at the south end (SO 734823), the 1¼m continuation of the trackbed as a private farm track down to the junction with the SVR.

Stretford Bridge–Horderley: W, NI, mainly DR, 1½m, access at SO 417858 or from Cheney Longville, just north of Craven Arms. This is part of The Onny Trail (named after the local river), a 1990s project, which reuses a section of the Bishop's Castle Railway, closed in 1935. The path is a permissive trail, with poor signage, and seemingly free from promotional leaflets. The Bishop's Castle Railway Society includes a very brief description and sketch map on its website (www.bcrailway.co.uk/railway-onny.htm).

The Bind (near Billingsley)–near Highley: W, NI, DT, 2m, SO 726838–SO 753817. In the late eighteenth century, coal mines and a blast furnace were opened in the parish of Billingsley, which is just west of the start of this walk. Coal and iron travelled out on a horse-drawn tramway, which ran alongside the north bank of the Borle Brook, a tributary of the River Severn; on reaching the Severn, the goods were trans-shipped into boats and travelled downstream. The tramway lasted no more than fifteen years but survives as a footpath, which includes shallow embankments and cuttings. On reaching the Severn, turn left (north) along the Severn Way to reach Highley station (½m).

Somerset

Somerset is a 'late developer' in terms of reusing its old railways. In 1999, the extent of railway paths in the county was maybe a dozen miles, but now the situation has improved immensely. There are plans to reuse the old GWR line from Cheddar to Wells and eventually Shepton Mallet to form part of a cross-county route from the coast at Clevedon to Evercreech, but this is likely to require years of negotiation with private landowners; see www.thestrawberryline.org.uk for details. Apart from Axbridge–Cheddar (see below) and Axbridge–Yatton (see under Avon), short sections of the Strawberry Line network are now open between Draycote and Rodney Stoke, and Wells and Dulcote.

Axbridge–Cheddar: C, W, UT, DR, 1½m, ST 440546–ST 454531. This trail connects at Axbridge with the Cheddar Valley Railway Walk to Yatton, now known as the Strawberry Line (see entry under Avon). The two trails start from the west and east ends of Axbridge respectively. At Cheddar, a start has been made on an extension to Wells, but this is far from complete: a ¼ of a mile is open at Cheddar, and a further ½ mile between Haybridge and Wells. Somerset CC has devised a trackbed-based route for the Cheddar–Wells link, but a stalemate has developed. In December 2014, the local authority would not grant planning permission until funding was in place, but the backers would not provide funding until planning permission had been granted.

Brushford–Nightcott: W, UX, DR, 1¾m, SS 920256–SS 895258. Part of the GWR's former branch line from Taunton to Barnstaple. The significance of Brushford is that it was once the home of Dulverton station, which, in true railway fashion, was over 2 miles distant from the town whose name it bore. The route is now part of the Exe Valley Way, but is consistently muddy due to the canopy of trees that has developed since the railway closed.

Glastonbury–Shapwick: C, W, UT, DR, 5m, ST 486392–ST 412418. A quiet Sustrans route which reuses part of the former Somerset & Dorset Railway's branch line from Evercreech Junction to Highbridge and Burnham. The westernmost exit is from Shapwick station site (ST 423411). Although one can walk beyond here for nearly another mile, the trackbed after that is in private ownership. The end of public access is marked by a locked gate immediately after the railway's old bridge over the South Drain. The remains of the little known Glastonbury Canal survive alongside the eastern part of this route.

Highbridge–Burnham: CIP, W, UT, DR, 1½m, ST 319472–ST 303488. This is not quite a 'normal' railway path, but is included as it was part of the former S&DR network. The course of the old branch line to Burnham can be picked up in Newtown Road, which starts on the west side of Church Road (the A38) in the centre of Highbridge. Newtown Road leads to Lakeside Track, a cycle trail, which has been built on or immediately adjacent to the old railway formation and can be followed through Apex Park, passing some attractive lakes en route. At the western entrance to the park (ST 310480), Lakeside Track joins Marine Drive which proceeds west to Burnham seafront, also mostly on the course of the old S&DR. Completists should cross Marine Drive and walk west via Willis Court, which is built on the former trackbed and rejoins Marine Drive at ST 308484. It is then just ¼ mile to Burnham seafront, where the Somerset Central Railway's trans-shipment jetty still projects into the Bristol Channel, although the rails have long since gone, and the height of the jetty has been reduced. Burnham-on-Sea station was situated opposite the Somerset & Dorset public house, which remains on the corner of the High Street and Abingdon Road. The traffic lights at the junction of the High Street, Marine Drive and Pier Street mark the western end of the old station, while the nearby pay-and-display car park, just off Marine Drive, has been built over the old station yard. In 2015 the Burnham Buffer Stop Memorial Project installed a set of railway buffers at the seaward end of Pier Street, where the railway line used to end.

Ilminster–Chard: C, W, UT, DR, 5½m, ST 347147–ST 329088. A Sustrans route completed in 2004, part of NCN33, which reuses the southern section of the GWR's former branch line from Taunton to Chard. Just off the southern end of the trail, Chard Central station (on Great Western Road) is of note, while out in the country there is much evidence of the Taunton Stop Line, a series of inland defences designed to hold back the Germans in the event of an invasion during the Second World War. The trail ends on the A30 just opposite the local Tesco supermarket, which occupies the site of the former Chard Town station.

North Molton–South Molton: W, UX, DT (part), 2½m, SS 742296–SS 721271. A pair of tramways from local mines, the New Florence Mine and the Crowbarn Mine, used to provide traffic to South Molton station on the Taunton–Barnstaple line (closed 1966). The New Florence Mine Tramway ran along the west bank of the River Mole, and the footpath listed here provides 1m of walking along the trackbed from south of North Molton Sewage Works to just above Bicknor Bridge. Further details can be found on Historic England's website, www.pastscape.org.uk.

Radstock–Great Elm (near Frome): C, W, UT, DR, 5½m, ST 691544–ST 751498. Starts in Avon but is mostly in Somerset; part of NCN24, Colliers Way. Community group 'Frome's Missing Links' is working on an extension from Great Elm, which will take this trail on to Frome town centre and railway station.

Roadwater–Comberow Top: W, UP, DR, 2¾m, ST 032383–ST 023345. Part of the West Somerset Mineral Railway, which starts just south of the former Roadwater station. The trackbed is used as a (very)

Above Left: This fine girder bridge over the Staffordshire & Worcestershire Canal at Tettenhall used to carry the GWR's Kingswinford branch from Oxley East Junction (near Wolverhampton) to Kingswinford Junction (near Stourbridge). There are no prizes for guessing why the locals call this 'Meccano Bridge'. Nowadays, the majority of this line can be enjoyed as the Kingswinford and Pensnett Railway Walks. (Phil Earnshaw)

Above right: This atmospheric photograph is recent but looks a century old or more. The two viaducts in the foreground connect the three Oxley Junctions north-west of Wolverhampton: that in the foreground carried the Wombourne line, now a popular railway path, while that behind is still in use for the main line to Shrewsbury. (Jenny Hartshorne)

minor public road as far as Pitt Mill, a paper mill, after which it becomes a farm track with permissive access to walkers. Exmoor National Park has established a waymarked trail, presumably permissive as well, through the tiny community of Comberow and on to the mighty Comberow Incline, which is ¾ mile long and has a ruling gradient of 1 in 4. At the top, ENP has also stabilised the remains of the winding house, which can now be viewed. Permissive access has been negotiated over a further section of the trackbed between ST 018343 and ST 009346, where Burrow Hill Engine House can be viewed.

Washford–Watchet: W, UX, DR, 2m, ST 049414–ST 070435. A further section of the West Somerset Mineral Railway, which for most of its length runs parallel to the preserved West Somerset Railway. The WSR has stations at both Washford and Watchet, which is very convenient if you prefer to walk one way and ride back the other. Gardens now occupy the trackbed in Watchet, but there is a signed diversion via Whitehall and a footpath that leads

into Mill Lane. At the junction of Mill Lane and West Street, turn left to view the WSMR's former Watchet station, where the platform has been enclosed to form a skittle alley for the local Royal British Legion. A local restaurant now uses the nearby engine shed.

Yeovil Pen Mill–Yeovil Town–Hendford: C, W, UT, DR, 1½m, ST 569162–ST 562159–ST 548153. Yeovil Country Park, once part of the GWR's branch line from Yeovil to Taunton and now part of NCN26. The site of Yeovil Town station is occupied by a new development, necessitating a short diversion. The western end of the trail finishes a few yards short of the site of Hendford Halt, which served the nearby Westland Helicopter factory (which is still there). From Hendford, the trackbed now accommodates the public road past the factory, then Bunford Lane, then the A3088 that uses the old formation as far as Cartgate roundabout on the A303, just short of Martock. From Cartgate to Muchelney, the line is privately owned, and in some places extremely overgrown, but a further 1-mile section is open to cyclists and walkers between Muchelney and the site of Langport West station (ST 422248–ST 414266).

Staffordshire

Aldersley (near Wolverhampton)–Pensnett Pools (near Dudley): C, H, W, UP, DR, 9½m, SJ 899012–SO 918884. The Kingswinford Railway Walk and the Pensnett Railway Walk. The old stations at both Tettenhall and Wombourne have been restored, the former being used as a café and the latter as a rangers' office.

Biddulph–Chell Heath–Milton (near Burslem): C, W, UX, DR, 7½m, SJ 878568–SJ 879529–SJ 897499. A continuation of the railway path from Congleton to Biddulph (see below). In recent years, Stoke-on-Trent City Council has made big improvements to the surface.

Cobridge (near Burslem)–Kidsgrove: C, W, NI, DR, 5½m, SJ 877490–SJ 840545. The Potteries Loopline Greenway, now part of NCN5, which reuses most of the former Potteries Loop Line from Etruria to Kidsgrove. At Pinnox Line Junction (SJ 865508), a connecting railway path heads south-west towards the Trent & Mersey Canal at Longport.

Congleton–Biddulph: W, UP, DR, 5m, SJ 865633–SJ 878568. The Biddulph Valley Way; starts in Cheshire, q.v. Connects with the route to Chell Heath and Milton (see above).

Froghall Wharf–Shirley Common: W, NI, DT, 1½m, SK 028477–SK 048480. This is the western end of a tramway, which once linked Caldon Low Quarry with the Caldon Canal at Froghall Wharf. A minor road leads from the wharf to the foot of a mile-long incline – the first of three on the line. The trackbed is shown on the OS Explorer map as 'Staffordshire

Moorlands Walks', which belies its history. While this particular line was built in 1847, others serving the quarry go back to a wooden waggon way of 1778. The trail ends at the junction of the A52 with the lane to Lower Shaw-wall, but it is worth studying the Explorer map to identify more of the former quarry lines from Caldon Low. Part of the 1804 plateway from the quarry has also become a public footpath; this is believed to be that which heads south-east from Froghall Wharf to near Whiston (¾m), again involving a steep incline (SK 028477–SK 035472).

Hulme End–Waterhouses: C, W, UP, DR, 8m, SK 103594–SK 091501. The course of the former narrow gauge Leek & Manifold Railway, donated to the local authority by the LMSR after closure. The scenery along the route is outstanding. Take care on the 1½-mile section south of Swainsley (which includes Swainsley Tunnel), because this has been turned into a road, albeit a narrow and usually quiet one.

Leek–Rushton Spencer: W, UX, DR, 5½m, SJ 971568–SJ 930634. Part of the scenic Churnet Valley line, which used to provide a direct link from Macclesfield to Uttoxeter. The trail continues a little way south of the start point given in Leek but peters out by the northern portal of Leek Tunnel.

Newcastle-Under-Lyme–Silverdale: C, W, UT, DR, 2½m, SJ 853463–SJ 814466. Part of the NSR's former line from Newcastle-Under-Lyme to Market Drayton, now part of NCN551.

Newport–Stafford: C, W, UT, DR, 10½m, SJ 759184–SJ 910233. The conversion of this long cross-country line started in 1991 and was finally completed in 2014, by which time £2 million had been invested in the project; the former railway is now the Way for the Millennium and part of NCN55. It starts from Castlefields (a housing estate ½ mile out of Stafford) and ends at the A41 bypass in Newport. See also entry under Shropshire, where the trail ends.

Oakamoor–Denstone: W, UX, DR, 4m, SK 053446–SK 099410. A further section of the Churnet Valley line, forming part of NCN54. The station at Alton, designed by the engineer of the NSR in the style of Augustus Pugin, is particularly noteworthy; it is now owned by the Landmark Trust and can be rented for holidays. It is hard to believe that this line was closed when one of its intermediate stations served the tourist honeypot of Alton Towers.

Steep Holm

While Steep Holm's railway remains are less than the 2-mile threshold required for inclusion in this gazetteer, it is unusual that the island should have had any kind of rail transport at all. Steep Holm was taken over by the military authorities in 1941, like its near neighbour, Flat Holm (see entry under Wales). The purpose was to protect the sea approaches to Bristol and Cardiff, to which end army engineers installed four 6in First World War naval guns with their attendant emplacements, look-out posts and ammunition stores. In order to deploy the necessary building materials around the island, the army built a jetty linked to the island's plateau via a switchback railway laid with 60cm gauge track that had been captured from the Germans during the First World War. The railway included three inclines from the jetty, which were cable-operated with diesel-powered winches used to haul the wagons. Virtually this entire network, track included, remains in place today, and visitors can follow the railway's zigzag course uphill from the jetty. The island is privately owned with trips available (weather permitting) from Knightstone Harbour in Weston-super-Mare from April to October. Further details are available from the island's website, www.steepholm.org.

Suffolk

Hadleigh–Raydon: C, H, W, UX, DR, 2½m, TM 030422–TM 060404. The western end of the GER's rural branch line from Bentleigh to Hadleigh, now known as The Hadleigh Railway Walk.

Haughley Junction–Brockford & Wetheringsett: W, NI, partly DR, 6m, TM 042627–TM 129659. This trail, the Middy Railway Footpath, was opened by Mid Suffolk District Council in 1995, but uses local rights of way to join together short sections of trackbed and is not a railway path in the usual sense of the term. The Mid Suffolk Light Railway Society has established a railway centre at Brockford & Wetheringsett station, where an admission ticket entitles visitors to walk a further section of trackbed in its ownership.

Southwold–Blythburgh: W, UX, DR, 3½m, TM 505766–TM 453755. The eastern end of the narrow gauge Southwold Railway, which closed in 1929. A modern footbridge carries walkers over the River Blyth on the piers of the railway's original swing bridge. After this crossing, follow the trackbed until the trail descends from the embankment to avoid a missing bridge, whose concrete abutments are visible to the right (north-west). Follow the footpath to TM 481748 where it meets the B1387 Walberswick–Blythburgh road and turn right (west). About 200yds past the entrance to Eastwoodlodge Farm, a trail veers off right (north-west) to the southern edge of a wooded area (the Walberswick National Nature Reserve), rejoining the trackbed at TM 477749, initially on a low embankment, then descending a steep, winding cutting. The trackbed becomes a public footpath at TM 467748, passing through Deadman's Covert to emerge on an embankment, which runs alongside the reed beds on the south side of the Blyth Estuary. This footpath continues to Station Road, Blythburgh, at TM 453755.

Sudbury–Lavenham: This is actually three separate routes (the Valley Walk, the Melford Walk and part of St Edmund Way) which are close enough to form a longer walk of about 9m, with nearly 7m on the southern section of the old railway from Sudbury to Bury St Edmunds.

- **Sudbury–Long Melford:** C, W, UT, DR, 2½m, TL 861447–TL 874458. A popular walking and cycling trail known as the Valley Walk. Arriving in Long Melford from the Sudbury direction, head north along the B1064 to pick up the Melford Walk, which is signed off this road at the site of a demolished rail-over-road bridge.
- **Long Melford:** W, UX, DR, 1¼m, TL 861447–TL 874458. The Melford Walk, a linear route along the trackbed to the east of the village, which includes a number of intact railway bridges. At the north end (which comes out in Bull Lane), turn right to reach the A134; St Edmund Way lies about a mile north along this road on the east side. However, rather than walking along this busy main road, consider this route: (1) Follow the minor road to Acton Place as far as TL 882460; (2) Turn left here on to a bridleway (Roydon Drift) and follow this to TL 876468 just north of Lodge Farm on the A134; (3) At TL 876468, turn right on to a footpath which meets St Edmund Way just before it joins the old railway for the final 3 miles into Lavenham.
- **North of Acton Place–Lavenham:** W, UX, DR, 3¼m, TL 884475–TL 916497. Part of St Edmund Way incorporating the Lavenham Walk at its eastern end. In spring 2015, the site of Lavenham station (TL 917498) was redeveloped and a new path installed under the Bury Road Bridge. The route that St Edmund Way takes between TL 910495 and the old station is indirect, but it does lead walkers to a place which connects with

Lavenham's streets instead of dropping them on the village's western periphery.

Surrey

Surrey has lost few of its railways due to its proximity to London, hence the short list below. A further short railway walk (c. ¾m) that is worth a mention is that within Brookwood Cemetery, where the course of the former London Necropolis Railway can be traced fairly easily. The old line is joined immediately outside the southern exit from Brookwood station.

Horton Country Park, near Epsom: H, W, UP, DR, 2m, access at TQ 191617 off Horton Lane, to the west of Epsom and Ewell. This is Surrey's least known railway path, actually a network of contractor's lines installed to help build the Horton group of hospitals, once the largest facility in Europe for the care and treatment of the mentally handicapped. After the hospitals were built, the line was retained to deliver coal and other supplies. The railway was closed in 1950, with the hospitals following years later. In 1973,

Just west of Southwold, the Southwold Railway crossed the River Blyth via a swing bridge. The swing bridge is no more, but its abutments and piers have been reused to accommodate the new river crossing shown here being impressively busy. (Neil Hebborn)

the local council purchased two of the redundant hospital farms to create Horton Country Park. An excellent leaflet entitled 'Days of Steam' (based on Alan A. Jackson's *Railway Magazine* article of 1981) can be downloaded from www.epsom-ewell.gov.uk; this makes tracing the lines relatively easy, since it includes a reproduction of a large-scale OS map from 1933. Most of the main line to West Park Hospital survives, together with parts of the branches to Long Grove and Horton Hospitals.

Peasmarsh (Guildford)–Baynards: C, H, W, UP, DR, 9m, SU 993465–TQ 078349. The northern end of the popular Downs Link path, which continues into West Sussex, q.v. Connects at Peasmarsh with the towpath of the River Wey Navigation via a new bridge installed in 2006 to replace one demolished shortly after the railway closed.

Tongham–Ash Junction: W, UP, DR, 1½m, SU 887492–SU 909502. Part of a former through route from Guildford to Winchester and Southampton. Passes the privately owned Ash Green station near the east end. Note that there is no access to or from the trackbed at Ash Junction, but there are several access points in Ash Green village, one from the bridge by the old station.

Sussex, East

Barcombe Mills–Anchor Lane: W, UP, DR, 1m, TQ 430149–TQ 440160. A permissive route on part of the former Lewes to Uckfield line. It starts at Barcombe Mills station and extends for a mile northwards, where a right turn leads to the delightful Anchor Inn on the River Ouse. For many years, Barcombe Mills station was open to the public as a tea room, but it is now a private residence with leylandii gradually enveloping the site. There are plenty of footpaths in the area, which provide access from the Anchor Inn to

Isfield, where there is another finely preserved station, this one the home of the Lavender Line steam railway.

Near Devil's Dyke–Hangleton: C, W, UT, DR, 1¼m, TQ 268091–TQ 270075. See entry under Sussex, West.

East Grinstead–Groombridge: W, UX, DR, 9m, TQ 400379–TQ 521368. The Forest Way, which just east of East Grinstead passes a former home of Dr Richard Beeching, who famously brought the axe to many branch lines in the 1960s. In recent years, the surface of the trail at the East Grinstead end has been much improved. Beyond Ashurst Junction (TQ 521368) where the trackbed ends, there is a link into Groombridge village.

Polegate–Heathfield: C, W, UT, DR, 10½m, TQ 584052–TQ 578217. The popular Cuckoo Trail, now part of NCN21, which has been extended from Heathfield station site through Heathfield Tunnel for about ½ mile to the north. An aspiration to accommodate more of NCN21 on the old trackbed towards Eridge appears to have come to nought, no doubt because East Sussex County Council owns little of the route. Note that Heathfield Tunnel is open only during 'the summer' which, unhelpfully, the ESCC website leaves undated.

Rye–Camber: W, UX, DT, 2½m, TQ 925206–TQ 955188. The Rye & Camber Tramway (1½ miles). Virtually all of the extant trackbed of this 2½-mile long, 3ft gauge line can now be walked, although some sections have been lost, thanks in part to former gravel workings. It is best to start at the Rye end of the line, where the trackbed can be accessed just off the A259 at grid reference TQ 925206. Two footpaths start here, so take care to follow the northerly one that passes the southern boundary of the local school. Nearly a mile of the route, including Halfway House station, has been lost beneath Northpoint Beach, which is now a lake for water sports, but a diversion around the southern edge of the lake can be followed to TQ 942195, where the line is rejoined. From here, the trackbed survives as a concrete road, with the original rails still evident in places. (The army laid the concrete during the Second World War, when numerous supply dumps were built in the Rye area.) Golf Links station survives at TQ 944191, where the rails of a passing loop can still be seen. Shortly after this, there's a revelation: Rye Golf Club has opened a permissive footpath across the rest of the trackbed, which survives as a shallow, grassy embankment across its golf links. The line continues to the site of Camber Sands station (presumed to be at TQ 955188), but there is no trace of the timber structure, which once stood here. A few yards to the south, a kissing gate leads on to a sandy footpath from the nearby dunes; turn left here to reach Camber Road, which connects Rye with Camber. There is a bus stop to the right along Camber Road, called 'Camber Farm Lane', from which buses can be caught back to Rye (hourly Monday to Saturday, two-hourly Sunday).

Rye–Rye Harbour: W, UX, DR, 1m, TQ 920199– TQ 936192. Part of the former Rye Harbour Branch. This 1½-mile standard gauge branch left the Ashford–Hastings line just west of Rye station. It can be joined on the southern edge of Rye at grid reference TQ 920199, where a kissing gate leads on to a narrow waymarked path enclosed by bushes. This is the trackbed, which soon opens out on to a shallow embankment across sheep pastures, with fine views of Camber Castle to the south. The old railway can now be followed, with very minor diversions, as far as the former level crossing on Harbour Road (TQ 936192). Do not turn back here, but continue by road to Rye Harbour, turn left at the T-junction where Harbour Road ends, and walk past the William

the Conqueror pub to the water's edge. Turn left here and you will see the railway trackbed heading back towards Rye. Look around carefully, and you will see another grassy embankment nearby, which carried a branch off of the branch. While you are here, do not be surprised to see railway trackbeds heading off at 90 degrees to each other: there were three wagon turntables in Rye Harbour, which explain how this seemingly impossible feat was achieved. There is a bus stop near the end of Harbour Road, from which buses can be caught back to Rye (hourly Monday to Saturday, no service Sunday).

Rye Harbour–Pett Level: W, NI, DT, 4½m, believed to be TQ 938189–TQ 935184 and TQ 941180–TQ 912166. This line has not been explored in detail, since two railway ramblers discovered it by accident when visiting the area and studying a 1936 edition of the Ordnance Survey's 1in map of Hastings. The line started immediately north of the Church of the Holy Spirit in Rye Harbour and then negotiated a large 'S' bend to reach the beach at TQ 940177. From here, it followed the coast in a south-westerly direction to TQ 904147 on the seaward edge of Pett Level. The line was built in 1934 to a gauge of 2ft and covered a distance of 5 miles. It was used in the construction of sea defences along Winchelsea Beach, but this work was completed in 1946, when the line was abandoned. Study of the modern Explorer map (number 125) indicates that footpaths follow the route from TQ 938189 to TQ 935184, and from TQ 941180 to TQ 944178. At the latter point, the trackbed reaches the coastal path, where the tramway turned south-west towards Hastings. A comparison of the old and new maps suggests that the coastal path follows the course of the old tramway as far as Pett Level Road on Winchelsea Beach (TQ 912166).

Sussex, West

Baynards–Christ's Hospital: C, H, W, UX, DR, 6m, TQ 078349–TQ 139296. This route is a continuation of the Downs Link, which starts at Peasmarsh (see entry under Surrey). The section within West Sussex begins with a diversion over the top of Baynards Tunnel, whose northern portal has been buried, and then follows the old line (originally from Guildford) all the way to what used to be platform 5 of Christ's Hospital station. Here for many years, a locked gate barred access to the modern platform 2, which is served by trains from Bognor Regis to London Victoria. If it remains locked, there is now a link path that goes underneath the railway and leads to the station forecourt for platform 1 (southbound) or the next leg of the trail to Shoreham-by-Sea (see below).

The LBSCR line from Chichester to Midhurst lost its passenger service in 1935 and became a dead end in 1951 when a storm and blocked culvert combined to bring down an embankment south of Midhurst. The southern section is now a railway path called Centurion Way, with the Lavant area featuring a number of sculptures such as the 'Lavant Track Gang'. The figures are made from old gas cylinders, sleeper chairs, rail keys (for ears) and shovels reputed to have come from the Russian army. (Jenny Vinter)

Chichester–Lavant–West Dean (no exit currently): C, W, UT, DR, 5½m, SU 857048–SU 856086–SU 857126. A path dating from 1995, extended twice and known as Centurion Way since it crosses a Roman road south of the palatial Lavant station. Starts at the western edge of Chichester alongside Bishop Luffa School. At Lavant, it is necessary to follow a residential road built on or near the old railway for just under a mile. The trackbed, which is never more than a few yards away, is rejoined at SU 855094. A report from the Planning Committee of the South Downs National Park included the following: 'This proposal [for the 2015 Binderton–West Dean extension] comprises part of a larger ambition to create a shared pedestrian/cycle lane from Chichester to Midhurst including a link to the South Downs Way.' Currently, there is no exit at the north end pending an agreement between various agencies about how to get trail users safely across the busy A286 and into West Dean village, so pro tem anyone heading there should leave the railway path at Binderton (SU 855107), turn west along a short link to the A286 and then turn north along the separate roadside cycle path (a good example of this type of facility). It is just a matter of time before the arrangements at West Dean are improved, for the village includes the famous West Dean House and Gardens, a pub, an enterprising village shop, a primary school and, just beyond all that, the Weald & Downland Open Air Museum.

Chichester–Selsey (parts only): The following fragments are listed here because it is remarkable that anything of this cheaply built Colonel Stephens railway should survive at all. These sections can be linked by following local public footpaths, albeit with some circuitous detours. In the 1990s, Selsey resident George Smith went to a lot of trouble waymarking this route as the Selsey Tram Way, but unfortunately few of these signs still survive. In March 2001,

Chichester District Council allocated funds to a Chichester–Selsey cycle trail, which was expected to reuse parts the old tramway. Phase 1 was started in 2006, but this is a very long-term project, and all has gone quiet in the current economic climate. As an aside, the Chichester–Selsey line was really a railway, but is known as the Selsey Tramway because it was built to light engineering standards under the 1896 Light Railways Act.

- **Stockbridge Road, Chichester–Chichester Canal:** W, UP, DR, ½m, SU 856037–SU 861030. Starts as a signed public footpath and leads on to the embankment, which runs alongside and above the Chichester Canal, south of the city basin.
- **Hunston Lift Bridge–opposite site of Hunston station:** W, UX, DR, ½m, SU 860021–SU 859015. A short length of trackbed now absorbed into the local footpath network. The concrete abutment of the former lift bridge over the Chichester Canal can be seen at the north end, where the railway used to cross the canal. The canal towpath provides a convenient link between this and the section above.
- **Sidlesham–Ferry:** W, UX, DR, ¾m, SZ 860973–SZ 857963. A section of trackbed alongside the picturesque Pagham Harbour Nature Reserve, which had to be embanked following a breach of the sea wall between Selsey and Bognor in 1910; the rail replacement bus service at the time was a horse-drawn carriage. The 1910 inundation created the modern nature reserve.

Christ's Hospital–Shoreham-by-Sea: C, H, W, UP, DR, 17½m, TQ 143281–TQ 207059. The southern leg of the Downs Link, which has seen much resurfacing work in recent years, delivering marked improvements. There are signed diversions around Partridge Green (short), Bramber (fairly long) and Botolphs (short).

Nr Devil's Dyke–Hangleton: C, W, UT, DR, 1¼m, TQ 268091–TQ 270075. This is the railway part of a cycle trail from Devil's Dyke to Hangleton. The section from TQ 268091 to TQ 261102 (Devil's Dyke station) is privately owned, so please do not trespass. Diligent explorers can find some evidence of the line in the urban section from Hangleton to Aldrington station, but this is not an easy task without old maps and photographs. Steam locomotives on this line had a steep climb, as cyclists and walkers will discover.

Three Bridges–East Grinstead: W, UX, DR, 6m, TQ 289367–TQ 388382. The Worth Way, which has been much improved in recent years including complete resurfacing in September 2015 between East Grinstead and Gullege. A feasibility study carried out by Sustrans for the local authorities regarding a possible East Grinstead town trail along the former St Margaret's Loop (which starts at TQ 388382) unfortunately came to nought. East Grinstead's first railway station, now a funeral directors, is just east of the end of this trail at TQ 392383.

Tyne & Wear

Allerdene (Team Valley)–Wrekenton–Pelaw: C, W, NI, DT, 4m, NZ 255586–NZ 272595–NZ 295623. This trail follows most of the trackbed of the Teams Colliery Waggonway, which connected coal mines at Ravensworth Park (in the Team Valley) with coal staithes at Pelaw Main on the River Tyne. It is a rather hilly route, thanks to the waggonway's inclines, and includes two fairly short on-road sections.

Blackhill (Consett)–Swalwell: W, UP, DR, 10½m, NZ 099514–NZ 200621. The Derwent Walk, which starts in Durham, q.v. Most of the minor rail-over-road bridges on this trail have been demolished, but by way of compensation it includes four substantial viaducts.

Consett–Chester-le-Street–Washington: C, W, UT, DR, 18m, NZ 099493–NZ 273535–NZ 313550. The Consett & Sunderland Railway Path, the westernmost 14½ miles of which are in Durham, q.v.

Hebburn Colliery–Wardley–Springwell Bankfoot: C, W, NI, DR, 4½m, NZ 321652–NZ 306617–NZ 285590. Part of the Bowes Railway Path, which connects at Springwell with the historic Bowes Railway. See also the entry for Springwell Top–Marley Hill (below).

Marley Hill (Andrews House Station)–Dunston: C, W, NI, DT, 3m, NZ 209573–NZ 232614. The Tanfield Railpath, which follows the trackbed and inclines of the Tanfield Railway. There are three inclines altogether: Lobley Hill at 1 in 18, Fulgar Bar (Baker's Bank) at 1 in 20, and Sunniside at 1 in 50. Published sources give various figures for the gradients, but these are the ones published by Gateshead Council, which ought to know.

Monkseaton Metro Station–near Seaton Delaval Hall: W, C, HIP, NI, DR, 3m, NZ 347721–NZ 317762. Part of the NER's Monkseaton to Morpeth line. Continues into Northumberland.

Newburn (Newcastle)–Wylam Bridge: W, NI, DR, 4½m, NZ 163655–NZ 110642. See entry under Northumberland, where this path ends.

South Gosforth–Wallsend: C, W, UT, DT, 2m, NZ 256682–NZ 279673. A section of waggonway reopened as a cycle trail in October 2009. The waggonway, known variously as the Coxlodge Waggonway, the Kenton & Coxlodge Waggonway and the Gosforth & Kenton Waggonway, was opened in 1808 and connected the South Gosforth area with coal staithes on the River Tyne at Wallsend. The new route is 3 metres wide and has been fully lit, signposted and landscaped; it finishes near Wallsend Golf Club.

Springwell Top–Marley Hill (Andrews House Station): C, W, NI, DR, 4½m, NZ 278575–NZ 210572. A further section of the Bowes Railway Path. Starts at the western end of the current Bowes Railway operation and provides a trackbed-based link to Andrews House station on the Tanfield Railway. Forms part of the Great North Forest Trail. Cyclists should note that this is a hilly route and not suitable for racing or road tyres.

Sunderland (High Newport)–South Hetton: C, W, UT, DR, 8m, NZ 381541–NZ 378452. Part of NCN1. Starts from near the big sports complex on Silksworth Lane, Sunderland, where you can practise everything from tennis to snow sports. NCN70 also passes this complex, facing the town centre in one direction and East Herrington in the other; despite extensive landscaping, this trail has something of a railway look about it, e.g. the occasional bridge, and could be part of the local Hetton Colliery Railway. (There's something to research on a cold winter's night.) Sunderland–South Hetton connects at South Hetton with the Haswell to Hart Countryside Walk (see entry under Durham). If you are using the trail from the South Hetton end, you may find it easier to start from the bridleway which heads north off of Front Street at NZ 378453.

Wallsend–Byker: C, W, NI, DR, 4m, NZ 305663–NZ 267645. Formed from most of the NER's line from Percy Main to Byker, this route keeps close to the River Tyne, unlike the still operational line between these two communities, which now forms part of the Tyne & Wear metro system. The trail forms part of Hadrian's Wall Path and NCN72. East of Wallsend, further sections of the NER line have been linked together to create a cycle trail to Percy

Main but, in disued railway terms, this part of the route is fragmentary and the section listed here is the part most worth following. If you want to explore what remains between Wallsend and Percy, follow the eastward signs for NCN72.

Washington–Sunderland: C, W, NI, DR, 5½m, NZ 322542–NZ 395565. This trail follows part of the old Penshaw–Sunderland line. On reaching South Hylton, it runs alongside the Tyne and Wear metro, which was extended to this point (via Sunderland) in 2002. The trail ends by Park Lane station in Sunderland city centre.

Warwickshire

In addition to the routes listed below, Warwickshire includes the Lias Line Cycleway (NCN41) from Rugby to Warwick (21½m). This uses two short sections of the old Rugby–Leamington Spa railway (Draycote–Birdingbury and Offchurch–Radford Semele) plus a lot of country lanes, but there are aspirations to open up the whole of the line between Rugby and Radford Semele (11½m), where the cycle trail switches to the towpath of the Grand Union Canal to access Leamington and Warwick. Railway Paths Ltd owns the trackbed except for *c*. 60yds west of the B4455 crossing (SP 375661), where a footpath runs parallel on the north side. It may take the construction of HS2 to get things moving, for John Grimshaw Associates have planned the 'HS2 Cycleway' which will follow the approximate course of the new line. Their plans show the cycleway using the Daventry line from Southam & Long Itchington to Marton Junction before joining the 'main' line and heading west to Radford Semele; the trackbed from Marton Junction back to Bilton (on the edge of Rugby) is shown as a potential feeder route. As things stand, the line can be walked from New Bilton to Radford Semele (SP 489755–SP 354649), but it is very wet and muddy in places (especially cuttings), which would make a cycle ride very challenging. There is a single missing bridge east of Offchurch at SP 375661, where the old railway crosses the Fosse Way: take care here because it is a fast road.

Alcester–Wixford–Salford Priors: W, NI, DR, 3½m, SP 084570–SP 086545–SP 080521. Part of the old MR line from Barnt Green to Evesham, this is an unlikely survivor as a railway walk. Anyone tracing the route will need the local OS Explorer map since a few detours are required, but generally speaking a public footpath runs on or immediately alongside the line from just south of Alcester to the A46 near Salford Priors. Access at the Salford Priors end is from the public footpath at SP 078512. What is so unusual is that parts of this old railway have become a public footpath – an outcome that hardly ever occurred with closed railways.

Draycote–Birdingbury: C, W, DR, 1¼m, SP 448707–SP 430690. A short section of the former LNWR line from Rugby to Leamington Spa (see above). In 2010, Sustrans was reported to be extending this by 3m to Bilton Lane (SP 475746) near Cawston, west of Rugby, but nothing came of it, perhaps due to the start of government austerity measures. At about this time, a group of local residents formed the Cawston Greenway group, which is working to convert this part of the line into a viable trail. At Draycote, Railway Paths has erected a sign, which states that the trackbed towards Rugby can walked or cycled on a permissive basis.

Kenilworth–Berkswell: C, W, UP, DR, 4m, SP 298732–SP 257768. The Kenilworth–Berkswell Greenway, once the LNWR's Coventry-avoiding line, and now variously part of NCN52, NCN523 and the 'Coventry Way'. At the Kenilworth end, a fine new bridge

(SP 297735) has been installed over the A429 at Crackley.

Newton–Rugby–Rainsbrook: C, W, NI, DR, 4½m, SP 532789–SP 517725. The Great Central Walk, a linear nature reserve following the former GCR through the centre of Rugby. The demolished bridge over the Oxford Canal is negotiated by a diversion, which conveniently passes Rugby railway station. Access to the northern (i.e. Newton) end is at SP 532788, and to the southern end at SP 517725, off Onley Lane. The remains of Rugby Central station can be seen off Hillmorton Road at SP 514745.

Nuneaton–near Higham on the Hill: C, W, NI, DR, 1½m, SP 357929–SP 367950. The Weddington Country Walk, part of the former LNW and Midland Joint Railway from Nuneaton to Market Bosworth and Shackerstone, whence separate lines continued to Coalville and Moira. Ends at Hungry Hill, just north of the A5, with a link via a minor road into Higham on the Hill.

Rugby Station–Rugby Brownsover Road: C, W, UT, DR, 1m, SP 506762–SP 496775. This trail opened in 2012 and can be found about 500yds west of Rugby station – aim for the new Network Rail bridge over the tracks. It reuses the start of the former LNWR line from Rugby to Nuneaton, and includes the eleven-arch Grade II-listed Leicester Road Viaduct as well as a double-track bridge further south over the Oxford Canal.

Stratford-Upon-Avon–Long Marston: C, W, NI, DR, 6m, SP 195549–SP 155479. Part of the former GWR Stratford–Cheltenham line – starting just south of Stratford station and continuing to a point just north of the rail-connected military depot at Long Marston. See also entry for Cheltenham (Gloucestershire).

West Midlands

Aldersley (near Wolverhampton)–Pensnett Pools (near Dudley): H, W, UP, DR, 9½m, SJ 899012–SO 918884. The Kingswinford Railway Walk and the Pensnett Railway Walk. For further details, see entry under Staffordshire.

Harborne–Rotton Park: W, UP, DR, 2¼m, SP 035850–SP 045874. Most of the short Harborne branch, an early Birmingham commuter line.

Ryecroft–Pelsall: C, W, UT, DR, 2¼m, SP 016999–SK 025030. Part of the former LNWR route from Lichfield Line Junction to Pelsall, where separate lines diverged to Hednesford and Lichfield; now part of NCN5. There is a diversion off the line in the Goscote area. There are many disused railways in this area, several of which have provided short contributions to local cycle trails. Brownhills West station on the Chasewater Railway is about 2 miles north of Pelsall.

Near Sandwell Junction–Swan Village: C, W, NI, DR, 2½m, SP 022898–SO 994922. The West Bromwich Parkway, part of the former GWR line from Birmingham Snow Hill to Wolverhampton. The Parkway used to have exclusive use of the old trackbed until the opening of the Midland Metro. At Swan Village, the trail continues northwards for another ½ mile to Black Lake (SO 991931), just a few yards west of the old railway/modern Metro lines.

Wiltshire

Chippenham–Calne: C, W, UP, DR, 5m, ST 928739–ST 995708. The reuse of this rural branch, now part of NCN4, required the construction of three new bridges: two to replace railway structures which were removed after the line closed and one to cross the

A4. The surface is usually firm but could do with some attention in the vicinity of Stanley Bridge. For many years the trail began inconveniently in D'Arcy Close, about ½m east of Chippenham station, but in early 2015 a new path was opened around the north-eastern perimeter of the now redeveloped Chippenham Cattle Market. This permits walkers (but not cyclists) to access the trail via Cocklebury Road, the footpath that begins at ST 924739, and the new 'perimeter trail' that begins at ST 925740.

Ludgershall–Collingbourne Ducis: W, UX, DR, 2m, SU 260510–SU 245536. A permissive route once managed by MAFF (Ministry for Agriculture, Fisheries and Food), and also a 'detached' part of the Midland & South Western Junction Railway (see next entry). The views over the rolling Wiltshire downland are most attractive, but be warned that the route ends in Collingbourne Ducis at the site of a demolished underbridge that took the railway over Mill Lane. As you approach this, look out for a path that leads off on the right hand side. Follow this and you will reach Mill Lane via only a slight gradient; turn left and the main road through the village is just 50yds ahead.

Midland & South Western Junction Railway: This cross-country line, known as 'Swindon's other railway', has fared remarkably well in north Wiltshire, with the majority of its course from Marlborough to the county border being preserved as either a railway path or, in the Blunsdon area, as a preserved railway. To make it easy for walkers and cyclists to trace the route (which is about 25 miles long including diversions), the following entries are listed in order, from south to north:

The GWR branch line to Calne is now an attractive rural trail, opened at considerable cost when one considers the lost bridges, which had to be replaced. However, several of the railway's original bridges survive, including this one just out of Chippenham which has a pleasing vernacular appearance, recalling bridges on the local canals. (Author)

- **Marlborough–Chiseldon and Chiseldon–M4:** C, W, UT, DR, 9½m, SU 198686–SU 192793 and SU 184801–SU 179811. The largest single section of the M&SWJR, now known as the Chiseldon and Marlborough Railway Path. At Marlborough, the trail will soon start from the site of the former M&SWJR station (SU 193687) now that Wiltshire CC is no longer using it as a depot; the start point shown here is tucked away in the town's backstreets. North of Chiseldon, the trackbed has been converted into a cycle trail as far as the M4, where the motorway takes over for about a mile as it skirts around the south of Swindon. The path crosses the motorway via a public footpath, which it then follows into Swindon via Coate Water.
- **Swindon Old Town–Rushey Platt (near Toothill):** C, W, UT, DR, 2m, SU 157834–SU 132838. This section starts from near the site of the M&SWJR's Swindon Town station. Only part of a platform remains from this once important railway centre.

Above left: *Many know of Swindon's affiliation with the Great Western Railway, but few know of its connection with the Midland & South Western Junction Railway, which operated a cross-country line from Andover to Andoversford with onward connections to Southampton and Cheltenham. This is the M&SWJR's trackbed, now a cycle trail, just west of its Swindon Town station. (Author)*

Above right: *South of South Cerney, the trackbed of the former M&SWJR includes no fewer than four of these brick-built road-over-rail viaducts. Each one comprises nine or ten arches, and photographers can have great fun taking arty shots from within the piers, which are hollow. (Author)*

- **Rivermead (West Swindon)–Elborough Bridge (near Haydon Wick):** C, W, NI, DR, 2m, SU 127852–SU 122873. Leaving urban Swindon behind, this section of the M&SWJR terminates near the southern end of the restored Swindon & Cricklade Railway, which has reinstated the line between Haydon Wick and Hayes Knoll. (The railway's headquarters are at the intermediate station of Blunsdon.)
- **Hayes Knoll–Cricklade:** C, W, NI, DR, 1¼m, SU 104913–SU 099932. A Sustrans cycle trail, continuing from a point just north of the Swindon & Cricklade Railway. The S&CR hopes to extend to Cricklade, so this trail may one day be accompanied by a running line.
- **Cricklade–South Cerney:** W, NI, DR, 3½m, SU 091938–SU 048978. Wiltshire's last section of the M&SWJR, which continues into Gloucestershire. Passes through the Cotswold Water Park (old water-filled quarries) where, not surprisingly, the trackbed is often wet. The north end of this section includes four striking, brick-built road-over-railway viaducts.

Yorkshire, North

Grosmont–Goathland and Goathland–Moorgates: CIP, HIP, W, NI, DR, 5m, NZ 827050–NZ 833014 (footpath) and NZ 835013–SE 845994 (bridleway). Known locally as the Rail Trail, this right of way follows the course of the old Whitby & Pickering Railway and includes the Beck Hole Incline. Stations on the North Yorkshire Moors Railway serve both Grosmont and Goathland. If you are walking as far as Moorgates, you will need to cross Goathland via Beck Hole Road and The Green.

Ingleby Greenhow (near Battersby)–Blakey Junction: C, W, UX, DR, 11m, NZ 592061–SE 683990. Part of the former Rosedale Railway and now incorporated into the Lyke Wake Walk for part of its length. The section of trackbed listed here has been dedicated as a public bridleway, which is popular with mountain bikers, but note that a few very short sections have been washed out. At Blakey Junction the line divided with separate branches going to Low Baring (SE 708978, 3½m) and Bank Top (SE 720950, 3½m) above Rosedale Abbey. While no public right of way is shown on the map above Blakey Junction, there is no practical impediment to walking these trackbeds, and local ramblers' websites include reports of doing so. The views from the trackbed around Rosedale are spectacular, as are some of the railway's cuttings and embankments.

Stamford Bridge–Gate Hemsley: C, W, UT, DR, ½m, SE 712552–SE 705556. This section of trackbed includes the notable Stamford Bridge Viaduct, which accounts for so short a path appearing in this list. For further details, see entry under Humberside.

Starbeck (near Harrogate)–Ripley: C, W, NI, DR, 2¾m, SE 325564–SE 287598. Cycle trails occupy two sides of the railway triangle just east of Harrogate where the line to Northallerton branched off from the still operation Leeds–York line. These cycle trails meet at the apex of the triangle at Old Bilton (formerly Bilton Road Junction, SE 314575), where NCN67 continues over Nidd Viaduct (SE 307583) to Pateley Bridge Line Junction (SE 302594), where it follows the Pateley Bridge branch as far as the A61 south of Ripley (SE 287598). Back at the Harrogate end, the cycle trail on the north-west chord of the triangle runs from Old Bilton (SE 314577) back to Dragon Junction (SE 311565), with NCN67 providing a westward link into the town centre.

Wetherby–Spofforth: C, W, UT, DR, 2½m, SE 405487–SE 365507. The Harland Way, part of NCN67 and formerly part of the NER Church Fenton–Harrogate line. The route starts in West Yorkshire and includes the whole of Wetherby railway triangle, which is bounded by SE 405487, SE 396483 and SE 398492.

Whitby–Scarborough: W, UP, DR, 23½m, NZ 893107–TA 030887. The scenic Cinder Track, named after the material on which this former NER branch line was laid. Previously known as the Scarborough and Whitby Railway Path and now part of NCN1, this route includes, just west of Whitby, the massive Larpool Viaduct that consists of thirteen spans crossing the River Esk at a height of 120ft. If you can sample only part of it, the section from Whitby to Robin Hood's Bay is hard to beat. This is one of the greatest railway walks in the UK with only two short diversions, at Ravenscar (around the closed tunnel) and Scalby (around redevelopment) respectively. Access in Whitby is from Southend Gardens, and in Scarborough is off Commercial Street. In 2011, there were fears that the northern end of the trail would have to be closed to permit reinstatement of the railway to serve a new potash mine south of Whitby. The North York Moors National Park Authority gave planning permission for this in June 2015, but the potash will now be removed via a 23-mile tunnel to Wilton International Complex between Redcar and Middlesbrough, so this popular railway path is safe.

York–Osbaldwick: C, W, UT, DR, 2m, SE 603534–SE 632521. Part of the former Derwent Valley Light Railway, now incorporated into NCN66.

York (Woodthorpe)–Barlby: C, W, UT, mainly DR, 9½m, SE 581484–SE 631359. This route comprises most of the York and Selby Path. Formerly part of the East Coast Main Line, it became a railway path when the Selby coalfield was extended beneath the trackbed in the 1980s, necessitating the construction of a high speed rail diversion – the first section of new main line to be built in the UK for decades. Between Riccall and Barlby, the trackbed accommodates a new road, with cyclists and walkers catered for by an adjoining cycle track, which leaves the old railway formation at Barlby and continues to Selby via minor roads.

YORKSHIRE, NORTH

Yorkshire, South

Ardsley–Cudworth (West Green): C, W, NI, DR, 2½m, SE 373056–SE 375085. A branch off the Wombwell–Barnsley trail (see below).

Beighton–Killamarsh–Staveley (Inkersall Green)–Arkwright Town: C, W, NI, DR, 9½m, SK 446836–SK 449824–SK 425723– SK 426705. Part of the Trans Pennine Trail which reuses a section of the late lamented Great Central Railway. The southwards extension to Arkwright Town is fairly recent, with the trail now ending in the former pit yard south of the A632 rail overbridge. Only the first 2 miles of this route are in South Yorkshire, the rest lying in Derbyshire.

Dunford Bridge–Penistone–near Wortley: C, W, UT, DR, 10½m, SE 157023–SE 251032–SK 297988. A long-distance trail based on two former GCR lines, that from Dunford Bridge to Penistone being part of the famous Woodhead route across the Pennines (see entry for Hadfield–Woodhead under Derbyshire). At Penistone, the route switches on to the connecting line that led to Wortley, Deepcar and Sheffield Victoria. Dunford Bridge to Penistone is part of NCN62, the Trans Pennine Trail, while Penistone to Wortley is part of NCN6.

Harlington–Conisbrough Viaduct–Warmsworth: C, W, UP, DR, 3½m, SE 488016–SK 526992–SK 537994. This is another part of the Trans Pennine Trail, NCN62, which can be picked up at the south-east corner of Harlington village and leads to the western edge of the Doncaster conurbation. It uses part of the former Dearne Valley Railway, which ran from Brierley Junction, north of Grimethorpe, to Black Carr West Junction, south of Doncaster. The modern trail diverts from the trackbed in the vicinity of Denaby Ings Nature Reserve, but that is a small price to pay for what lies near the south-eastern end of the route – Conisbrough Viaduct. This gigantic structure comprises a central girder section with fourteen arches to the north and seven to the south; it is 1,527ft long and was constructed from 15 million bricks. Following years of unofficial use as a footpath, Sustrans laid a tarmac path across it which links with the TPT at the north-western end.

Laughton Common–Thurcroft Colliery: C, W, UT, DR, 2m, SK 507864–SK 502889. The Thurcroft Colliery branch opened on 22 September 2006 as part of the National Cycle Network. At the moment this route is of purely local significance, i.e. it connects only with minor roads and footpaths rather than other cycle trails.

Meadowhall Station (Sheffield)–near Ecclesfield: C, W, NI, DR, 2m, SK 391913–SK 370939. This is the start of the Chapeltown Greenway, which (according to plans first published in 2003) is intended eventually to reach Chapeltown. The route is based on part of the old GCR Tinsley to Barnsley line, but currently stops at Butterthwaite Lane, Ecclesfield; land access issues appear to be preventing any further progress to the north.

Tilts–Bentley–Warmsworth: C, W, UT, DR, 5¼m, SE 571086–SE 559061–SE 549013. This route across the west side of Doncaster was opened at a cost of £180,000 in 2003 and now forms part of NCN62. It uses the former Brodsworth mineral line, and includes a large bridge over the River Don just north of Warmsworth.

Wombwell (Broomhill)–Barnsley: C, W, NI, DR, 5½m, SE 421021–SE 352060. Part of the Trans Pennine Trail, NCN62, and NCN67. Connects at SE 391043 with the Wombwell–Silkstone Common trail (see below), and at SE 373056 with the Ardsley–Cudworth trail (see above).

Wombwell–Silkstone Common: C, H, W, NI, DR, 7½m, SE 394040–SE 282036. The Dove Valley Trail – an early (if not the first) railway path in South Yorkshire, now forming yet another part of the Trans Pennine Trail.

Yorkshire, West

Sustrans is constructing a route called The Great Northern Railway Trail, which it describes as a 'work in progress'; the objective is to convert the Keighley to Queensbury line into a railway path between Cullingworth (near Oakworth) and Queensbury. There are even plans to extend south by reopening the 1½m Queensbury Tunnel to Holmfield. Currently, the completed sections of this trail (part of NCN69) are fragmentary, but already Cullingworth to Harecroft is open (SE 066364–SE 076355, ½m, including Hewenden Viaduct) and Thornton to Queensbury (SE 091327–SE 105310, 1m, including Thornton Viaduct). Several of the viaducts on this line are owned by Railway Paths, which is keen to see them reused.

If you fancy a bit of detective work in the hills above Hebden Bridge, you might like to track down the remains of the Hardcastle Crags Railway, which is as scenic as it is obscure. It lasted from *c.* 1901 to 1912 and was used in the construction of the three reservoirs at Walshaw Dean. The National Trust's website (search for 'Railway walk at Hardcastle Crags') includes a walk over part of the line, starting at Gibson's Mill Courtyard (SD 973298) and extending north to opposite Black Dean (SD 963313), where the piers of the railway's viaduct can still be seen marching across Hebden Water. Along the way, you will pass the remains of Hell Hole Quarry, which provided the stone for the dams. The navvies lived in a huge community at Slack known as Dawson City, which was ruled by two women – 'the Queens of Dawson City'.

Garforth–Aberford: CIP, HIP, W, UP, DR, 3m, SE 413338–SE 433369. This route is based on the Aberford Railway, which the Gascoigne family opened in 1834 to carry coal from their collieries near Garforth to Aberford on the Great North Road. The old railway can be picked up from the north end of Ash Lane, off the modern A624 east of Garforth station, from where it's an easy walk to Aberford thanks to a falling gradient. The section to SE 421358 is a public footpath (UX); the rest a bridleway (UT).

Garforth–Allerton Bywater: C, W, UT, DR, 3½m, SE 411324–SE 421280. Part of the Leeds Country Way, also NCN697, based on a section of the former NER line from Garforth to Kippax and Castleford.

Huddersfield–Deighton (near Mirfield): C, W, UP, DR, 2m, SE 143178–SE 168197. Part of a Sustrans route known as the Calder Valley and Birkby Bradley Greenways, which reuses the former MR goods line from Huddersfield (Newtown Goods) to Mirfield. Includes Bradley Viaduct. The trail continues – although mainly off the trackbed – to Mirfield, where there is a signed connection to the Spen Valley Greenway (see entry for Ravensthorpe).

Methley–Stanley: C, W, UT, DR, 2m, SE 384256–SE 356247. Part of the former Methley Joint Line, which ran from Methley Junction to Lofthouse Junctions via Stanley; now part of NCN67. In autumn 2014, a further ¾m of this line was opened at its east end, running from Ramsden Street in Cutsyke to Lumley Hill near Whitwood Junction (SE 422245–SE 411251). Wakefield Council plans to continue west along the trackbed from Lumley Hill to near the village of Methley Junction, replacing the missing bridge over the Normanton–York railway line (SE 410252) and then opening the viaduct over the River Calder (SE 404255) where a connection will be made with the intended River Calder Cycle Route.

When complete, this extension will be 1¾ miles long and include some notable engineering features.

Ravensthorpe (near Mirfield)–Low Moor: C, W, UT, DR, 7½m, SE 234203–SE 170277–SE 165282. The Spen Valley Greenway, opened in May 2001 using the trackbed of the former line from Mirfield to Low Moor. Now part of NCN66. Access from Ravensthorpe is off the minor road at SE 236199.

Savile Town (Dewsbury)–Ossett: C, W, NI, DR, 2m, SE 249206–SE 273201. This is the new Dewsbury and Ossett Greenway, which includes part of the Kirklees Way. Its engineering features include the substantial Headfield Viaduct at Savile Town, and the 179yd Earlsheaton Tunnel (SE 255208), which cost £1.3 million to restore. Watch out for the hairpin bend at SE 252211 where there is a change of direction.

Thornton-in-Craven–Foulridge: W, UX, DR, 5m, SD 910482–SD 888426. The county councils, on either side of the Lancashire–Yorkshire border, own this part of the former L&YR line from Skipton to Colne. The two councils only permit walkers to use the trackbed at their own risk. At the Foulridge end, the access point is beyond Lancashire CC's ownership, but the link on to the towpath of the Leeds & Liverpool Canal is walked regularly and in 2013 was being improved, as it was previously rather steep.

Wetherby–Spofforth: C, W, UT, DR, 2½m, SE 405487–SE 365507. The Harland Way, part of NCN67, but formerly part of the NER's line from Harrogate to Church Fenton. For further details, see entry under North Yorkshire, where the trail ends.

Wetherby–Thorp Arch: C, W, UT, DR, 2¾m, SE 413485–SE 441462. A further section of the NER Harrogate–Church Fenton line, this time on the east side of Wetherby. Part of NCN66 and now extended south into Thorp Arch Trading Estate.

A Brief History of Railway Closures

CLOSING OF ERIDGE TO HAILSHAM LINE

As and from MONDAY 14th JUNE 1965, the passenger service on the line between ERIDGE and HAILSHAM, via HEATHFIELD, will be withdrawn and the following stations closed to passengers:-

ROTHERFIELD AND MARK CROSS
MAYFIELD
HEATHFIELD
HORAM
HELLINGLY

HEATHFIELD, HORAM and HELLINGLY will remain open for freight traffic, and will be served by trains to and from HAILSHAM.

'Bus facilities in the area are provided by Southdown Motor Services Ltd.

This is the sort of sign that struck fear into a community's heart in the 1950s and 1960s. A lot of these notices went up in the latter decade because the now infamous Beeching Report listed five and a half pages of railway lines to be closed, covering some 5,000 route miles. (Robert Greenall)

It is never kindness to perpetuate a state of decay. You are only prolonging the agony.

Lord Beeching

Tramways and railways have been closing for almost as long as they have existed. If you think about it, especially in the context of mineral lines, it makes perfect sense. All the time that there is coal, granite, china clay or whatever to exploit, the rails remain, but as soon as the reserves are exhausted, the need for rail-based transport disappears, and with it the rails, sleepers, sidings, passing loops, locomotives and rolling stock leaving nothing but empty trackbeds. In what is now rural Shropshire,

the tramway and subsequent railway that conveyed coal from Billingsley down to the River Severn (and later the Severn Valley Railway) are cases in point; they were the transient by-products of another industry. On the Isle of Purbeck where china clay was (and still is) excavated from open cast pits, the systems were even more transient – their tracks were moved regularly in order to service the areas being worked, a practice which made them like giant model railway layouts. The 2ft 9in Seaton Tramway provides a modern illustration of the portability of narrow gauge systems: until 1969, it was based at Eastbourne before an over-winter move to its new home in east Devon, where it now occupies most of the former Seaton branch of the London & South Western Railway.

The First World War brought the first noticeable changes to a pattern of organic growth and contraction. The little East Southsea branch closed in August 1914, a victim of Portsmouth's rapidly expanding tram network and a government directive that required all railways unable to support themselves financially to cease operating; according to Dr Edwin Course, its rails were used to make ammunition. In 1915, Hallatrow to Limpley Stoke (south of Bath) closed, followed in 1917 by the Basingstoke & Alton Light Railway and the Bideford, Westward Ho! & Appledore Railway, the latter pair being requisitioned for war service by the Minister of Munitions. However, most lines that were closed during the war were reopened afterwards. For example, Hallatrow to Limpley Stoke and Basingstoke to Alton came back to life, in 1923 and 1924 respectively, finding subsequent fame in the movies *The Titfield Thunderbolt* (1953) and *Oh! Mr. Porter* (1937). By coincidence, both of these films are about railways of the 'financially challenged' type.

After the war, another, more insidious change became apparent – the transformation of the motor vehicle from a luxury hobby into a reliable workhorse. As a result, local bus services were claiming their first railway victims by the 1920s, a notable example being the delightful little Southwold Railway, which steamed into history in 1929 after fifty years of service in rural Suffolk. The modern Southwold Railway reports that an abandonment order was applied for at the time but only granted as recently as the 1990s, a delay which may go some way towards explaining why the trackbed between Blythburgh and Southwold became an early railway path.

The Wall Street Crash of 1929 and the subsequent Great Depression turned up the heat on the railways, and it is in this decade that the first significant swathes of railway closures occurred, at least of passenger services. (At this time, the complete closure of lines was rare thanks to profitable freight operations.) The London & North Eastern Railway carried out a cull of passenger services on minor lines on 22 September 1930 which claimed, amongst others, the highly scenic route from Alnwick to Coldstream, and the East Anglian byway from Denver (near Downham Market) to Stoke Ferry. Many readers may never have heard of the latter, but part of it survived until 1981 thanks to a British Sugar factory at Wissington. Other closures at this time included the Leek & Manifold Railway (1934), the Selsey Tramway (1935), the Ringwood to Christchurch branch (1935) and the Lynton &

This is Lumb Viaduct on the former L&YR line from Stubbins Junction, north of Ramsbottom, to Accrington. It doesn't look like this any more thanks to the efforts of Railway Paths and its partners, who have incorporated it into a new trail, but this photograph illustrates what a permanent way looks like after decades of neglect. To the right of the parapet is the deck, to the left a sheer drop. (Author)

When railways are closed, the permanent way is normally lifted and, if not worn out, reused; otherwise it usually goes for scrap. The Ponts Mill area north of Par is an exception to this rule, for both narrow and standard gauge tracks remain in situ, including this narrow gauge example, which possibly originates from Treffry's Tramway. The royal train used to be stabled at Ponts Mill – on standard gauge, of course – until its siding became too overgrown to reach. (Author)

Barnstaple Railway (1935). This quartet make an interesting group: the Leek & Manifold Railway operated a narrow gauge line over one of the most scenic routes anywhere in these islands; the Selsey Tramway was one of many cash-strapped independent lines operated by the eccentric Colonel Holman Frederick Stephens, who kept his empire running with cast-offs from the larger railways; the Ringwood to Christchurch route was once part of the main line to Bournemouth; and the Lynton & Barnstaple Railway was another highly scenic and much lamented loss from the narrow gauge scene. (It is now being rebuilt as the 'last great narrow gauge adventure'.) However, in the context of railway closures, it is the Leek & Manifold Railway that is of the most interest because in 1936 its owner, the London, Midland & Scottish Railway, donated its

trackbed to the local authority for use as a country path; it opened as a trail in July of the following year.

It is impossible to tell how many more railways might have closed by gradual, economically induced contraction because the Second World War intervened. From 1939, the hostilities effectively put railway closures on hold: the multiple routes from the big manufacturing centres were a boon when any of them might suddenly be disrupted by a bombing raid, while in the south of the country unprecedented levels of traffic traversed even the most secondary routes in the run-up to D-Day. The branch line from Midhurst to Chichester (closed to passengers in 1935) saw some of this traffic, with dock-bound ammunition trains being stabled overnight in its tunnels which were fitted with large blast doors to reduce the risk that a returning German bomber might offload unspent bombs on its home run and score a lucky hit; a couple of these rusty shields still hang beside the portals of Cocking Tunnel.

If the 1940s extended the working lives of railway byways, the 1950s ushered in a very different era. By now, increases in private motoring and road-hauled freight were combining with ever more extensive bus services to rob local lines of their traffic, thereby creating ever-rising losses. The railways were also worn out after the exertions of two world wars when they were operated under government control. Salvation appeared to come in 1955 with the government's 'Modernisation Plan', which promised investment and development with the trade-off of a small number of line closures. The idea was that upgrades and efficiencies would win back traffic and challenge road transport on price, but the programme was badly managed, failed to achieve its objectives, and earned the railways a reputation for poor financial management. Meanwhile, a new tranche of branch lines chuffed into history, including Fareham to Alton (1955), Blackburn to Rose Grove via Padiham (1957), and Bristol to Frome (1959).

These three are lucky survivors in that parts of their routes can now be walked and cycled, but unfortunately the railway industry as a whole was not so lucky: its annual losses continued to rise – from £15.6 million in 1956 to £42 million in 1960.

Many people with even a modest knowledge of twentieth-century railway history know the name of Dr (later Lord) Richard Beeching, who burst upon the public consciousness in March 1963 with the publication of his infamous report, 'The Reshaping of British Railways', now more commonly known as the 'Beeching Report'. Beeching had been a member of the Stedeford Committee, convened in 1961 by Harold Macmillan's Conservative government to review Britain's railways, which – as seen above – were haemorrhaging money; he was part of the government's 'fresh talent' from industry, and his strong views on how to stem the railway's losses (by the wholesale closure of unprofitable lines) led to him being offered the post of Chairman of the then nascent British Railways Board. By the time that copies of his fateful report left Her Majesty's Stationery Office, Beeching had had two years to analyse the problem and devise an action plan. The implementation of this plan led to the closure of more railways in the UK than has been witnessed before or since. This is not the place to discuss the rights or wrongs of what Beeching did, but it must be pointed out that the situation in the 1960s was dramatically different to what it is in the twenty-first century. Then, private motoring was emptying trains and creating ever larger railway losses; now, the nation is increasingly short of rail capacity and closed lines are being rebuilt. Beeching could not see into the future and deserves to be judged in his historical context: when he stood down as Chairman of the British Rail Board in 1965, he had cut the industry's annual loss from £180 million to £120 million.

What is most regrettable about Beeching's chairmanship of BR is that it introduced some distinctly anti-rail attitudes into railway management: for example, in the years following 1965, lines were closed which Beeching had not actually listed for closure in his report. Only in 1989, when Michael Portillo as Minister of State for Transport refused to let BR close the Settle–Carlisle line, did this approach finally get its comeuppance; but by then the UK's railway industry had been managed for twenty-six years partly on the basis that it was not small enough.

How much did all this cost in terms of lost route miles? When interviewed by Hunter Davies in 1981, Dr Beeching stated that he had been responsible for the closure of one third of Britain's 18,000 miles of railway. Even that figure was something less than the peak of 19,585 miles which had existed on 1 January 1923, when over 100 Victorian railway companies were 'grouped' into the 'Big Four': the Great Western; the London, Midland & Scottish; the London & North Eastern; and the Southern. An even more dramatic grouping took place on 1 January 1948 when the Big Four were nationalised to form British Railways or 'British Rail' from 1965. The final statistic is about BR as a whole and comes from the September 1984 edition of *The Journal of Transport Economics and Policy*: between 1 January 1948 and 31 December 1982, the UK's state-owned railway operator closed 8,144 miles of railway. That's a lot for a small island.

IRELAND

Introduction

Most counties in Ireland have done little with their disused railway lines, the most common use being the conversion of convenient sections into roads. A number of proposals for rail trails were mooted in the 1980s but few, if any, were built at that time. Where railway paths were constructed, they tended to be short, as for example between Westport and Westport Quay (County Mayo) and north of Bandon (the Bandon Railway Path, County Cork). Both of these trails are well below the 2-mile limit for inclusion in this gazetteer.

Rather than list a large number of county titles above the announcement, 'No railways paths' or 'No railway paths of any significance', this section of the gazetteer lists only those counties where there is something to report – and therefore something of railway interest to walk or cycle. However, the future might be kinder to Ireland's old railways, since governments on both sides of the border now recognise the green credentials of 'cycle tourism'. In the north, Sustrans has been establishing routes for the National Cycle Network, a development that did not go unnoticed in Dublin. An Irish Tourism report published in August 2006 acknowledged that old railways could play a vital role in providing safe, traffic-free routes for cyclists – and, of course, walkers. This was followed in August 2010 by the publication of the *National Cycle Network Scoping Study*, which took plans a further step towards realisation.

Currently, interest in new railway paths is focussed largely on the west of the country, where Irish Rail and the Irish government have been keen to reinstate the western rail corridor. However, this has not been an unqualified success, with the reinstated line from Ennis to Athenry (reopened in 2010) attracting low passenger numbers, thereby creating losses and the need for an annual subsidy. While parts of the line remain unused, farmers and other landowners are beginning to encroach on Irish Rail's property, especially around level crossings. There is concern that, in time, this will lead to claims of 'adverse possession' over the land, and some observers see the creation of railway-based cycle trails (even if only temporary) as a way of asserting Irish Rail's ownership of the route, and of preserving its integrity. Adverse possession claims are a serious risk in Ireland. For example, on 27 April 2013 *The Irish Times* reported an angry confrontation at the County Limerick–Kerry border near Abbeyfeale. Thirty farmers claiming adverse possession over part of the trackbed obstructed walkers and cyclists intending to use a newly converted section of the Great Southern Trail. Sections of the western rail corridor that have been highlighted as suitable for greenway use are Athenry to Sligo, Collooney (near Sligo) to Claremorris, and Kiltimagh to Castlebar. Irish Rail's position is that it is willing for closed railways to become greenways, but only on the strict understanding that these routes will revert to rail if so required in the future.

It is some compensation for the lack of railway paths that some of Ireland's canal towpaths have been improved for use by cyclists, with walkers benefitting also from their improved all-weather surfaces.

Antrim

The former railway path from Bushmills to Giant's Causeway (2 miles) is no longer available, since the line was reopened in spring 2002 and now sees regular steam trains every weekend between Easter and the end of October (daily in July and August). The line has been relaid to a gauge of 3ft, like the Portrush, Bushmills & Giant's Causeway Tramway that preceded it.

Belfast–Comber: C, W, NO, DR, 7m. The Comber Greenway, part of NCN99, which reuses the old railway line from Belfast to Comber via Dundonald; continues into County Down. The route was completed in September 2008 but soon fell under the threat of conversion into a guided busway. However, in 2012 Northern Ireland's Department for Regional Development accepted that 'the route is better used as a greenway rather than a busway'.

Dundrum–near Clough: C, W, NI, 1½m, J409371–J417389. Dundrum Coastal Path. A highly scenic section of the former Belfast & County Down Railway between Newcastle and Downpatrick; part of NCN93. At the north end, it includes a causeway over Inner Dundrum Bay.

Randalstown: C, W, UT, DR, ¼m. This short railway path between Station Road and New Street exists thanks to the enthusiasm of the local community, and includes a massive viaduct over the River Maine. There are plans to create an off-road trail to Toome, some 12m further west along the north coast of Lough Neagh, using the trackbed of the former Belfast & Northern Counties Railway.

Cork

Blackrock–Crosshaven: W, NI, DR, 12m but only c. 6m on old trackbed. This route utilises parts of the former Cork, Blackrock & Passage Railway, although not continuously but in at least four separate sections. These sections are believed to be Blackrock to Passage, Glenbrook to Monkstown, Monkstown towards Raffeen, and near Frenchfurze to Crosshaven. The trackbed is difficult to trace around Carrigaline, where it used roads through the town before running on to an embankment, which led to a now demolished viaduct. However, there are some notable remains, namely many bridges, several platforms, a short tunnel at Blackrock, and a viaduct at Rochestown. The line has some fine views over Lough Mahon and the Owenboy River, and is well worth exploring.

Timoleague–Courtmacsherry: C, W, NI, DR, 2¾m. The trackbed of the former Timoleague and Courtmacsherry Extension Light Railway is now open as a traffic-free trail for walkers and cyclists; it was the last roadside railway to operate in Ireland, closing (together with the rest of the extensive west Cork network) on 31 March 1961. The trail follows the south side of the tidal estuary of the River Arigideen, which provides some fine views.

A view looking north along the Foyle Valley Greenway with the now disused narrow gauge Foyle Valley Railway running alongside. The greenway as a whole is 21 miles long, but only 5 miles of it reuse former railway infrastructure; it won a European Award of Excellence in 2003. (Author)

Derry/Londonderry

Derry/Londonderry–near Newtownhamilton (near Carrigans): C, W, NI, DR, 5m. Part of the Great Northern Railway's former line from Derry/Londonderry to Strabane and Omagh, now part of the Foyle Valley Greenway. The route passes the now closed Foyle Valley Railway Museum in Derry/Londonderry and offers occasional views over the River Foyle.

Donegal

Falcarragh–Creeslough: W, NI, DR, 6m. Part of the former Londonderry & Lough Swilly Railway, traversing the rocky terrain to the north of Muckish Mountain. Note that there are stepping stones over the Agher River. This line was an early closure, losing its passenger service in 1940 and its freight service in 1947.

Down

Belfast–Comber: C, W, NO, DR, 7m. See entry under Antrim.

Kerry

Glenbeigh–Caherciveen: C, W, NO, DR, 17m. In February 2015, a scheme to convert part of the abandoned Great Southern & Western Railway's branch from Farranfore to Valentia Island into a greenway finally got the go-ahead when Kerry CC voted to proceed with compulsory purchase orders to acquire the trackbed. The Dublin government has committed €3.4 million to the project, which it is claimed has the potential to be one of the world's 'most iconic' walking and cycling routes, being on the scenic Ring of Kerry.

Tralee–Fenit: C, W, NF, DR, 8½m. In 2009, Kerry CC obtained a licence agreement from Irish Rail, owner of the 8½-mile-long former Fenit branch, to turn it into a dedicated walkway and cycleway directly from the heart of Tralee to the deep-water port of Fenit. The council is convinced that, with views of Tralee Bay and the Slieve Mish mountains, the cycle path will boost tourism and provide an important local amenity. The first mile of the route, between Rock Street (in the heart of Tralee) and Bracker O'Regan Road, opened in April 2014, but members of the Tralee–Fenit Greenway Group claimed on Facebook that there was a 'lack of will to see this fantastic project through to completion'. Tralee's mayor, Mr Pat Hussey, argued that the government was committed to 'amenity trailways', as demonstrated by it's funding for the Glenbeigh–Caherciveen Greenway (see above).

Tralee–Limerick: C, W, UP, DR, 53m. See entry under Limerick.

Limerick

Tralee–Limerick: C, W, NF, DR, 53m. It must be emphasised that this route – the Great Southern Trail – is not yet open throughout, but it is on its way to becoming a most impressive long-distance trail. Several sections are open already, including the very scenic stretch from Abbeyfeale to Rathkeale (22 miles). This was completed in early 2011, with a mass walk and cycle ride over the line taking place on 18 June that year. The railway-based section of the route may have to end near Rathkeale, where the trackbed meets the in situ Limerick–Foynes freight line, which was last used in October 2000 – although the port company at Foynes wants to see it reopened. In 2015, Irish Rail 'de-vegetated' the branch, and inspected the track and structures, with a view to re-establishing freight operations. If this goes ahead, the Great Southern Trail will not be able to reach Limerick via the old railway, but even Tralee to Rathkeale will be an impressive 46 miles.

Mayo

Westport–Newport–Mulranny–Achill: C, W, NI, DR, 28m. This route is now the 'World Class 42km Great Western Greenway', much of which was still being developed as recently as 2009. The trail is based on the Midland Great Western Railway's branch line from Westport to Achill, although the railway never actually reached Achill Island but stopped just short on the mainland side of Achill Sound. As one might expect of Ireland's west coast, the views are tremendous. There is a fine red sandstone viaduct of seven arches just to the north of Newport, said to be the highest viaduct in Ireland; it has now been incorporated into the trail after years of use as a short local walkway. Note that Mulranny is also spelt as Mallaranny, something to watch out for on maps and signs.

Waterford

Dungarvan–Waterford: C, W, DR, NI, 27m. In 2010, this was just a 1½m trail from Dungarvan to Ballyfandle, but even then the 2006 *Strategy for the Development of Irish Cycle Tourism (South East Regional Report)* had stated that, 'The further conversion of this disused railway corridor to shared-use will make Dungarvan a Mecca for cycling in the region'. Today this old railway (once part of the Great Southern & Western Railway's former line from Mallow to Waterford) is the Deise Greenway, which now has its own website at www.deisegreenway.com. The trackbed from Dungarvan to Waterford has been given to Waterford County Council under licence, so presumably the route and its infrastructure are still owned by Irish Rail. The trail was set to be open throughout in 2016; it includes viaducts at Durrow and Kilmacthomas, and a ruler-straight tunnel at Ballyvoyle.

New Routes for Old

People will walk and cycle if given safe places to do so.

John Grimshaw

When a state railway operator decides that it doesn't want to operate 8,144 miles of railway, what does it do with them? The obvious answer is 'sell them', and that works well in an area like East Anglia, which has the lowest elevation in the UK, and where the most significant railway engineering structures were often bridges over rivers. Here, old railways can be absorbed easily back into the landscape. However, it's a different story in much of Scotland, Wales, Northumberland, the Peak District, the Lake District, the west of England, etc. From 1948 onwards, British Railways (or more correctly its Property Board) continued to sell unwanted railway land until, eventually, all the viable property had gone and only a rump remained. That rump consisted of viaducts, tunnels, underbridges, overbridges, embankments, cuttings, mountainside ledges and a range of miscellaneous structures such as culverts and one-sided retaining walls which no purchaser in his or her right mind would ever have paid good money for. In 2016, the Historic Railways Estate and Railway Paths Ltd (of whom more later) retained responsibility for over 7,000 such structures spread around the United Kingdom. It is obvious that Dr Beeching and his contemporaries never thought of that particular legacy.

Between the 1960s and 1980s, demolition was seen as a good way to deal with this problem, and in the 1960s especially many railway bridges over roads, rivers and canals were removed; it was not just unwanted steam locomotives that fed Britain's scrap metal industry. By the early 1980s, attention began to focus on unwanted viaducts, and two in particular came to illustrate the problems with which the railway industry had saddled itself. These were Smardale Gill Viaduct in Cumbria and Hockley Viaduct near Winchester. In both cases, the initial solution was to 'reach for the Semtex'. However, Smardale Gill Viaduct is situated in the North Pennines Area of Outstanding Natural Beauty, where it is not good form to blow up an unwanted fourteen-arch viaduct. Gradually, it became apparent that the costs of obtaining consent to demolish, protecting the environment and clearing up the mess afterwards made it cheaper to repair the structure. The thirty-three-arch Hockley Viaduct, which crosses the scenic Itchen Valley, presented a different problem to those who would demolish it. A team from the University of Southampton under Dr Edwin Course obtained permission to drill behind the brickwork and came back with samples of mass concrete, which had been unsuspected. The viaduct, built in 1890–91, proved to be the oldest surviving mass concrete structure of modern times, predating 'Concrete Bob' McAlpine's viaducts on the West Highland Line by about seven years. In view of these developments, it is not surprising that both of these imposing structures now form part of modern railway paths. Many more historic viaducts, like Smardale Gill, are now listed – and that puts demolition out of the question.

The fundamental problem with disused railway lines is that they once formed part of a communication system, and therefore any cohesive (as opposed to piecemeal) reuse must serve the same purpose. With hindsight, it appears extraordinary that it took so long for this to happen, especially when one considers the eye-watering mileage of railways that was closed down between 1963 and 1967. Maybe the nation as a whole was in a state of collective shock, or so entranced with new motorways and ever improving cars that it simply forgot about trains as a relic from a bygone age.

The rather obscure branch line from Hooton to West Kirby on the Wirral saw its last train, a freight working, in May 1962, nearly a year before Dr Beeching burst upon the scene. Local residents concerned at the gradual loss of Wirral countryside spotted the potential of the old railway to become a country park and began a campaign to convert it into a 'green walkway'. Their eventual success in 1969, when Cheshire County Council purchased the majority of the trackbed from BR's Property Board, owes much to the energy of the late Captain Laurence Beswick, who helped to create Britain's first rail trail since the Leek & Manifold Railway became a path in July 1937. This established an important new precedent.

The following year, 1970, saw the publication of Dr J.H. Appleton's report for the Countryside Commission, *Disused Railways in the Countryside of England and Wales*. The fact that this was produced at all suggests that officialdom perceived a 'problem' with disused railways in the UK, and possibly even some opportunities. Appleton's report was heavy on description (its content contained few surprises for anyone who was already walking old railways), but it did raise the possibility that some trackbeds might be reused for recreational purposes. The very year that it was published, Surrey County Council and Hambleton Rural District Council purchased the Surrey part of the Guildford to Horsham line for conversion into a trail. (It is now part of the Downs Link railway path from Peasmarsh to Shoreham-by-Sea.)

It was cars eventually, or rather the sheer number of them on the roads, that forced disused railways firmly into the public eye. In July 1977, a group of cycling enthusiasts in Bristol, concerned at ever increasing dependence on the car, formed an organisation called 'Cyclebag'. The group urged Avon County Council to improve conditions and facilities for local cyclists, but in 1979, disappointed at the council's response, took direct action by leasing from British Rail part of the former Midland Railway's line from Bath to Bristol and turning it into a cycle trail. Initially, the trail linked the backstreets of Bath with Bitton, barely 6 miles away, but it rapidly attracted huge numbers of walkers and cyclists, leading to gradual expansion east and west until, eventually, Bath and Bristol were linked by a continuous railway path. By the time that Avon CC ceased to exist in 1996, over 2 million journeys were being made on the old railway every year.

In 1982, a very different report into disused railways appeared. Entitled *A Study of Disused Railways in England and Wales: Potential Cycle Routes*, it comprised a core report supported by no fewer than thirty-three separate 'annexes' which set out with detailed engineering drawings how a selection of these apparently useless trackbeds could be turned into multi-use trails. The organisation behind this substantial work was John Grimshaw and Associates. John Grimshaw was already a leading member of Cyclebag and, when that organisation evolved into the charity Sustrans in 1984 (the name stands for 'sustainable transport'), he became its first chief executive.

Under Grimshaw's energetic leadership, Sustrans rapidly became a major force in reusing the nation's abandoned railways, and its efforts helped to galvanise local authorities up and down the country to do the same. A number of councils had purchased disused railways on the basis that they would be 'useful' for future road improvement schemes, only to discover that traffic levels never grew sufficiently to justify the huge cost of a major road improvement project. Turning such acquisitions into trails became a way of doing something constructive with an otherwise useless asset. (The railway-based part of Hampshire County Council's Test Valley Way started life in this way.)

What is noticeable about Grimshaw is his ability to achieve the seemingly impossible. Until the early 1990s, it had been assumed that only those old railways in public ownership could ever be converted into trails. It came as a surprise, therefore, when the Plym Valley Railway Path and Cycle Route (now part of NCN27 linking Ilfracombe and Plymouth) opened as a continuous trail, despite being owned by a range of different organisations including the National Trust and the Maristow Estate. Subsequent Grimshaw initiatives included the C2C route from Whitehaven to Sunderland, a coast-to-coast trail based substantially on old railways, and the National Cycle Network, which not only reuses old railways but also links them back into the hearts of communities. Additionally, he suggested the Trans Pennine Trail (a coast-to-coast network of rail trails between Hornsea and Southport) and wrote the initial report, although the project was then delivered by a consortium of local authorities led by Barnsley Metropolitan Borough Council, which manages it still.

By the 1990s, things were really beginning to happen. In 1994, the government's Planning Policy Guidance Note 9 (PPG9) instructed local authorities to improve facilities for walkers and cyclists, and specifically advised them to look at old railways as a means of achieving this. Although PPG9 no longer exists, its principles continue in modern planning guidance. In 1998, Railway Paths Ltd was established as a sister charity to Sustrans. It came about in a rather indirect manner: when the railways were being privatised, the government did not want to lumber Railtrack Ltd (the precursor to Network Rail) with maintenance responsibilities for rail-less structures which had not seen a train for forty years or more. RPL took on the stock of ex-railway structures, which it considered potentially useful for walking and cycling, while the rest went to British Rail Board Residuary Ltd. (When BRBR was abolished in September 2013, its property portfolio was transferred to the Historic Railways Estate of the Highways Agency.) Today, RPL is busy restoring bridges, viaducts and tunnels, and feeding them into new path projects around the country.

In the twenty-first century, the development of rail trails continues apace. Improvements to the National Cycle Network are one of the main drivers of this, but there appears to be a wide recognition nationally that disused railways can and should fulfil a new transport role. Perhaps the most telling proof of this is the number of restored tunnels, new bridges and even new viaducts which have been opened in the last decade to reconnect once isolated and useless sections of trackbed so that they enable people once more to travel along an old railway corridor – separated from road traffic again, but now under their own steam, on foot or by bicycle.

Left: Into the light! On Saturday 6 April 2013, the Somerset & Dorset Railway between Lower Bristol Road in Bath and Midford was reopened as the Two Tunnels Trail. This photograph depicts some of the many walkers and cyclists passing through Lyncombe Vale, i.e. between the two tunnels, on the opening day. (J. Bewley/Sustrans)

Below: Lundy Island, some 22 miles off the north Devon coast, is hardly the place where one would expect to find many railway remains, or indeed any at all; but over the years it has seen three tramways come and go. This is the lower tramway on the east side of the island, looking south towards the inclined plane where Lundy granite was taken down to sea level and transferred to ships for the journey to the mainland. (Author)

A striking view of Meldon Viaduct on Devon County Council's Granite Way from Okehampton to Lydford, formerly part of the LSWR main line from Waterloo to Plymouth. The valley floor here was once a hive of activity due to lime making and granulite quarrying. (Ivor Sutton)

When Meldon Viaduct was restored in 1996, viewing platforms were installed on either side of the structure, which enable visitors to take some very striking photographs. Its piers and trusses are of wrought and cast iron respectively, making it one of only two such viaducts remaining in the UK. The other is at Bennerley on the Derbyshire–Nottinghamshire border, which should appear in the next edition of this gazetteer. (Author)

Below: The High Peak Trail in Derbyshire reuses much of the Cromford & High Peak Railway, which was built on canal principles with inclined planes operated by stationary engines to connect the various level sections. Middleton Top Engine House is the only complete survivor from this system; its large beam engine is still steamed at least once a month between Easter and October. (Peter Martin)

Right: This country station on the Monsal Trail, formerly the MR's main line from London St Pancras to Manchester Central, is Great Longstone. The station was little used and closed to passengers on 10 September 1962, but uniquely trains would still stop for a local nursing sister whenever she needed a train to or from Buxton, where she worked. (Jonathan Dawson)

Walkers and cyclists who get out and about during the winter may end up with near frozen body parts, but occasionally they witness atmospheric scenes, which the masses never see. This is Newmachar Curve on the GNSR's line from Dyce to Fraserburgh, now the Formartine and Buchan Way, and part of NCN1. (Phil Earnshaw)

Outwood Viaduct, now part of the Outwood Trail and NCN6, crosses the River Irwell near Radcliffe on the former L&YR line from Bury to Clifton Junction. After restoration, this Grade II-listed structure was reopened for walkers and cyclists in 1999. (Phil Earnshaw)

Above: As the former M&SWJR approached Marlborough from the north, it negotiated a long curve around the eastern side of this attractive Wiltshire town. This overbridge near Poulton Farm is one of several on this part of the line, which now serves as the Chiseldon & Marlborough Railway Path and NCN482. (Author)

Right: Rayne station on the former GER line from Braintree to Bishop's Stortford now accommodates the Booking Hall Café and, as can be seen, is a popular stop for walkers and cyclists using the railway path built along the trackbed. (Steve Harris)

Above: The NER's station at Ryehill & Burstwick was the halfway point on the company's branch line from Hull to Withernsea, which closed to passengers in 1964 and to freight in 1965 – yet another victim of the Beeching cuts. Today, all but the easternmost 4 miles of the line may be walked and cycled. (Peter Martin)

Right: The little station at Sandford & Banwell is a perfect example of the Bristol & Exeter Railway's architecture in miniature. The Grade II-listed buildings now serve as a railway museum open from Easter to October on the popular railway path from Cheddar to Yatton. (Author)

Above: This is a very rare railway artefact – a catch pit on an inclined plane. This example is on Sheep Pasture Incline on the Cromford & High Peak Railway, now the High Peak Trail. If wagons broke free on the way up or down, a pointsman would divert them into the pit where they would smash to pieces in relative safety. The device was installed after just such a runaway, when the escaping train contained a load of explosives for use in quarries up the line. (Peter Martin)

Left: Shillingstone station used to be a country stop on the famous Somerset & Dorset Railway from Bath to Bournemouth, but is now a major feature on the North Dorset Trailway, which will one day link Stalbridge with Poole. Passengers awaiting trains had a fine view over nearby Hambledon Hill. (Author)

Slaggyford station was the penultimate stop on the scenic NER branch line that ran from Haltwhistle to Alston. The South Tyne Trail now uses the trackbed, but trains will return if the South Tynedale Railway's current extension project succeeds. (Mark Jones)

Taken on the launch day for new artworks on the Spen Valley Greenway, this is part of the 'Swaledale Flock' of eleven steel Swaledale sheep created by sculptor Sally Matthews. There is a feast of public art on this trail, which uses the old railway from Ravensthorpe to Low Moor, a densely populated urban area with distant views of the local moors. (Jez Toogood/Sustrans)

Below: In the nineteenth century, cities rated their importance by the number of railway stations they possessed. St Albans had three – Abbey, City and London Road, the latter (seen here) being situated on the GNR's branch line from St Albans Abbey to Hatfield. The building is now a business centre in a new housing estate, which accounts for its excellent state of repair. (David Brace)

Right: Some old railway structures are too large to capture easily on camera, and the Spey Viaduct east of Garmouth on NCN1 and the Moray Coast Trail is a case in point. This is the main bowstring section, which is approached from either side by a 300ft three-span approach viaduct. (Bob Prigg)

Above: The Ystwyth Trail links Aberystwyth with Tregaron. This view near the delightfully named Strata Florida reveals several key features of the bygone rural railway: the steep-sided cutting, the sharp curve and the overbridge in the distance. Only rails and a train are missing. (Bob Morgan)

Right: It can be easy to miss the lineside features on a railway path, especially fifty or more years after closure when vegetation can hide them. These steps just east of the old station site in Sturminster Newton still convey a public footpath up and over the railway, but the railway is now part of the North Dorset Trailway. (Author)

Left: Tettenhall station in Staffordshire, like its neighbour at Wombourne, survives almost completely intact. After several years in use as an office for rangers on the Kingswinford Railway Walk, the building was converted in 2014 into a tea room called 'Cupcake Lane', which is very handy for anyone walking or cycling the old line. (Maurice Blencowe)

Below: The restored Thornton Viaduct in West Yorkshire is currently at the western end of a short railway path from nearby Queensbury, but Sustrans and the local authorities aspire to make it part of the Great Northern Railway Trail which, when complete, will link Queensbury with Cullingworth, near Oakworth. (Author)

To think of tramways as cheap minor enterprises is to miss the point: if a tramway required a large engineering feature, it could rise to the challenge. This is Treffry Viaduct – actually a combined viaduct and aqueduct – south of Luxulyan on Treffry's Tramway, which linked Bugle (in Cornwall's central china clay district) with Par. Today, virtually all of this line can be traced on foot. (Author)

Right: The charming station at Thorpe Thewles (NZ 402244) on the former line from Stockton to Sunderland via Wingate is now the Station House Visitor Centre on the Castle Eden Walkway and NCN1. The station closed to passengers in 1931 and to freight in 1951, but the line itself remained open for freight until 1968. (Robert Greenall)

Below: The MR's station at Warmley in Bristol's outermost suburbs now serves as Warmley Waiting Room, a popular coffee shop, café and tea room – highly convenient for anyone walking or cycling the Bath and Bristol Railway Path. The sculptures on the platform, entitled 'Brief Encounter', are by Steve Joyce. (J. Bewley/Sustrans)

Above: This scene on the high Durham moors reveals how remote and exposed was the railway, which once served Waskerley; the company that built it was the early Stanhope & Tyne Railway, but the trackbed is now used by the Waskerley Way. As part of the C2C route, Durham County Council has had to strengthen the surface, which here has been diverted off the sagging railway embankment on the left. (Wendy Johnson/Sustrans)

Right: This is a perfect example of being in the right place at the right time. The photographer is standing on the trackbed of the West Somerset Mineral Railway just before it enters Watchet at the very moment that 7828 Norton Manor steams overhead with a train bound for Bishops Lydeard on the preserved West Somerset Railway. (Bob Spalding)

Above: The Somerset & Dorset Railway afforded some fine views south of Bath, which is one of the reasons why the line was held in such high regard by enthusiasts. While some of the views have now vanished due to half a century of unchecked vegetation growth, those on the permissive section of trail between Midford and Wellow are as extensive as ever. (Author)

Left: The short railway path from to Keswick to Threlkeld is a feast of railway engineering, featuring many bowstring bridges over the River Greta. One of these is seen in the foreground with the short Wescoe Tunnel behind. (Richard Lewis)

Above: The GNR's line from Lincoln to Boston, now largely the Water Trail Way, must have been a relatively easy project for the company's engineers thanks to the level terrain, but they hit a problem when they needed to cross the Old River Witham at Bardney Lock; this long brick and steel viaduct was the result. The River Witham is in the foreground with the old river disappearing beneath the viaduct's piers. (Phil Earnshaw)

Below: A small group of ramblers walks through a pool of light on the railway path from Shanklin to Wroxall, which re-uses part of the former Isle of Wight Railway's lost line to Ventnor. The island is a rambler's, and a railway rambler's, paradise. Apart from an excellent network of well-maintained footpaths and bridleways, the local authority has opened up at least a part of every disused railway line on the island. (Author)

Above: This is the new viaduct at Woolfold Gap under construction in 2011 as one of Sustrans' Connect2 projects. Now that it is complete and open, a continuous railway path – part of NCN6 – exists between Greenmount and Bury, reusing all but the very ends of the L&YR's former Holcombe Brook branch. (Martin Philpott/Sustrans)

SCOTLAND

Introduction

The 1974 county names are used for consistency with the rest of the gazetteer, but the new authority names are shown in brackets where known.

In recent years the Scottish councils have created 'core path networks', and opened paths where there was no access before. While the quality of the work is uneven, the good news is that they have upgraded many former railway routes and waymarked them as part of this work. The Borders region in particular has benefitted from this work, with a number of very attractive old lines now being open to walkers.

Trespass

A long-standing popular view was that Scotland had no trespass law, as expressed by Tom Johnstone, the Secretary of State for Scotland, in 1942:

> Any member of the public is at liberty to walk over any land in Scotland provided he does so without damage to crops or fences and does not commit a breach of the various Poaching Acts. This applies to the whole country with the exception of private gardens or grounds, which form the curtilage of a dwelling house or other private residence.

Exactly a quarter of a century later, the then minister Dr Dickson Mabon took an almost opposite position:

> There is very little difference in the law of trespass in Scotland and England. In both countries, it is a civil offence against the personal right of property.

There was certainly scope for confusion there! Fortunately, in 2003, the situation was regularised by the Land Reform (Scotland) Act with the result that 'Scotland now has one of the best arrangements in Europe for public access to land and water for its citizens and visitors' (Ramblers' Association). Stephen Lewis, a fellow railway walks author, summarises the current situation thus:

I think it could be argued that Scotland does not have a law of trespass but more a law of access. My reasoning for this is that the public has a legal right of access with various eminently sensible and reasonable exceptions to most land ... [The] current Scottish Outdoor Access Code ... is an excellent document in plain English and does not contain the word 'trespass' at all! The key piece of legislation is the Land Reform (Scotland) Act 2003. In a nutshell, access to dismantled railways is definitely covered unless the trackbed passes through such things as gardens, cropped fields and some farm yards/buildings etc. with the emphasis being on 'responsible use' and ensuring no damage is caused by the person exercising their right of access.

Copies of the Scottish Outdoor Access Code can be downloaded from Scottish Natural Heritage's website (www.snh.org.uk).

To summarise the situation, it is safe to regard access to old railway land as permissible under the code, except where it passes through 'gardens, cropped fields and some farm yards/buildings etc.'. Obviously, walkers should also follow the Country Code and respect private property at all times.

Borders

The 2¼m trail from Galashiels to Melrose along the course of the Waverley line was part of NCN1, but now only a fragment exists at the Melrose end thanks to the rebuilding of the Borders Railway (the modern name for the Waverley line) between Millerhill, outside Edinburgh, and Tweedbank. On the plus side, a new alignment has been found for NCN1 along the same general corridor. There are calls for the Borders Railway to be extended further south, first to Hawick and then to Carlisle, and this cannot be ruled out

because the reopening of the first 30 miles has been such a success. Further extensions would mean a reduction of the short trail over Leaderfoot Viaduct, north of St Boswells, and the complete loss of the longer trail from Shankend to Stobs.

Biggar–Broughton: CIP, W, NI, DR, 5m, NT 043372–NT 112360. Part of the former Symington, Biggar & Broughton Railway; access the start via a track off Boghall Road, Biggar, which starts at NT 038370 and heads east. The railway followed the shallow valley of Biggar Water (a burn), which explains why there are few relics, structures or even substantial earthworks.

Coldstream–East Learmouth: W, NI, DR, 1m, NT 863394–NT 865378. Connected to the Coldstream–West Learmouth trail at Coldstream Junction. Despite Coldstream being just inside the Borders, the town's station was on the south side of the River Tweed and therefore in Northumberland, q.v.

Coldstream–West Learmouth: W, NI, DR, 1¾m, NT 863394–NT 846379. Actually in Northumberland, q.v.

Duns–Manderston: W, NI, DR, 1¼m, NT 791532–NT 809536. Part of the NBR line from Reston to Ravenswood Junction, now reused by the Duns Paths Project. The trail starts in Duns Industrial Estate and proceeds to a bridge just south of Manderston House Estate.

Kelso–Carham: W, NI, DR, 4m, NT 735335–NT 791370. Part of the NBR and NER line from Roxburgh to Coldstream, which stops just short of the border with Northumberland. This route has been upgraded as part of the Kelso Walks Project. It starts at a flight of steps off the Kelso bypass and then proceeds past Sprouston station to the remains of Carham station.

Kelso–Roxburgh: H, W, NI, DR, 2¼m, NT 723327–NT 697305. This is the westward continuation of the route above, now waymarked as part of the Kelso core paths network. It starts at the south-west end of the Kelso bypass and continues through the Teviot Valley to the site of Roxburgh Junction, crossing the magnificent Roxburgh Viaduct to join the Jedburgh branch. One old goods platform survives just prior to the viaduct. This walk can be linked with the Borders Abbeys Way south of Roxburgh to continue down the Jedburgh branch as far as Jedfoot (see entry for Roxburgh).

Leaderfoot Viaduct–Ravenswood Junction: W, NI, DR, 1¼m, NT 574345–NT 579333. This short railway path east of Melrose is included because it contains the wonderful Leaderfoot Viaduct, which can be accessed immediately to the north of the access point at NT 574345. The viaduct was renovated by Historic Scotland, the Railway Heritage Trust and the former British Rail Property Board between 1992 and 1995. The viaduct comprises nineteen arches, each of 43ft span, and the views from it are magnificent. By September 2010, the walk had been waymarked; it crosses first the Melrose bypass (to join the Waverley route immediately after Ravenswood Junction) and then the A68, continuing as far south as the first bridge.

Lyne–Neidpath Viaduct–Peebles: W, NI, DR, 2¾m, NT 209401–NT 233402–NT 244403. This section of the former CR line from Symington to Peebles is now part of the Tweed Path. Originally, only the section from Lyne to Neidpath Viaduct was open, but by 2015 walkers could continue through the 600yd curved and unlit South Park Tunnel (bring a torch) to reach South Park Crescent in west Peebles. By diverting through streets around the site of the town's former CR station (NT 250403), one can follow a further section of trackbed, now a tarmacked path, which uses the old railway bridge under the A7062 and continues along the south bank of the River Tweed as far as the former river bridge at NT 254402; the loss of the railway bridge is no hardship thanks to the 1905 Priorsford suspension bridge, which leads across to the north bank. The CR's Symington–Peebles branch is included in the Upper Tweed Railway Path Project, part-financed by the Scottish government and the EU, which David Gray and John Grimshaw (a former CEO of Sustrans) are working on.

Peebles–Cardrona–Innerleithen: C, W, UT, DR, 6m, NT 261403–NT 300391–NT 331362. In August 2013, Paul Whitehouse, Environment and Climate Change Minister in the Scottish Parliament, formally opened the new Tweed Valley Railway Path between Peebles and Innerleithen; it is based on part of the former NBR line from Leadburn to Galashiels, and cost over £1 million to construct. The route includes a

Neidpath Viaduct, also known as Queen's Bridge, once carried the CR's Symington–Peebles line over the River Tweed. It is a fine piece of architecture, being built from ashlar blocks on a curve of 440yds radius, which required the eight arches to be skewed and constructed with helical courses. It is now part of the growing Upper Tweed Railway Path Project. (Phil Earnshaw)

new bridge over the River Tweed at NT 308380, just east of Cardrona, and utilises an old railway tunnel under the A72 at Eshiels, east of Peebles.

Roxburgh–Jedfoot Bridge: C, W, NI, DR, 6m, NT 697305–NT 662241 (Roxburghshire). Part of the Borders Abbeys Way, which reuses most of the former NBR branch line from Roxburgh to Jedburgh. At the Roxburgh end, the local OS map shows the Abbeys Way leaving the trackbed at NT 696287, but local sources advise that it can be followed to NT 697305, just east of the site of Roxburgh station. There is a diversion west of Nisbet due to a bridge over the River Teviot at NT 667251 having been demolished.

Shankend–Stobs: H, W, NI, DR, 2¾m, NT 521060–NT 507093. This is another railway path based on part of the former Waverley route, this one forming part of the Hawick Paths Project. The trail can be joined just north of the listed Shankend Viaduct (repaired in 2007) and followed to just south of Stobs station with an exit by a gate on to Stobs Camp. Abandoned platelayers cottages are passed en route.

Bute

Port Bannatyne–Ettrick Bay: C, W, NI, DR, 1¾m, NS 065673–NS 035665 (Argyll). This trail follows part of the former Rothesay & Ettrick Bay Light Railway, which opened in 1882 between Rothesay and Port Bannatyne; in 1902, it was extended across the island to Ettrick Bay, and electrified, although closure came early on 30 September 1936. The line followed the A814 from Rothesay Pier to west of Port Bannatyne, and then ran alongside the B875 to Ettrick Bay. This trail uses the railway's trackbed alongside these roads.

Central

Aberfoyle–Cobleland–Buchlyvie: C, W, UT, DR, 5½m, NN 521010–NS 532989–NS 564941 (Stirling). The NBR's branch line from Buchlyvie to Aberfoyle, now part of NCN7 and recently extended southwards from Cobleland to Buchlyvie.

Balquhidder–Glenoglehead: W, UX, DR, 4½m, NN 576214–NN 558282. If the importance of railway paths were measured by multiple titles, then this one would score well since it is variously the Glen Ogle Trail, part of the Rob Roy Way and part of NCN7. The start at Balquhidder is not currently shown on the OS Explorer map but can be walked or cycled on a mountain bike. Along the way, several formidable gates will be encountered but they are designed to be effective against deer, not people, and all open easily. Sustrans made improvements to the route in 2001 so that walkers and cyclists would not have to use the nearby A84. The company's work opened up the listed Kendrum Burn Viaduct near Lochearnhead, where a new steel span was installed to replace one that had been demolished earlier. This span is dedicated to the memory of Nigel Hester, a music teacher and organist who was killed nearby on the A9 in a tragic accident. The other notable viaduct on the route – Glen Ogle Viaduct – is further north at NN 570264. There is a low-level route from Balquhidder, which uses part of the Balquhidder–Crieff branch (NN 584223–NN 585230), but you pay the price at the north end when it passes Craggan and climbs up a steep zigzag to reach the upper railway.

Blanefield–Dumgoyach Bridge–Gartness: W, UX, DR, 5¾m, NS 549797–NS 503869. Part of the former NBR line from Kirkintilloch to Gartness, virtually all of which is now open (see entry for Strathblane). Dumgoyach Bridge to Gartness is part of the West Highland Way long-distance path, but walking is permitted on the trackbed (which has been used for a water pipeline) from Blanefield.

Bridge of Keltie (near Callander)–Drumvaich: C, H, W, UT, DR, 1¾m, NN 649069–NN 668049. Nothing came of the proposed Callander–Doune trail reported to the author in 2010, but not all is lost. RR member Keith Potter reports: 'This section of the old railway served for many years as the haul road for an apparently closed gravel quarry at Cambusbeg, and is now used mainly for forestry access.' Signs warning of various forestry-related hazards suggest that the public are welcome to use the route. It is dead straight for almost the entire length and is easy going for walkers and cyclists, although perhaps less so for horse riders due to the hard surface. At the eastern end, one can exit the quarry to the nearby A84. A little to the south-east was the non-passenger crossing station of Drumvaich where the stone building, which combined staff housing with a signal box, has been sympathetically restored as a holiday cottage; it is worth seeing. To the south-east at Doune, NCN765 now uses 1½m of the old trackbed towards Dunblane (NN 729017–NN 751018).

Callander–Strathyre–Kinghouse: C, W, UP, DR, 11½m, NN 627081–NN 560171–NN 565206. Part of the CR's former line from Dunblane to Balquhidder, now part of NCN7 and the Rob Roy Way. The path is wheelchair-friendly from Callander to St Bride's Crossing (NN 587093). As it nears Strathyre, the trail runs along the west side of Loch Lubnaig, with excellent views, but there are a couple of diversions off the trackbed in this area. The railway-based part of the trail used to stop at Strathyre, but in 2014 a lengthy diversion to the east of the A84 was finally abolished when another 2½m of the trackbed was reused. At the south end of this route, a further ½ mile of the line can be walked to the east of Callander (NN 637077–NN 644073), but at the latter

point the trail turns south to join the nearby Old Military Road (A84).

Dalchonzie–St Fillans: C, H, W, UT, DR, 2½m, NN 740231–NN 699245 (Perth & Kinross). Although reported as a rail trail by Scottish railway ramblers, this route is given no designation on the local OS map other than 'Dismantled Railway', so use of the trackbed is informal. However, a community group called LERP (Loch Earn Railway Path) is running a scheme to extend the trail from St Fillans to Lochearnhead for walkers and disabled users, which would bring its length up to 11½m. In October 2014, Public Contracts Scotland published a notice to the effect that a consultant had been appointed to

North of Callander, the Rob Roy Way uses sections of the former Callander & Oban Railway. This is the start of the route as it leaves Callander, the upper quadrant signal indicating that the road ahead is clear. It is more than likely that the signal is an import, possibly from the town's now empty station site, but it leaves trail users in no doubt that they are setting off along an old railway. (Author)

There are times when riding a bicycle along an old railway almost conveys the sense of rail travel, especially if – as here on the western side of Loch Lubnaig – the telegraph poles remain and flick by at regular intervals. This former CR line is now part of the Rob Roy Way from Callander to Strathyre. (Author)

way to get to the start of this route is to continue north along the Balquhidder–Glenoglehead route after it leaves the old railway trackbed. Like the route to Glenoglehead, this is a further part of the Rob Roy Way and NCN7; it crosses the A84 at NN 558283, near where there is an off-road car park. The path arrives in Killin near the famous Dochart Falls and the town's Breadalbane Folklore Centre. At the other, i.e. north end of the town, the extension of the branch to Killin Pier can be picked up at NN 575333 and followed to NN 580342, by the old Killin Pier on Loch Tay. There are two good viaducts in Killin, one over the River Dochart, the other over the River Lochay.

Strathblane–Kirkintilloch: C, H, W, NI, DR, 7½m, NS 564792–NS 656742 (East Dunbartonshire). Another part of the former NBR line from Gartness to Kirkintilloch, now converted into a cycle trail – the Strathkelvin Railway Path – that continues into Strathclyde. The end of the trail at Strathblane is less than a mile from the start of the Blanefield–Gartness route. In October 2009, Sustrans and East Dunbartonshire Council completed a £130,000 six-year programme to upgrade the route.

identify the works required, and that his report was expected to provide the basis for an application to secure funding for construction from 2015 to 2016.

Upper Gartness–Croftamie: C, H, NI, DR, 1½m, NS 497867–NS 473861. Part of the NBR's former line from Stirling to Balloch. Starts at Upper Gartness on a minor lane heading west alongside the old railway, but switches on to the trackbed at NS 492867. The Upper Gartness end of the trail is only ¼ mile from the start of the Blanefield–Gartness route.

Dollar–Tillicoultry–Alloa: C, W, UT, DR, 6m, NS 966976–NS 916966–NS 888931. The Devon Way based on the western half of the former NBR line from Alloa to Kinross. West of Tillicoultry, the trail runs for ½ mile alongside the A908 to avoid a missing river viaduct. This section, i.e. from Tillicoultry to Alloa, has been 'landscaped' more than the Dollar section, especially through Sauchie.

Dumfries & Galloway

Apart from the routes listed below, Dumfries & Galloway can offer the National Trust's Threave Estate Walk south-west of Castle Douglas, which includes a 1-mile section of the G&SWR's Dumfries to Kirkcudbright line (NX 737606 to NX 749617,

Killin Junction–Killin–Killin Pier: C, W, NI, DR, 2½m, NN 555307–NN 570323–NN 580342. The easiest

where a bridge over the River Dee is missing). This forms part of various circular walks on the estate, which range from 2 to 9 miles in length.

Big Water of Fleet Viaduct–Gatehouse of Fleet Station: W, NI, DR, 1½m, NX 560644–NX 545625. This is an official path, although at the eastern end access to the viaduct (owned by Railway Paths) is on a permissive basis; the excellent views and massive twenty-arch viaduct make for a stunning short walk. The trackbed once formed part of the Port Road, the name given by railwaymen to the Portpatrick & Wigtownshire Joint Railway, which – together with the Dumfries to Castle Douglas section of the G&SWR's Kirkcudbright branch – once provided a direct rail link between Dumfries and Stranraer. Modern trains have to travel the long way round via Ayr.

Creetown–Graddoch Bridge (near Palnure): C, W, UT, DR, 2m, NX 469604–NX 462631. Part of NCN7, which reuses a further section of the Port Road, west of Gatehouse of Fleet. The route is managed by Dumfries & Galloway Council and is known as the Creetown and Blackcraig Cycleway.

Dumfries–Locharbriggs: C, W, UT, DR, 3½m, NX 976765–NX 993808. Part of the former CR line from Dumfries to Lockerbie, now managed by Dumfries & Galloway Council and known as the Caledonian Cycleway.

Dumfries–Maxwelltown: C, W, UT, DR, 2m, NX 973773–NX 948751. The last section of the Port Road to close, which survived for many years as a freight-only stub to the ICI chemical works at Maxwelltown. The track was lifted in 2006, after which Dumfries & Galloway Council in conjunction with Sustrans converted the route into part of NCN7. In July 2008, the route was extended over the Queen

of the South Viaduct in Dumfries, thereby linking the east and west parts of the town.

New Galloway–Loch Skerrow: W, NI, DR, 3½m, NX 661705–NX 609680. This part of the Port Road is a good path to Loch Skerrow, although you need to return the same way as the official path ends at the loch; the trail crosses Stroan Viaduct at NX 647700. Most of the Port Road is now privately owned, which explains why only isolated sections are open officially.

Fife

Dunfermline (Rumblingwell)–Slack Cottage–Clackmannan: W, UX, DR, 11m, NT 082881–NS 956912–NS 919925. This is virtually the whole of the NBR's former line from Dunfermline Upper to Clackmannan via Oakley, now designated the West Fife Way and part of NCN76 and NCN764. A mile to the east of Rumblingwell, i.e. beyond central Dunfermline, a further mile of the same line has been reclaimed between Headwell and Queen Margaret station (NT 097877–NT 115883). Queen Margaret station is near Townhill Junction, where this branch diverged from the NBR's line from Cowdenbeath to Dunfermline Lower, Kincardine and Alloa.

Leslie–Glenrothes (Woodside)–Markinch: C, W, UP, DR, 3¾m, NO 245013–NO 287007–NO 299014. The NBR's former branch line from Leslie to Markinch, now called The Böblingen Way (after Glenrothes' twin town), which starts/ends at the south end of the car park at Markinch station. The route includes viaducts at Leslie and Balbirnie but deviates slightly from the course of the trackbed on the south side of the new town. Also, in 2011, there was a gap between the A92 at Woodside (NO 287007) and the A911 at the west end of Balbirnie Viaduct (NO 290012) – hopefully, a connection will be installed in future, although the roads will need to

FIFE

be crossed safely and a way devised through housing developments at Woodside. Following closure of the Markinch–Auchmuty branch in the late 1980s, the eastern part of this route now connects with a short extension from Auchmuty Junction (NO 292013) to the A92 approaching Auchmuty (NO 284015). This too may be extended in future.

Vantage–Drumcooper: W, UX, DR, 1¼m, NT 150857–NT 154876. This short walk follows part of the Fordell Railway, a colliery waggonway of 4ft 4in gauge dating from *c.* 1770. It ran from Cowdenbeath and Crossgates to St David's Harbour on Inverkeithing Bay, serving a number of coal mines.

Wormit–Tayport: W, UX, DR, 4½m, NO 397263–NO 455292. Sustrans converted the Wormit to Tayport section of the NBR's Wormit to Leuchars line into a cycleway in 2004. Named the Tayport–Tay Bridge Cycle Route, it was officially opened by the Minister for Transport on 5 July that year. Deviations are necessary through local streets at West Newport

(NO 420273–NO 423275, ¼m) and East Newport (NO 424283–NO 435290, 1m).

Grampian

The Grampian region of Scotland now has a network of railway paths to rival the best anywhere in the British Isles, while superb scenery makes this an area that repays exploration. There are enough railway paths here to fill a week with cycling, although walkers will need rather longer.

Ballater–Cambus o'May–Dinnet–Aboyne: C, H, W, UT, DR, NO 372962–NO 423973–NO 460987–NO 528986, 11m (Aberdeenshire). The western end of the GNSR's branch line from Aberdeen to Ballater, now better known as the Deeside Way; recently extended from Dinnet to Aboyne and now part of NCN195. See also entry for Duthie Park to Culter and Banchory.

Dufftown–Craigellachie–Ballindalloch: W, UT, DR, 18m, NJ 321418–NJ 149363. The Speyside Way, a long railway path built on part of the GNSR's former line from Keith to Boat of Garten. This is a highly scenic route and was featured in the BBC's *Railway Walks* series in 2008. A notable feature is the number of distilleries formerly served by the branch, several of which are still operational. Aberlour and Knockando were two of the stations en route – names that need no introduction to a whisky connoisseur. If you are looking for Ballindalloch on a map, look for Cragganmore (NJ 167367); Ballindalloch Castle is ½ mile to the east as the crow flies and gave its name to the local station, no doubt as part of a deal with the local landowner. At the end of the section listed here (i.e. at NJ 149363), the Speyside Way leaves the trackbed and follows a separate course to Cromdale, where a further mile-long section of the railway is used (NJ 082299–NJ 070287). Another diversion

Carron station on the modern Speyside Way is an attractive stone-built structure, which still boasts an external station clock, although it is many years since the hands turned. This is whisky-making country, the local distillery being Dailuaine – a name little known to all but the most expert of whisky buffs since most of its production goes into the Johnnie Walker blends. (Phil Earnshaw)

then leads on to Grantown-on-Spey, where the trackbed is rejoined again (see below).

Duthie Park (Ferryhill, Aberdeen)–Peterculter–Banchory: C, W, UT, DR, 7¼m, NJ 938046–NJ 843004–NO 706957. The eastern end of the Deeside Way based on a further section of the Ballater branch (see above). The section between Peterculter (or 'Culter' to locals) and Banchory was opened in 2006. The local OS map shows a 1¼-mile gap east of Culter (NO 828999–NO 806996), where the trackbed is not accessible and the route diverts on to a minor lane; please follow local waymarking signs. Improvements to the route continue, with Aberdeen City Council installing a new high-quality bridge over Holburn Street, near the start of the trail, in 2009.

Dyce–Maud–Fraserburgh: C, H, W, UP, DR, 40m, NJ 884128–NJ 999679 NJ 997665. This route starts at Dyce railway station and enables walkers and cyclists to follow the whole of the former GNSR's branch line to Fraserburgh. Like the Maud–Peterhead route (see corresponding entry), it is part of the Formartine and Buchan Way, and – like that route again – many bridges along the way have been replaced by ramps. This is Scotland's longest continuous railway path and is used in places by NCN1.

Forres–Grantown-on-Spey: C, W, NI, NJ 036576–NJ 024283, 23m (Morayshire). This is the Dava Way, opened in July 2005 and named after Dava Moor and the intermediate settlement of Dava. Initially, a few sections diverted from the old HR trackbed, but the organisations behind the trail (the Cairngorms National Park and others) have worked hard to secure access agreements, which now reduce this to a minimum. At Grantown-on-Spey, energetic cyclists and walkers can switch to the Speyside Way (see entries for Dufftown and Grantown-on-Spey).

Divie Viaduct on the Dava Way is situated almost exactly halfway between the trail's two end points at Forres and Grantown-on-Spey. This fine structure carries the former HR line over the River Divie on seven arches at a maximum height of 477ft. (Phil Earnshaw)

Garmouth–Cullen: C, W, UT, DR, 11m, NJ 337641–NJ 510671. Part of the GNSR's line from Elgin to Tillynaught, much of this line has been reused in NCN1 which, from west to east, threads together the following sections of trackbed:

• **Garmouth–B9104 (north of Bogmoor):** C, W, UT, DR, 1¼m, NJ 337641–NJ 354642. Includes the magnificent 1,010yd Spey Viaduct at the west end.

• **Lower Auchenreath–Porttannachy:** C, W, UT, DR, ¾m, NJ 372641–NJ 386641.

• **Portgordon–nr Buckpool:** C, W, UT, DR, ¾m, NJ 393641–NJ 405647.

• **Portessie–Findochty:** C, W, UT, DR, 1½m, NJ 440662–NJ 463676.

• **Portknockie–Cullen:** C, W, UT, DR, 1½m, NJ 491683–NJ 510671. Three viaducts carry the line above Cullen; the largest is at the west of the town.

This large single-storey station is Maud Junction, where the Formartine and Buchan Way, which comes up from Dyce, near Aberdeen, offers walkers and cyclists the choice of continuing to either Peterhead or Fraserburgh. It is now home to the Maud Railway Museum, which opens between Easter and October, usually on the second full weekend of each month; admission is free. (Bob Prigg)

Grantown-on-Spey–Nethy Bridge: C, W, NI, DR, NJ 036262–NJ 001206, 4½m. A further section of The Speyside Way, which leaves the trackbed one station short of the junction with the HR at Boat of Garten. See also the entry for Dufftown (above).

Inverbervie–Gordoun: C, W, UT, DR, 1m, NO 833724–NO 830710. This short cycle trail is the northernmost mile of the former NBR branch from Montrose to Bervie. Although the town at the end of the line is called Inverbervie, its station was named Bervie, possibly because the town is situated on Bervie Bay. The 1911 *Encyclopaedia Britannica* gave the town's name as 'Bervie, or Inverbervie'.

Lossiemouth–Spynie (near Elgin): W, UP, DR, 4m, NJ 239709–NJ 231647 (Morayshire). Most of the GNSR's branch line from Elgin to Lossiemouth. Although this route is not shown as a cycle trail on the current OS map, pages and downloadable documents on the Moray local authority website confirm that it is open.

Maud–Peterhead: C, H, W, UT, DR, 13½m, NJ 926479–NK 124465. This cycle trail reuses the whole of the GNSR's branch line from Maud Junction to Peterhead and now forms the eastern arm of the Formartine and Buchan Way. A number of bridges have been removed and replaced by ramps.

Highland

Although not an official railway path, the Lochaber Narrow Gauge Railway, which skirts around the lower slopes of the Nevis range east of Fort William deserves a mention. This was a 25-mile long 3ft gauge network that was built to construct and later service a 15-mile tunnel from Loch Treig to Fort William. The purpose of the tunnel was, and is, to convey water to the Lochaber Hydro-Electric Power Scheme, which generates electricity for the Lochaber aluminium smelter in Fort William. The railway was opened in 1925 and remained in use until 1977, by which time the Forestry Commission had constructed many access roads in the area, and a section of the line had been washed away during storms in 1971. The trackbed is best followed from east to west, and can be found most easily near Fersit at NN 348779, south of Tulloch station on the still operational West Highland line to Fort William; it heads off initially in a north-westerly direction and is clearly labelled 'dismantled tramway' on the local OS Landranger sheet, number 41. Do not be surprised to find sleepers and rails left in places, especially on some of the bridges and viaducts. The trackbed ends near Fort William just east of the Ben Nevis Distillery and Lochaber Smelter, but the variety of tracks and trails here makes it difficult to pick out the start of the line if you are travelling in the other direction, i.e. from west to east. Julian Holland describes a walk over this unusual railway in *The Lost Lines of Britain* (AA Publishing, 2010), but choose a clear day to explore it.

Aberchalder–North Laggan: C, W, NI, DR, 3½m, NH 339030–NN 303983. Access from Aberchalder is at NH 339060, and from North Laggan at NN 300982. This is part of the NBR's former branch line from Spean Bridge to Fort Augustus. The trail is actually a mixture of General Wade's Military Road and the old railway, the former at the north end, the latter at the south end. However, the two routes are extremely close and run parallel to each other. Basically, if you are not actually on the Fort Augustus branch, you are right next to it. There is a long, low viaduct near Aberchalder and a fine crenellated bridge en route, while the remains of Invergarry station are passed at the southern end – see if you can spot the subway by which passengers gained access to the station's island platform. The route forms part of the Great Glen Way, which was opened by Prince Andrew in 2002. To the north and south of the section described here, the Way follows the towpath of the Caledonian Canal, which is a bonus for those who enjoy exploring waterways as well as old railways.

Dornoch–Embo: W, NI, DR, 1½m, NH 802906–NH 814927. The 'Visit Dornoch' website advertises a 3m walk along the trackbed of the Dornoch Light Railway, which almost certainly means 1½m each way!

Fortrose–near Avoch: C, W, UT, DR, 2m, NH 727567–NH 699554. Part of the HR's branch line from Muir of Ord to Fortrose. The route is a very popular link between Fortrose and Avoch, but curiously is not indicated on the local OS map, which still shows it as a disused railway. Publications by Transition Black Isle confirm that the route is open as a cycle trail.

Lothian

The network of railway paths in Edinburgh has been finished in tarmac, which makes the routes look more like lanes than former railways. However, plenty of bridges have been retained (vital for the 'grade separation' of path users from road traffic), while a few demolished bridges have been replaced by new ones. Overall, the extent of Edinburgh's railway path network makes the city one of the best places anywhere in the UK for getting around on a bicycle – an achievement that owes much to the hard work of Spokes, the Lothian cycling campaign (see www.spokes.org.uk).

Balerno–Slateford: C, H, W, UT, DR, 4¼m, NT 167670–NT 216704 (City of Edinburgh). Practically all of the CR's former loop line from Ravelrig to Balerno Junction near Slateford; now part of NCN75.

Bathgate–Plains: C, W, UT, TP, 13m, NS 971683–NS 802672. After the then freight-only line from Bathgate to Drumgelloch was closed in 1982, Sustrans installed a multi-use trail on it. This trail was itself closed, and removed, in October 2008 to permit relaying of the railway as a double-track passenger line, but Network Rail invested £7.3 million to construct a new cycle trail parallel to the new railway; both opened in December 2010. As a result, this is not a conventional railway path but a rail-side path, which makes one-way trips very easy, i.e. walk/cycle out and catch the train back from an intermediate station.

Edinburgh (Holyrood Park Road)–Brunstane: C, W, UT, DR, 2¾m, NT 269727–NT 312725. This section of NCN1 was formerly part of the Innocent Railway – the Edinburgh & Dalkeith, the first line into Edinburgh, planned in 1824–26 and built in 1827–31. The line was built to serve collieries and used a gauge of 4ft 6in. The wagons were hauled by horses but with a stationary engine working the incline that passed under Holyrood Park Road. A passenger service soon followed and, from 1832–45, the railway carried 200,000 to 300,000 passengers per year – more per mile than the Liverpool & Manchester Railway.

Dalkeith (King's Gate)–Lasswade–Penicuik: C, H, W, UX, DR, 8m, NT 321677–NT 321658–NT 240598 (Mid Lothian). The Penicuik to Musselburgh Foot and Cycleway. This trail used to run only from Bonnyrigg to Esk Bridge, just outside Penicuik, but has now been extended at both ends. It reuses the whole of the NBR's Penicuik branch, plus part of the same company's line between Millerhill and Dalhousie. The short connecting branch from Glenesk Junction to Dalkeith terminus is also open.

East Calder–Uphall: W, NI, DR, 2m, NT 090681–NT 065706. This line was a freight-only branch of the NBR, serving East Calder (Goods). Just after leaving East Calder, the trail crosses Camps Viaduct over the River Almond, which offers impressive views. The trail ends just east of Uphall station on the still-open line to Bathgate, although a non-railway extension can be followed into Uphall proper.

Elphinstone (Crossgatehall)–West Saltoun: C, H, W, UP, DR, 6m, NT 368689–NT 454666 (East Lothian). The Pencaitland Railway Walk, one of Scotland's earliest rail-to-trail conversions, formed from part of the NBR's branch from Smeaton to Gifford. At the Elphinstone end, the Dalkeith–Penicuik trail (see above) is less than a mile to the west.

Bilston Glen Viaduct is a difficult structure to photograph because trees surround it and the gorge below is steep sided. Fortunately, RR's doughty photographer was not deterred and came back with this striking image through the girders. Note the branches, which will make even this view disappear in the summer. (David Brace)

Longniddry–Haddington: C, H, W, UT, DR, 4¼m, NT 446763–NT 502740 (East Lothian). Most of the NBR's former branch from Longniddry to Haddington, now converted into a cycle trail.

Murrayfield–Leith: C, H, W, UT, DR, 4m, NT 233730–NT 260768 (City of Edinburgh). The CR's North Leith branch, now part of NCN1. At the Leith end, near Trinity, there is a five way choice of railway paths, with short railway-based links going off to Wardie, Heriot Hill and Bonnington, as well as Murrayfield and Leith. Near Craigleith, just north of the former Craigleith station, this trail connects with:

- **Branch to Davidson's Mains:** C, H, W, UT, DR, 1¼m, NT 224745–NT 205755 (City of Edinburgh). The start of the CR's Barnton branch.

Ratho Station–South Queensferry: C, H, W, UT, DR, 4½m, NT 125728–NT 129782 (City of Edinburgh). A cycle trail formed from most of the NBR's Ratho–Dalmeny line. Starts by a roundabout on the M9, north-east of Ratho station, but rapidly heads off into the countryside.

Roslin–Loanhead–Gilmerton (Lasswade Road): C, W, UT, DR, 3m, NT 279640–NT 283656–NT 292673 (Midlothian). This is the central section of the NBR's Glencorse branch, including the 150ft-high Bilston Glen Viaduct at NT 281648. The branch ran from Glencorse to Millerhill, the 4 miles nearest Millerhill being retained to serve Bilston Glen Colliery, which closed in 1989. (Passenger services were withdrawn in 1933.) The trail originally terminated at Loanhead, but by 2014 had been extended under the Edinburgh Bypass to reach Lasswade Road, south-west of Gilmerton. Midlothian Council wanted the trail extended north-east to the A7 (NT 309689, within Edinburgh's boundary) and by October 2016 clearance work on the extension had started. Just before the route passes under the

Edinburgh Bypass, a ½-mile trail comes in from Straiton Farm to the west (NT 275665–NT 283667), which reuses an old railway incline. At the Roslin end, the Dalkeith–Penicuik trail is a short distance to the south.

Tranent–Cockenzie: W, NI, DT, 1¼m, NT 402729–NT 402753. The 2½m Tranent and Cockenzie Waggonway, opened in 1722, can claim to be the first railway in Scotland; the northern end remains in use as a path by walkers, cyclists and horse riders, although the local OS map does not show it as a dedicated footpath or bridleway. The Coast Alive website provides the following:

> There is still much to be seen today of the historic Tranent–Cockenzie waggonway. Almost the whole of the route of the 1722 waggonway is clearly visible, and indeed most of its length is used as a public path by walkers, cyclists, and horse-riders … At Cockenzie Harbour many old stone sleepers are still in position, and above Meadowmill a long length of the waggonway was used as a siding for National Coal Board coal wagons into the 1960s. This meant that parts of the route were used as a railway for about 240 years!

Raasay

Here's a surprise. The small island of Raasay is situated just off the east coast of Skye and is hardly the first place one would go looking for old railways. However, Raasay had an iron works during the First World War, and a narrow gauge railway ran from the iron ore mine to the kilns above the pier – a railway, moreover, which from 1916 was worked by German prisoners of war. By the end of the war, almost 200,000 tons of raw ore had been produced, but within six months of hostilities ending, production was reduced before stopping altogether.

Raasay Iron Ore Mine–South Raasay Pier: W, UX, DR, 1½m, NG 565366–NG 554341. The line is more or less downhill all the way, and dead straight; you cannot miss the piers of the former viaduct at NG 562359.

Skye

Here's another surprise. The island of Skye used to boast several short industrial lines, the longest of which was a 2½-mile-long 3ft gauge railway built by the Skye Marble Company in 1904. Originally horse-drawn, the line was steam-worked from 1909, the motive power being a 0-4-0 tank engine called *Skylark*. The marble was transported from quarries at Kilchrist to Broadford Pier, but both the line and the bridge over the A87 (at the Broadford end) fell into disuse in the 1920s.

Broadford Pier–Kilchrist: W, UP, DR, 2½m, NG 642235–NG 621197. The former Skye Marble Company's line, now known as 'The Broadford Marble Line' (see www.walkhighlands.co.uk/skye/marble-line.shtml). In 2010, Skye's Heritage Trail Project and the Broadford Environmental Group installed a new span over the Broadford River using one of the original abutments of the old railway bridge at Broadford as part of their plan to create a 'heritage footpath' along the former Marble Company's trackbed, linking the pier with the original quarries at Kilchrist. Halfway up a mountain, these quarries occupied a very lonely spot, which nonetheless was equipped with a platform for loading and unloading; it survives to this day. The project, backed by a sizeable consortium of community and local government interests, also restored a section of 3ft gauge track on the pier and installed an information board.

Strathclyde

During the late 1980s, Sustrans constructed several long routes out of Glasgow, e.g. to Balloch, Greenock and Irvine, reusing old railways wherever possible. This helps to account for this region's very good railway path network. Note that the Balloch–Glasgow route consists of only two-thirds railway path, but its start and end points are listed below as a convenient way of joining the railway parts together in a single walk or ride. Although mainly urban, there is plenty of transport interest along this route, which in places also uses the towpath of the restored Forth & Clyde Canal.

Balloch–Scottish Exhibition and Conference Centre (Glasgow): C, W, UT, DR, 20m, NS 391819–NS 563656. This cycle path was opened in 1989 and initially linked Loch Lomond with Glasgow, but is now the start of the Sustrans long-distance Glasgow to Inverness cycle route (Lochs and Glens North). The trail comprises a mixture of route types, with the first few miles south of Balloch following the west bank of the River Leven. The railway-based sections are as follows:

- **Dumbarton–Bowling–Old Kilpatrick:** C, W, UT, DR, 4¼m, NS 405754–NS 437738– NS 465727. Part of the former CR line from Dumbarton to Glasgow, now incorporated into NCN7. East of Bowling, the cycle trail is formed from a mixture of the old railway and the towpath of the Forth & Clyde Canal, which run side by side.
- **Yoker–Partick:** C, W, UT, DR, 2¼m, NS 518684–NS 552663. Another section of NCN7 formed from the former CR Dumbarton to Glasgow line.

Coatbridge–Airdrie: W, UX, DR, 1¼m, NS 740658–NS 758663 (North Lanarkshire). Just before Airdrie, this connects with the following short link:

- **Branch to Burnfoot:** C, H, W, UP, DR, ½m, NS 748661–NS 755665 (North Lanarkshire).

Coatbridge (Calder)–Hillhead (near Calderbank): C, W, UT, DR, 1¼m, NS 745645–NS 765637 (North Lanarkshire). Part of NCN75, based on a section of the former CR line that linked Baillieston with Newhouse. This area used to be a complicated web of railways operated by the CR and NBR.

Connel Ferry–Ballachulish Ferry: The first section of the Oban to Fort William cycle trail was opened between Ballachulish Ferry and Kentallen in 2008, and a lot of progress has been made since then. It looks as if the route could end up using about one half of the former 28-mile-long CR branch line from Connel Ferry to Ballachulish. (Oban to Connel Ferry remains open as an operational railway, so the trail follows an entirely new route between these places.) All this is part of the 48-mile Caledonia Way, which Sustrans describes as a 'largely traffic-free route [which] follows the spectacular coastline between Oban and Fort William. The route has lengthy sections of fine, traffic-free path, and some sections on quiet minor roads, but there remain a few short sections where cyclists have to use the main road [the A828].' Unfortunately, the main road sections can be unpleasant and are best avoided by all but the most experienced cyclists; an example is the section from Dalnatrat to Duror, where negotiations for a better route have been described as 'protracted'.

- **Barcaldine–Creagan Roundabout:** C, W, UT, DR, 3m, NM 945412–NM 976440 (Argyll & Bute). The trackbed through Barcaldine lies on the east side of the village but was not available so the trail takes a diversion via Barcaldine House, which usefully joins two trackbed sections together. North of Creagan roundabout, the A828 occupies the trackbed for ¼ mile but a good-quality, segregated roadside cycle track leads on to the next trackbed-based section at Inverfolla.

- **Inverfolla–North Dallens–Appin House:** C, W, UT, DR, 4½m, NM 959450–NM 929491–NM 934498 (Argyll & Bute). This section is on the trackbed all the way, with views across the Sound of Shuna to Shuna Island. It finishes a short distance north of Appin House, but once again a good quality, segregated roadside cycle track continues on to Dalnatrat.
- **South of Duror–South of Kentallen:** C, W, UT, DR, 1¾m, NM 988547–NN 004564 (Highlands). The grid reference at the Duror end marks the point where the trail leaves the A828, but it is soon back on the trackbed which it then follows as far as Lagnaha Farm.
- **Kentallen–Ballachulish Ferry:** C, W, UT, mainly DR, 4m, NN 014584–NN 054594 (Highlands). This is another scenic coastal section with good views across Loch Linnhe. It connects at Ballachulish Ferry with a cycle trail to Ballachulish alongside the A82, which has subsumed much of the old trackbed. At Ballachulish, a trail continues on to Glencoe, but east of Ballachulish the route is an entirely new roadside trail with no railway antecedents.

Cumnock–Logan: W, NI, DR, 1¼m, NS 573195–NS 588203. The great feature of interest on this short trail is the thirteen-arch Cumnock Viaduct, which passengers on the Kilmarnock–Dumfries line get to see from the carriage window.

Darvel–near Loudounhill: W, UX, DR, 1½m, NS 573378–NS 599376. RR Scotland came across this waymarked path in 2015; it uses part of the short-lived Darvel & Strathaven Railway near its western extremity. The trail ends where a high three-span girder bridge on sandstone piers (the latter still standing) once crossed a minor road to the south-west of the iconic Loudoun Hill. (This is about 300yds short of the former Loudounhill station, which was beyond a further demolished viaduct.)

Kilmarnock–Irvine: C, W, NI, DR, 5¼m, NS 419387–NS 339382. Part of NCN73, reusing virtually all of the former NBR line from Kilmarnock to Irvine.

Kirkintilloch–Muirhead: C, W, NI, DR, 4m, NS 657735–NS 696700. Part of the NBR line from Kirkintilloch to Bothwell, now converted into a cycle trail. In 2009, a new road was due to be constructed over part of the line south of Kirkintilloch, but there is another access (using part of the Lenzie–Bridgend Junction link line) from NS 655730.

Kirkintilloch–Strathblane: C, H, W, UT, DR, 7½m, NS 656742–NS 564792 (East Dunbartonshire). Part of the former NBR Kirkintilloch–Gartness branch,

The former branch line from Connel Ferry to Ballachulish closed to passengers in March 1966, but forty-four years later was being turned into a long-distance cycle trail from Oban to Ballachulish. This is the view to the south of Ballachulish Ferry station, where passengers could take a ferry across Loch Leven to North Ballachulish and the road to Fort William. (Author)

now converted into a cycle trail. Continues into Central Region, q.v.

Linwood–Mid Auchinleck: C, W, UT, DR, 8m, NS 433638–NS 335727. Part of NCN75, the cycle trail from Glasgow to Greenock, based on the NBR's Paisley–Greenock line. Connects at Linwood with the Paisley–Glengarnock route.

Paisley–Glengarnock: C, W, UT, DR, 12½m, NS 482635–NS 319534. The northern section of the NBR line from Paisley to Irvine, now part of Sustrans' Glasgow–Irvine route (NCN7).

Plains–Bathgate: C, W, UT, TP, 13m, NS 802672–NS 971683. This is the lavish new trail, which Network Rail constructed alongside the new Airdrie–Bathgate rail link in return for their turning the old Sustrans Drumgelloch–Bathgate route back into a railway. Continues into Lothian, q.v.

Upper Wellwood–Muirkirk–Glenbuck Loch: W, NI, DR, 4¾m, NS 675254–NS 696266–NS 750287. Thanks to the River Ayr Way, one can now walk almost 5m of the old railway through Muirkirk, where branches of the Caledonian and Glasgow & South Western Railways used to meet at an end-on junction. There is a ¾m detour around Muirkirk golf course and Kames Motorsport Circuit, west of the town's station site (NS 696266).

Whitecroft–Strone (near Greenock): C, W, UT, DR, 2m, NS 323740–NS 295748. A further section of NCN7 west of Mid Auchinleck, again reusing part of the NBR's Paisley–Greenock line.

Tayside

Bridgefoot–Dronley–North Dronley: W, UX, DR, 3m, NO 377352–NO 337367 (Angus). Part of the CR's branch line from Dundee to Newtyle, which opened in 1831 as the Dundee & Newtyle Railway – the first railway in the north of Scotland. Further north at the tiny community of Newbigging (NO 291426), more of this line can be walked as part of the Newtyle Path Network, which unfortunately is not shown on OS maps. The network includes several railway paths, the most notable being the well-signed Railway Loop Path around the west side of the village; this is a long, curving climb in the Swiss railway style to gain height. Maps of the Newtyle Path Network may still be available from the Post Office in North Street.

Montrose–Borrowfield: C, W, UT, DR, 2m, NO 722576–NO 712602 (Angus). A cycle trail based on the CR's short branch from Dubton Junction to the company's Montrose terminus.

Montrose (Broomfield Road Junction)–North Water Viaduct: C, W, UT, DR, 2¼m, NO 718591–NO 725622 (Angus). This new trail, part of NCN1, connects with the Montrose–Borrowfield route at NO 718591.

Ninewells–Lochee–Downfield: W, UP, DR, 4¼m, NO 355303–NO 389328 (Dundee City). Another part of the CR's branch line from Dundee to Newtyle. The path is wheelchair-friendly west of Lochee, where cyclists and horse riders are also permitted.

St Vigeans (near Arbroath)–Colliston: C, W, UT, DR, 2¾m, NO 639424–NO 619459. St Vigeans Nature Trail and part of the Arbroath path network, which finishes at the site of the former Colliston station. It is unsurfaced, but to use RR member Keith Potter's expression, 'should be manageable for all but the most highly-strung road bikes'.

Send in the Cranes

We build too many walls and not enough bridges.

Attributed to Sir Isaac Newton

In the late 1970s, the most powerful equipment used on a railway path would probably have been a vibrating roller, used to spray water on to limestone dust while compressing it into road chippings spread on top of old railway ballast. (Therein lies a story – quarry companies used to give away limestone dust, a byproduct of stone crushing, until Sustrans and local authorities were using so much of it that they had created a new market for a new product.) Nowadays, one might just see a very large crane on a railway path, lowering into place pre-assembled sections of a new bridge or viaduct.

That this has happened is due to a lot of local authority work and, most recently, Sustrans' Connect2 scheme, which was actually a programme of seventy-nine separate projects to reconnect communities severed by missing bridges, the construction of busy new roads, etc. Connect2 has an unusual history. In June 2005, the Big Lottery Fund and ITV announced a competition to find the winner of a £50 million grant: the thirty-three applications were whittled down progressively to thirteen, six and finally four, which went to a public vote conducted online and by telephone. The winner, announced on 12 December 2007, was the Connect2 scheme, which promised the broadest impact across the UK, as well as offering benefits to public health and local economies (of which more later). Sometimes, a Connect2 project would offer an improvement within a single community, but more frequently it would provide links between several communities, as happened spectacularly in the case of the Two Tunnels Trail at Bath where a fragmented railway was brought back to life as a multi-use trail.

The 'fragmented railway' was the northernmost 4 miles of the former Somerset & Dorset line, which in its heyday conveyed millions of passengers from the North and the Midlands to their annual summer holidays around Poole and Bournemouth. Thanks to Dr Beeching, this line ceased to operate from 7 March 1966, its 63¾ scenic miles being amongst the most regretted losses from the British railway network. While short sections of the trackbed south of Bath had been reused as trails, they were of local significance only because intermediate bridges had been removed, and the two tunnels along the way were blocked, one with its north portal walled up and filled with earth.

It is 2012 and a new steel span bridge has just been installed over Dartmouth Avenue in suburban Bath, thus bringing the Two Tunnels scheme another step closer to completion. The original bridge was a narrow structure, which was removed as part of a road improvement scheme shortly after the S&DR closed. (Tim Trew/Sustrans)

When Earlsheaton Tunnel was selected to form part of the new Dewsbury and Ossett Greenway, it needed a lot of remedial work, but by October 2012 the path-laying team were able to take possession. Since then, street lighting has been installed as well. (Graeme Bickerdike)

All that came to an end at 10.00 a.m. on Saturday 6 April 2013, when 100 VIPs cycled through the 'Two Tunnels' on their way from Bloomfield Road Open Space in Bath to Midford; they had each paid £175 for the privilege and thus raised a five-figure sum to start a maintenance fund for the new trail. This was the twenty-first-century equivalent of being at the opening of a new railway and even included a champagne breakfast on the newly laid deck of Tucking Mill Viaduct, a few miles to the south. At 12.30 p.m. the trail opened to the public, and people came in droves. The BBC reported that 2,000 attended the opening, but Sustrans put the number for the whole day at more like 10,000, with 8,000 travelling through the tunnels specifically. It was a momentous occasion.

Travelling from north to south along the Two Tunnels Trail today, one crosses Bellotts Road Viaduct (significantly altered), Dartmouth Avenue Bridge (new), Monksdale Road Bridge (new), Devonshire

Tunnel (excavated and restored), Combe Down Tunnel (restored) and Tucking Mill Viaduct (restored). After that, one passes the single platform of the old Midford station before crossing Midford Viaduct, which was restored as part of an earlier project in 2005. Bar a section between Wellow and Shoscombe, where the railway formation has been lost, one can now walk or cycle via the old railway from Bath to Radstock, where there are connecting railway paths to Frome, Midsomer Norton and Thicket Mead. At the Bath end, the Two Tunnels trail is just a few hundred yards from the long-established Bath to Bristol trail, which includes an extension from Mangotsfield northwards which it is hoped will one day reach Yate; currently, it stops on the west side of Pucklechurch. These trails comprise a significant regional facility.

Bath is not the only place that has seen developments like this in the last decade, and, although many of the headline-grabbing new connections have been Connect2 projects, this is not universally the case. Further south on the old Somerset & Dorset Railway, the Dorset local authorities have been working for decades to turn the old railway into a multi-use trail called the North Dorset Trailway; in the process, they have installed new bridges at both Fiddleford and Hodmoor, which enable local school children to cycle to and from school and avoid the difficult A350. Even in the New Forest – not the most obvious place to go looking for this type of work – two new bridges have been installed and a third repaired. The disused railway here was the old main line from Brockenhurst to Ringwood and beyond, which closed in 1964 and, under the terms of its Act, then reverted to the Forestry Commission as agent for the Crown. When BR was non-committal about the life expectancy of the underbridges at Long Slade Bottom on Hincheslea Bog and offered to demolish them, the commission was only too happy to accept. But come 2005 replacement spans were installed across the old abutments partly for the benefit of cyclists, and partly to prevent further erosion of the embankments by walkers negotiating the bridgeless gaps.

Around the country, major new engineering structures have been installed on old railways so that they can again serve a useful purpose. Many Scottish viaducts survived after closure because they were made of mass concrete, including Kendrum Viaduct near Lochearnhead on the CR's old line from Dunblane to Crianlarich; but Kendrum had the misfortune to include a central steel span, which was removed after closure for scrap. A new one was installed when NCN7 was established along the trackbed. In 2013, a new bridge over the River Tweed was opened at Cardrona so that the old railway between Peebles and Innerleithen could be reused as an off-road trail. For good measure, this route also uses an old railway tunnel at Eshiels that burrows beneath the A72.

It is the same in Wales. The spectacular section of NCN46 between Brynmawr and Abergavenny reuses parts of the LNWR's Heads of the Valleys Line and the Clydach Railroad, which preceded it. This has brought several viaducts back into use and, in between, mountainside ledges and blind viaducts that were extended outwards from the mountain face when the line was widened to take double track. If there were a book of 'Ten Railway Paths to Travel Before You Die', this would be in it. No one can travel through the Clydach Gorge without developing a sense of awe and wonder at what our Victorian ancestors achieved. And there is no shortage of railway history in Wales. It was here in 1804 that Richard Trevithick first ran a steam locomotive from Merthyr Tydfil to Abercynon along the Pennydarren Tramway, hauling five wagons of pig iron – not to mention seventy joyriders who clambered on to the wagons. His 'Pennydarren' locomotive reached a speed of 5mph and won him a prize of £500, a princely sum at the time. Trevithick's machine

unfortunately broke some of the tramway's cast-iron rails, but he proved that locomotive as opposed to stationary engines were viable. Nowadays, one can walk or cycle the Pennydarren Tramway in its new guise as the Trevithick Trail, and in 2012 the new Puddlers Bridge was installed south of Merthyr to provide a safe crossing of the busy A4060 dual carriageway.

The north is another area in which to see plenty of drama on railway paths. You don't have to be an engineer or railway historian to realise that the terrain often forced the Victorian railway builders to go over rather than under natural barriers. The Northern Viaducts Trust was a trailblazer in the region, having been set up in 1989 to restore Smardale Gill Viaduct; but it didn't stop there, moving on to Podgill Viaduct in 2000 and Merrygill Viaduct in 2005. All three of these mighty structures are near Kirkby Stephen on the famous Stainmore line which once linked Darlington with Tebay, a trans-Pennine route which carried coal and coke from the North East to the blast furnaces of Barrow, with iron ore going back the other way. Its summit on Stainmore was 1,370ft above sea level, which suggests what the weather might have been like up there, and why there were never many passengers. In Greater Manchester, the branch line from Holcombe Brook to Bury – now mostly reused in NCN6 – acquired a replacement viaduct in 2012 at Woolfold over the Kirklees Valley. As a result, the communities at Greenmount, Tottington and Brandlesholme now have an attractive off-road route into Bury town centre.

Further south in Derbyshire's Peak District, John Grimshaw played an important role in persuading the local authorities to open up four long-closed tunnels on the Monsal Trail, which used to be part of the Midland Railway's main line from Manchester Central to St Pancras – a route used in the 1960s by British Rail's prestigious 'Blue Pullman', which might have suggested that it was safe from closure.

When Bath's Two Tunnels Trail was opened on 6 April 2013, the first users were a hundred VIP guests who had paid £175 each for the privilege; the purpose was to set up a substantial maintenance fund for the route. Cycling through Combe Down and the Devonshire Tunnels, it was impossible not to think of the excitement of Victorians witnessing the opening of the railway in the nineteenth century. To provide some decadence, a champagne breakfast was served on the restored Tucking Mill Viaduct, just north of Midford. (Author)

As the Beeching-inspired trail of railway destruction began to slow down in the late 1960s, there was little or no interest in reusing or even exploring old railways. That would seem incomprehensible to this huge queue of cyclists, waiting to try out the new Two Tunnels Trail in Bath on its opening day in 2013. There were as many, if not more, walkers. (Author)

Viewed by Beeching as requiring only the removal of its stopping trains, it was closed entirely in 1968. The route regained its linear integrity for walkers and cyclists in May 2011, when Chee Tor, Litton, Cressbrook and Headstone Tunnels were finally reopened, in the process eliminating some awkward detours and bringing the trail's count of tunnels to six. (The public could already traverse large viaducts at Headstone and Millers Dale.) The tunnel openings led to a dramatic increase in the number of cyclists using the trail, with 50,000 having been counted by an automatic scanner by January 2012.

This overview of restoration and new construction on the UK's disused railway network is necessarily selective and brief, but it must mention Devon which has invested substantially in railway paths in order to make this most scenic but hilly of counties a 'must visit' destination for walkers and cyclists. Devon was already well endowed with such routes, especially around Barnstaple, but now there is hardly an old railway in the county which cannot be walked or cycled for at least some small part. In addition to the restoration of various disused bridges, viaducts and tunnels, two new bridges have gone in on the old branch line from Bovey Tracey to Moretonhampstead (which is not yet open throughout), and one on the immensely scenic Princetown branch (choose a bright day and walk south from Princetown: the views will not disappoint). However, the crowning achievement nationally was the opening in April 2012 of the new Gem Bridge south of Tavistock at a cost of £2.1 million. The name 'Gem Bridge' is a misnomer, for this is a new 650ft-long viaduct, which spans the Walkham Valley on four piers at a height of up to 85ft. It is the third structure to stand in this location, and was designed to imitate Brunel's original in which the deck was supported by fans of timber bracing built on masonry piers. If you are heading from Tavistock to Plymouth, it forms part of the 21-mile Drake's Trail. Or perhaps you would rather travel from Ilfracombe to Plymouth, when it forms part of the 100-mile Devon Coast-to-Coast route? If you want your walk or ride to have an international dimension, it is part of the Vélodyssey, a 750-mile cross-Channel link that starts with the Devon Coast-to-Coast but then uses the Plymouth–Roscoff ferry before continuing down the west coast of France to Spain.

Finally, with all the development that has taken place on the old Somerset & Dorset Railway in recent years, could there be a day when it will become a route between the Bristol and English Channels? All that it would take is a short link at Bath to connect properly with the Bath and Bristol Path (easy) and the reuse of the 'forgotten' section of trackbed between Midsomer Norton and Stalbridge (difficult). In the north, there are already four major coast-to-coast routes, the Trans Pennine Trail, the C2C, the Way of the Roses and Hadrian's Cycleway. Why should the south have less?

WALES

Introduction

Wales has long been a good place for the railway rambler, and it is getting even better. In the 1980s, when Sustrans was beginning to make an impact in reusing old railways as walking and cycling trails, a map was published which showed a network of proposed cycle trails throughout the south of the country. In the years that followed, much of this network was constructed, but on 10 September 2009 came news that many of the gaps were to be filled. Ieuan Wyn Jones, the country's Minister for Economy and Transport, announced that £7.6 million was to be invested to finish a £16 million project producing 100 miles of new walking and cycling routes for the Valleys Cycle Network. Following former railways and tramways, the scheme would link existing routes in the Swansea, Llynfi, Taff, Ely and Ebbw Valleys and would improve cycle access for areas including Merthyr Tydfil, Pontypridd, Llantrisant and Pontypool. When complete, the scheme would bring the National Cycle Network within 2 miles of an extra 636,000 people. Most of this extra route mileage is now open.

Clwyd

Connah's Quay–Hawarden Bridge–Chester–Mickle Trafford: C, W, NI, DR, 10m, SJ 300698–SJ 311695–SJ 420679–SJ 447691. A railway path opened in the late 1990s which links the Connah's Quay Dock branch with the western half of the old Mickle Trafford line (Hawarden Bridge to Mouldsworth). The extension from Newton (east of Chester) to Mickle Trafford was opened in October 2009, with access in Mickle Trafford from Station Lane. The trail finishes in Cheshire.

Corwen–Cynwyd: C, H, W, NI, DR, 1¼m, SJ 070433–SJ 056417. A bridleway with access at the Cynwyd end from SJ 057413. Part of the former GWR line from Ruabon to Dolgellau; now part of the North Berwyn Way.

Dyserth–Marian Mill: W, UX, DR, ½m, SJ 063829–SJ 063793. Connects with the route from Prestatyn to Dyserth. A privately built formation that was never actually laid with track; most easily accessible from the Dyserth end.

Greenfield–Holywell Town: W, UX, DR, 1¼m, SJ 197774–SJ 187760. The steeply graded Holywell branch.

Prestatyn–Dyserth: C, W, UP, DR, 2¾m, SJ 063829–SJ 063793. The LNWR's short Dyserth branch, once the preserve of steam-powered rail motors.

Towyn (near Kinmel Bay)–A547 near Porth Farm: W, NI, DR, 1¼m, SH 990794–SH 990776. Part of the former Kinmel Camp Railway, a standard gauge line built in 1916 to link Kinmel Camp to Foryd on the LNWR line from Chester to Holyhead. Start at the Towyn end following a public footpath westwards and turn south (sharp left) at SH 983792 on to the trackbed, which can then be followed as far as the A547 at SH 990776. A local informant reckoned that the route could be followed on to SH 983762 where the line crossed the A55 near Faenol Bach, but local maps show no evidence of this.

Dyfed

Once something of a desert for railway paths, the local authorities that took over from Dyfed County Council in 1996 have turned this part of west Wales into an area where the railway rambler will find much to enjoy.

Aberaeron–Llanerchaeron Estate–Crossway Wood (near Ciliau Aeron): C, W, NI, DR, 2¾m, SN 462620–SN 489597–SN 489597. The westernmost part of the GWR's former Aberaeron branch. The National Trust's tearooms at Llanerchaeron make an excellent refreshment/turnaround point if you've come from Aberaeron; the NT also offers a discount for walkers and cyclists wishing to visit the mansion or estate.

The section to Crossway Wood is a permissive route opened in 2013.

Aberystwyth–Allt-ddu: C, H, W, NI, DR, 20m, SN 583810–SN 692626. The northernmost part of the GWR's scenic cross-country line from Aberystwyth to Carmarthen, now designated the Ystwyth Trail that links Aberystwyth with Allt-ddu (for Tregaron) via Llanilar, Trawsgoed and Ystrad Meurig. That this route exists at all is a major achievement, for the railway closed in 1965 and was then left for forty years or more, which is why some parts of it still parallel the trackbed on minor roads, or take other road-based diversions. Further improvements are planned. For example, in 2011 the 2½-mile link from Allt-ddu to Tregaron followed the main road, the B4343, rather than the old railway, but in 2014 Ceredigion CC voted unanimously to move the path on to the trackbed so that it would come out in Tregaron at SN 679602, adjacent to Wynnstay Stores. When this is accomplished, it will extend the trail to around 23 miles in length.

Bwlch Glas Mine–Hafan Quarry: W, NI, DT, 1½m, SN 711878–SN 731880. This short walk follows the easternmost section of what is possibly the most obscure line in the whole of this gazetteer – the Plynlimon & Hafan Tramway, a narrow gauge line built to a gauge of 2ft 3in, which opened in 1897 and closed in 1899 when the company went into voluntary liquidation. Lead was mined at Bwlch Glas and stone quarried at Hafan. Bwlch Glas is situated about 14 miles north-east of Aberystwyth and is accessible via a narrow lane running east from Tal-y-bont on the A487 Aberystwyth–Dolgellau road. Wikipedia offers a decent history of the line; the scenery will not disappoint.

Cardigan–Cilgerran: C, W, NI, DR, 2½m, SN 181458–SN 187430. The northernmost section of the former

GWR branch from Whitland to Cardigan, now part of NCN82.

Llanelli–Cross Hands: C, W, NI, DR, 12m, SN 499003–SN 559132. Starts just north of Sandy Junction to the west of Llanelli and reuses virtually the whole of the Llanelly & Mynydd Mawr Railway. Now a well-used part of NCN47.

Kidwelly–Llangadog: C, H, W, NI, DR, 1½m, SN 408062–SN 424077. The Gwendraeth Valley Railway's freight-only line from Kidwelly to Mynyddygarreg is a bridleway along most of its length between Banc Pen-Dre in Kidwelly and Meinciau Road in Llangadog.

Kidwelly–Pembrey–Burry Port: C, W, UT, DR, 2½m, SN 418029–SN 443006. Part of the former Burry Port & Gwendraeth Valley Railway's line between Kidwelly Junction and Burry Port, which was extended by a mile in summer 2016 at a cost of £300,000.

Johnston–Neyland: W, UP, DR, 5¼m, SM 931112–SM 967048. Since 2002, this route – now part of NCN4 – has been extended north of Johnston to start near North Johnston. It runs for the first ¾ mile alongside the operational line from Haverfordwest to Milford before heading off towards Neyland at the site of Milford Haven Branch Junction. In practice, the most convenient place to pick up the trail is Johnston station.

King's Moor–Thomas Chapel: W, UX, DT, 2¼m, SN 122067–SN 103089. Part of the Saundersfoot Railway. See also the entry below for Stepaside–Saundersfoot–Ridgeway.

Parc y Llong–Cwm Mawr: W, NI, DR, 7¼m, SN 437065–SN 530127. This route survived as an operational railway until 1996. The now defunct Dyfed County Council maintained that a right of way existed alongside the line (a view corroborated by the Ordnance Survey), probably originating from its early days as a tram road.

Stepaside–Saundersfoot–Ridgeway: W, UP, DT, 3m, SN 138077–SN 137048–SN 127053. This path starts in a caravan park. If in difficulty, ask for directions at Stepaside Visitors Centre. The section between Wiseman's Bridge and Saundersfoot includes three tunnels on the Pembrokeshire Coast Path. At Saundersfoot, minor lanes lead to:

- **Wiseman's Bridge–Amroth:** C, W, NI, DT, 1m, SN 148065–SN 160071. Part of NCN4, which was improved in 2002, including a new balustrade

Anyone following the Pembrokeshire Coast Path through Saundersfoot may wonder why it includes three tunnels; surely they were a great expense and extravagance for a mere footpath? The answer, of course, is that the tunnels started life as part of a railway – the narrow gauge Saundersfoot Railway. (Richard Lewis)

against the sea. Sustrans states that this route used to be a tramway, but no corroboration has been found.

Flat Holm

The island of Flat Holm is situated in the Bristol Channel. While its railway remains are less than the 2-mile threshold required for inclusion in this gazetteer, this entry was considered worthwhile because it is unusual that the island should have had any kind of rail transport at all.

From 1941 onwards, a military railway was constructed on Flat Holm to carry provisions and ammunition, serving the needs of 300 soldiers who manned a range of heavy and light anti-aircraft guns, and a radar station. The railway was of 60cm gauge, being formed from pre-fabricated sections captured from the Germans during the First World War. While the track has all been lifted, parts of the trackbed can still be traced. Cardiff Council manages the island under the terms of a fifty-year lease from the Crown Estate, which expires in 2045. Day trips are available from Cardiff or Weston-super-Mare all the year round; see the island's website, www.flatholmisland.com.

Glamorgan, Mid

Bargoed–Parc Cwm Darran: C, W, UP, DR, 4½m, SO 149003–SO 110043. The Rhymney Railway's branch line from Bargoed to Darran and Deri, plus part of the onward extension (via an end-on junction with the Brecon & Merthyr Railway) towards Pant.

Bargoed–Cwmsyfiog: C, W, UT, DR, 1m, SO 151003–SO 155018. The start of the B&MR's branch to New Tredegar and Rhymney, now part of NCN468. See also entry below for New Tredegar.

Brynmenyn–Blaengarw: C, W, UT, DR, 5½, SS 907857–SS 900934. Most of the former GWR Garw Valley line, now part of NCN884. Enthusiasts plan to get the old line running again between Bryngarw Park on the edge of Brynmenyn and Pontycymmer, stating that at 4½ miles it will be the longest heritage line in South Wales.

Cefn Cribwr–Kenfig Hill–Frog Pond: C, W, UT, DR, 2¼m, SS 854834–SS 841819. Part of the former GWR line from Tondu to Pyle.

Dare Valley Country Park
Includes the following sections of old railway:

- **Cwmaman–Cwmdare:** C, W, NI, DR, 3½m, SO 008002–SN 980028. Part of the GWR Cwmaman branch.
- **Cwmdare–Gadlys:** C, W, NI, DR, 1m, SN 980028–SN 998026. Part of a Taff Vale Railway branch from Dare Valley Junction to Bwllfa Dare Colliery.

Hirwaun–Penderyn: C, W, NI, DR, 2½m, SN 959061–SN 951085. The former Penderyn Tramway, originally a horse-drawn route, which connected Penderyn's quarries with Hirwaun's blast furnaces. Opened in the mid 1780s, the line was converted to steam power in 1904 with diesels following. The line remained in use until 1982 and is now part of NCN46.

Hirwaun–Trecynon: C, W, NI, DT, 3m, SN 965052–SN/SO 000032. Part of the Hirwaun to Abernant tram road, last used in 1900. The first ½ mile at the Hirwaun end survives in very good condition, complete with stone sleepers, passing loops, boundary hedges and culverts.

Llwydcoed–Cwmbach: W, NI, DR, 2½m, SN 988051–SO 023027. Part of the former GWR line from Gelli Tarw Junction to Merthyr Tydfil, terminating near the southern end of the 1½-mile Merthyr Tunnel (details supplied by Cynon Valley Borough Council).

Merthyr Tydfil (Penydarren)–Abercynon: C, H, W, NI, DT, 7¼m, SO 056050–ST 085949. This is the Trevithick Trail, which starts from Milbourne Close on the south of Merthyr. The trail reuses as much as possible of the Penydarren Tramroad (also spelt 'Pennydarren', probably an Anglicised spelling), which was the first tramway on which a load of 10 tons of iron, plus various passengers, was hauled by a steam train on 21 February 1804. The designer of the locomotive was the Cornishman Richard Trevithick – hence the trail's name. On 21 February 2012, Sustrans Cymru opened the 'Puddlers Bridge' (SO 061041) over the A4060 on the southern edge of Merthyr, thus connecting two sections of the trail and eliminating a dangerous road crossing. En route, the trail passes the southern portal of Plymouth Tunnel, the first railway tunnel in the world.

Nantymoel–Brynmenyn: C, W, UT, DR, 6½m, SS 933930–SS 905847. The GWR's Nantymoel branch plus part of the connecting line from Tondu to Llantrisant via Hendreforgan; now part of NCN883 and NCN4. NCN4 heads east at Blackmill for Llantrisant, threading together these sections of the old Llantrisant line:

- **Llwyn-helig–near Hendreforgan:** C, W, UT, DR, 1m, SS 958868–SS 975875. A section of line that utilised the valley of the Ogwr Fach.
- **Near Thomastown–Ynysmaerdy, near Llantrisant:** C, W, UT, DR, 1¾m, ST 015865–ST 034839. In 2016, the OS mapping showed a gap south of Coedely roundabout on the A4419, but the Sustrans mapping showed the route as continuous throughout.

New Tredegar–Pontlottyn: C, W, UT, DR, SO 143032–SO 122060, 2m. Another part of the B&MR's line from Bargoed to Rhymney that has been incorporated into NCN468. The trail leaves the trackbed briefly at Abertysswg, but follow the NCN waymarking.

Senghenydd–Trecenydd: C, W, NI, DR, 2¼m, ST 115907–ST 140879. Part of the former Rhymney Railway's Senghenydd branch, now part of NCN475.

The Taff Trail
This is a 55-mile walking and cycling route from Brecon to Cardiff, which within Mid Glamorgan includes the following sections of old railway and tramway:

- **Pontsticill–Cefn Coed:** C, W, UT, DR, 3m, SO 061106–SO 032080. Part of NCN8, this trail uses the B&MR's line from Pontsticill to Morlais Junction, then the northern section of the joint B&MR and LNWR line from Pant to Merthyr Tydfil.
- **Pontygwaith–Abercynon:** C, W, UP, DT, 2½m, ST 081978–ST 085949. Part of the historic Penydarren Tramroad, including two stone-built single-span tramway bridges at Edwardsville, which are now scheduled ancient monuments. Now forms part of the Trevithick Trail (see entry above for Merthyr Tydfil–Abercynon).
- **Pontypridd–Castell Coch:** C, W, UP, mainly DR, 7m, ST 086892–ST 129836. Comprises sections of the Alexandra (Newport & South Wales) Dock & Railway, the Barry Railway and the Rhymney Railway. At intermediate Nantgarw where the Taff Trail reverses, a new ¾m link heads east to the western edge of Caerphilly (ST 126855–ST 137861). The surface on the ex-railway sections is excellent, but the link from the Rhymney Railway to Castell Coch involves a steep climb, which is unsuitable for prams, wheelchairs, etc.

Treharris–Gelligroes: C, W, UT, DR, 5½m, ST 101972–ST 176947. A relatively new trail, most of which is in Gwent, q.v.

Glamorgan, South

No substantial railway paths are known, but 8 miles of the Three Castles cycle trail are complete. This shares the same route as the Taff Trail and currently runs from Cardiff to Castell Coch. The Three Castles route includes part of the little-known Melingriffith Tramway (see below).

Tongwynlais–Melingriffith: C, W, UT, DT, 1½m, ST 131816–ST 143804.

Glamorgan, West

Afan Valley Country Park: A popular country park in a landscaped former mining valley with cycle hire available at Cynonville.

- **Cymmer–Blaengwynfi:** C, W, UP, DR, 2m, SS 860962–SS 885968. Part of the Rhondda & Swansea Bay Railway's line from Port Talbot to Treherbert. Currently, the mighty but sealed Rhondda Tunnel blocks further progress at Blaengwynfi. This is the longest disused tunnel in Wales at 3,443yds; it took five years to construct, from 1885 to 1890, with teams working from both ends. An extraordinarily well-supported campaign is under way to reopen it, so in the future it may be possible to cycle through and reach Treherbert again, as did passenger trains until 1968.
- **Cymmer–Glyncorrwg–North Rhondda:** C, W, UP, DR, 3½m, SS 860964–SS 874992–SN 887005. Part of the former South Wales Mineral Railway, now a good cycle trail south of Glyncorrwg. The valley here has been 'greened' and so gives no impression of what this area was like when the local pits were working.

- **Pontrhydyfen–Efail-fach:** C, W, UT, DR, 1m, SS 793940–SS 787954. This trail uses part of the PTR's Blaenavon branch.
- **Pontrhydyfen–Abercregan–Cymmer:** C, W, UP, DR, 5½m, SS 800942–SS 850966–SS 860964. One of two ex-railway routes between Pontrhydyfen and Cymmer, this one runs along the north side of the valley and uses the trackbed of the former SWMR.
- **Pontrhydyfen–Cynonville–Cymmer:** C, W, UT, DR, 5½m, SS 800942–SS 821952–SS 860962. This route runs along the south side of the valley and uses the trackbed of the former R&SBR.
- **Pontrhydyfen–Cwmavon:** C, W, NI, DR, 1m, SS 794937–SS 787922. A further short section of the PTR's Blaenavon branch, which ends on the north-east edge of Cwmavon where the cycle route uses a footbridge to cross from the south to the north bank of the river.

Briton Ferry–near Gelli-gaer: W, NI, DR, 1½m, SS 743949–SS 767951. A further section of the SWMR. This route is not shown as a right of way on the OS map, so confirmation or correction would be appreciated.

Bryn–Goytre: W, NI, DR, 3¼m, SS 819920–SS 781897. Another part of the PTR, in this case the company's former line from Maesteg (Neath Road) to Port Talbot Central.

Clydach–Cwm Clydach: W, NI, DT, 3m, SN 687010–SN 688052. The Lower Clydach Tramway, latterly an NCB branch line.

Onllwyn–Ystradgynlais: H, W, NI, DT, 3½m, SN 840105–SN 786098. If starting from Onllwyn, turn west (left) at SN 834106. Part of Claypon's Tramroad, now a scheduled ancient monument. There is no right of way over the short section from SN 796096 to SN 790097, but a bridleway and minor road offer a convenient detour to the north. At the Onllwyn end, the trackbed has been affected by open cast mining and subsequent land regeneration, but over Mynydd y Drum long sections can be followed, which still include many original stone block sleepers. A circular walk of 7m can be had by following this route in one direction and Coelbren–Y Gurnos in the other (see under Powys); the two trails intersect at SN 793097, just east of Y Gurnos.

Pontardawe–Ystalyfera: C, W, NI, DR, 3m, SN 733047–SN 766082. Part of the former MR line from Swansea to Byrnamman. While much of this line has succumbed to road improvements for the A4067, this section now forms part of NCN43.

Swansea Bike Path Network: A good-quality local network which reuses the route of the Swansea & Mumbles Railway and part of the abandoned section of the Central Wales line (which used to run through to Swansea rather than Llanelli, the modern-day destination).

- **Black Pill–Gowerton–Pontarddulais:** C, W, UT, DR, 7m, SS 619908–SS 592963–SN 595016. Part of the former LNWR from Swansea to Pontarddulais, now part of NCN4. The extension from Gowerton to Pontarddulais was opened in 2015 and comes as the culmination of twenty years of local campaigning. North of Gowerton, a short section of the trail runs alongside the B4296 where the railway trackbed has been built over. The end of the route is a little way south of Pontarddulais, so there is still scope for a trail into the town.
- **Swansea Marina–Mumbles:** C, W, UT, DT, 5m, SS 660924–SS 630875. The course of the Swansea & Mumbles Railway (actually a tramway) with extensive views across Swansea Bay; a further part of NCN4.

Gwent

Brynmawr–Llanfoist: W, CIP, DR, DT, 8m, SO 197121–SO 285133. This is one of the best railway paths in Wales, if not the whole of the UK. It runs through the Clydach Gorge reusing much of the LNWR's Heads of the Valleys line, which features superb scenery and imposing engineering works. Even by nineteenth-century standards, the construction costs must have been astronomical. The upper section is now complete from Brynmawr (SO 197121) to SO 235135, and then from SO 242139 to Llanfoist (SO 285133). The surface is tarmac except for the section just down from the upper tunnels (where it remains grassy ballast) and, for the most part, the line followed is the later railway rather than the original tramway. The tunnels are bypassed using the line of the tramway, some of which has been taken over by shared access to houses and a short stretch of public highway; the tramway gets around the upper tunnels by climbing dramatically high up a wooded cliff. One of the upper tunnels can be walked through but it is unsurfaced, unlit and pitch black in the middle due to the curve; if you intend to walk this, it is essential to bring a torch. Both lower tunnels are blocked. The missing section between SO 235135 and SO 242139 is apparently still under negotiation for access, although the lanes used to bridge the gap are quiet and only add a short 'dog leg' to the overall distance. The top end of the route at Brynmawr is very close to the two Darren Disgwylfa Tram Roads, which lead to disused quarries on the other side of the valley; see next two entries. (Details supplied by Tim Hewett and confirmed by the author.)

Near Brynmawr–Darren Disgwylfa Quarry: W, UX, DT, 2m, SO21124–SO 209135–SO 219148. This is the Upper Darren Disgwylfa Tramroad, now a public footpath, which was built by the Bailey family in 1811 to transport limestone from Darren Disgwylfa

Quarry down to Nantyglo Ironworks near Brynmawr. The views from the trackbed are impressive but, in practice, this is a route for experienced hill and mountain walkers only, especially at the west end: they will need good compass- and map-reading skills, as well as a fair run of dry weather to reduce the amount of water on the mountainside. The remains of the tramway are out there in the form of low embankments, shallow cuttings and stone sleeper sets, but it is no fun to have one's feet sink 2ft into waterlogged peat, which is likely to happen during the wetter months of the year. Walkers who wish to enjoy the spectacular countryside in this area the easy way should refer to the next entry.

Brynmawr–Pant-y-Rhiw: C, H, W, UT, DT, 4m, SO 197123–SO 200159. This is the Lower Darren Disgwylfa Tramroad, constructed between 1828 and 1830, and now a public road, albeit a very quiet one which serves only a handful of remote farms. While the uphill gradient from Brynmawr is very gentle, the height the tramway reaches is astonishing, and the views across the Clydach Gorge and the Usk Valley are superb, especially from Pant-y-Rhiw. At SO 200159, this route connects with the Llangattock Tramroad; see entry below for Pant-y-Rhiw–Llangattock. Locals advise that there are more old tram roads around Brynmawr, some of which have been incorporated into the local rights of way network.

Crosskeys–Gelligroes: C, W, UP, DR, 4½m, ST 214913–ST 176947. The Sirhowy Valley Country Park and part of NCN47 – perhaps one of the luckiest railway paths in Wales, given that a landslip closed it in August 2008 necessitating costly repairs. Part of the GWR's and LNWR's Sirhowy Valley lines, which met at an end-on junction at Nine Mile Point, where the old crossing keeper's cottage is now a visitor and information centre.

Gelligroes–Treharris: C, W, UT, DR, 5½m, ST 176947–ST 101972. This is a recent extension of the route above, which uses part of the former GWR line from Pontypool (Clarence Street) to Nelson & Llancaiach. Parts of the old railway formation have been encroached upon by new roads etc., but this trail – part of NCN47 – links them all together. The Treharris end, which is just in Mid Glamorgan, is only a mile or so from the Taff Trail at Edwardsville.

Hollybush–Blackwood: C, W, UT, DR, 4½m, SO 166035–ST 176980. Another section of the LNWR's Sirhowy Valley line (see entry for Crosskeys above). A further mile of this line can be walked and cycled from Peacehaven, just south of Tredegar, to Bedwellty Pits (SO 150073–SO 156061).

Machen–Bedwas: C, W, NI, DR, 2m, ST 208893–ST 184891. Part of NCN4 which reuses a section of the old B&MR's line from Machen to Rhymney. At the Bedwas (i.e. western) end, the OS map shows a footpath, cycle trail and RUPP running on or alongside the trackbed from ST 180892 to ST 163894.

Pant-y-Rhiw–Llangattock: W, NX, DT, 1m, SO 200159–SO 204158. This is the Llangattock Tramroad, now a public footpath, which was used to convey limestone from Darren Cilau Quarry (SO 202156) down to limekilns at Llangattock Wharf on the Brecon & Merthyr Canal. Both Darren Cilau Quarry and Llangattock Wharf are now scheduled ancient monuments. At Pant-y-Rhiw, this route connects with the Lower Darren Disgwylfa Tramroad (see entry above for Brynmawr–Pant-y-Rhiw). Be warned that the Llangattock Tramroad starts with two inclined planes, which are very steep and rough underfoot, so this is not a walk for the faint-hearted; to reinforce the point, the OS Landranger map marks the inclines as a 'Danger Area'. Stone remains, presumably of engine houses, survive at SO 200159 and SO 198161, where the route turns almost 90 degrees from a north-west to a north-east bearing. From SO 199163, the trackbed is almost level and used as a cattle drove; as it nears near Llangattock, stone sleeper sets can be seen in the ground.

Pontrhydyrun–Blaenavon: C, W, NI, DR, 11m, ST 295974–SO 229101. Part of NCN46. Reuses much of the old BR branch line from Llantarnam Junction to Blaenavon Colliery, which was formed by linking together separate sections of GWR and LNWR origin. The trail serves intermediate Pontypool and Abersychan, and at the northern end meets the preserved Blaenavon & Pontypool Railway.

Redbrook (Near Monmouth)–Whitebrook: W, NI, DR, 2¼m, SO 536101–SO 537068. Part of the Wye Valley Walk (see under Gloucestershire), including a GWR river bridge at Redbrook.

Railway stations come in all shapes and sizes, but few are more diminutive than Hadnock Halt on the GWR branch from Monmouth to Ross-on-Wye. Its working life was equally diminutive, opening in 1951 and closing with the line in 1959. One wonders if the railway ever recovered the cost of building it. (Author)

Symonds Yat–Hadnock Court (Near Monmouth): C, W, UT, DR, 2½m, SO 536101–SO 528146. Part of NCN423, which – if one doesn't mind a steep climb over Symonds Yat – connects with the Wye Valley Walk (see under Gloucestershire) coming up from Lydbrook Junction. Perhaps one day the local authorities will have mercy and open up Symonds Yat Tunnel.

Tintern–Black Morgan's Wood: W, UP, SR, 1½m, SO 529002–ST 539982. This trail starts on the east side of the A466 in Tintern on the so-called Wireworks Branch, whose long bridge over the River Wye is crossed about 30yds from the start. At SO 536001, the trackbed of the line to Chepstow is met: a detour to the left leads up to the southern portal of Tintern Tunnel, but the main route is to the right and is now a public footpath thanks to the Forestry Commission. Black Morgan's Viaduct is passed at ST 538987. The trackbed beyond ST 539982 is owned by Railway Paths, and there is a vigorous local campaign to convert it into a trail – so one day there might be another 2½m of trackbed to follow south to near Tutshill on the east of Chepstow.

Gwynedd

Bangor–Tregarth–Bethesda: C, W, NF, DR, 5¼m, SH 592726–SH 601679–SH 618669. Bangor and Bethesda were linked by two railways: a standard gauge LNWR branch line and a privately owned narrow gauge line that ran from Lord Penrhyn's quarries at Bethesda to Porth Penrhyn on the coast. This cycle trail (variously NCN5 and NCN85) uses Lord Penrhyn's line from SH 592726 to SH 587692 and the LNWR branch thereafter. In 2016, Gwynedd CC obtained funds to improve the trail, which formerly took a diversion around the closed 279yd Tregarth Tunnel. The new money will enable both the tunnel and the viaduct beyond it to be opened, after which the trail will revert to the original trackbed-based route on the west side of the A5, ending near Bethesda rugby ground.

Caernarfon–Aber Pwll (near Bangor): C, W, UT, DR, 6m, SH 482634–SH 536682. Most of the former LNWR line from Caernarfon to Bangor, now reused as part of NCN8. Starts in Caernarfon just north of the local Asda superstore. A couple of short sections have been lost near Llanfair Hall Farm and at Y Felinheli, but convenient diversions have been installed. In Caernarfon, follow the signs for NCN8 to pick up the trail to Bryncir (see next entry).

Caernarfon–Bryncir: C, W, UP, DR, 14m, SH 480626– SH 479447. Most of the former LNWR line from Caernarfon to Afonwen. The railway path (known as Lôn Eifion and a further section of NCN8) runs alongside the restored Welsh Highland Railway between Caernarfon and Dinas Junction before the WHR turns away to the east. South of Penygroes, this is as a lonely a railway path as one can find anywhere in Wales.

Bryncir station on the LNWR's former line from Caernarfon to Afon Wen served a tiny community, which still boasts the most westerly cattle market in Wales. The station's buildings are long gone, but the platform remains, as does this striking water tank, which was used to replenish locomotives at this, important crossing point. (Chris Parker)

Dolgellau–Morfa Mawddach: C, W, UP, DR, 7¾m, SH 714183–SH 628141. This is the Cambrian Railways' branch from Barmouth Junction (modern day Morfa Mawddach) to Dolgellau, where it made an end-on connection with the GWR's line from Ruabon. This is one of the great estuarial railway walks and was featured for good reason on 'Railway Walks' with Julia Bradbury in 2008. The route is now part of NCN8. At the seaward end, walkers and cyclists can continue into Barmouth via the town's famous viaduct in return for a modest toll.

Llyn Celyn (near Bala)–Trawsfynydd. The following sections of this remote GWR branch line are available:

- **Bryn Ifan–Arenig:** W, NI, DR, 1m, SH 850394– SH 836394. If you find yourself in Arenig, you

will inevitably end up asking yourself why the GWR built a halt there – it gives credence to the idea that railway companies developed a guilty conscience if they constructed more than 4 miles of line without a station of some kind. The trackbed can be picked up again north of Bryn Ifan, but there is not much point (other than the nice view) since it soon disappears into the waters of Llyn Celyn. One day, perhaps, the sub aqua branch of Railway Ramblers will follow the trackbed under water to the other side.

- **Near Pontrhydyfen–near Trawsfynydd:** W, UX, DR, 6¼m, SH 819391–SH 718359. The original permissive section from Cwm Prysor to Glanllafar has been extended almost to Trawsfynydd, as recently installed stiles and gates indicate. The notable Cwm Prysor viaduct is crossed at SH

775388. Few railway walks are more attractive or remote than this one, but the route was overgrown at the western end when last inspected. A ½m section of the line east of Cwm Prysor has been taken for a new alignment of the A4212 and there is no footway; take care here.

Ratgoed–near Aberllefenni: W, UP, DT, 1½m, SH 780121–SH 777101. Part of the Ratgoed Tramway, which carried slate down to Aberllefenni where connection was made with the Corris Railway. The scenery is superb, and there is an abandoned village just south of Ratgoed Hall to add interest.

Tryfan Junction–Bryngwyn: W, UP, DR, 2m, SH 503591–SH 495565. This slate-surfaced trail starts at Tryfan Junction on the Welsh Highland Railway and follows the trackbed of a branch of the North Wales Narrow Gauge Railway. After a mile, a large replica running-in board declares that one has arrived at Rhostryfan. Half a mile after that, the slate surface gives way to a grassy track that leads on to Bryngwyn. Signs at the start suggest that there is a

trail to the disused quarries at Moel Tryfan, which isn't quite correct. The incline leading up to the quarries is on open access land but, realistically, one needs an OS Explorer map east of Bryngwyn.

Powys

Coelbren–Y Gurnos, near Ystalyfera: C, W, UT, DR, 3½m, SN 835120–SN 783088. This path, the Tawe Uchaf Trail, uses much of the Neath & Brecon Railway's line from Colbren Junction to Ynys-y-Geinon Junction, but these are the railway company's spellings: the modern OS map gives Ynisgeinon and Coelbren respectively. A 7m circular walk can be had by following the N&BR in one direction and Claypon's Tram Road in the other (see entry for Onllwyn–Ystradgynlais under West Glamorgan).

Elan Valley (Caban Coch–Craig Goch): The long established railway path along the course of the contractor's railway in the Elan Valley has been

Below left: Cwm Prysor Viaduct on the scenic ex-GWR line from Bala Junction to Trawsfynydd is now open for walkers. The GWR built this line through remote countryside to capture a share of the lucrative slate traffic from Blaenau Ffestiniog. Unfortunately for the company's bank balance, this traffic persisted in staying on the LNWR to Llandudno Junction, or the Ffestiniog Railway to Minffordd. (Phil Earnshaw)

Below right: The route of the former North Wales Narrow Gauge/Welsh Highland Railway's branch between Tryfan Junction and Rhostryfan was formally opened as a public footpath on 21 May 2011. This is the start of the path at Tryfan Junction, which is served by trains on the preserved WHR. The trackbed can be followed beyond Rhostryfan after which it gets progressively more remote. (Chris Parker)

extended 3½ miles eastwards; see entry below for Rhayader, which route now incorporates this.

Llangurig–Skew Bridge: W, NI, DR, 1¼m, SN 909799–SN 927800. Part of the northern section of the ill-fated Manchester & Milford Railway, which was built and laid with double track but never opened. Only a single goods train ever used it.

Onllwyn–Ystradgynlais: H, W, NI, DT, 3½m, SN 840105–SN 786098. See entry under West Glamorgan.

Penwyllt–A4067 (south of Cray Reservoir): W, NI, DR, 2¼m, SN 857163–SN 870195. Part of the former Neath & Brecon Railway which now forms a 'permitted footpath' within the Brecon Beacons National Park. Further lengths of this line are situated on 'access land' where the public has a right to roam. The access land starts near Pen-y-Cae and incorporates this permitted footpath, thereby making it possible to follow the N&BR from south-east of Pen-y-Cae to the south side of Cray Reservoir, a distance of 6 miles (SN 853124–SN 885211). However, it is necessary to walk around the operational Penwyllt Quarry, which occupies the old line between SN 855154 and SN 854160. To get to the start point at SN 853124, follow the lane from Pen-y-Cae to Coelbren, and turn east on to a footpath at SN 851124; the nearby communications mast is a useful landmark. Follow this footpath to a bridge over the line at SN 853124 and there turn left (i.e. north) to follow the trackbed to Cray. Apart from the N&BR, there is also a former tramway in the area, since an extensive tramway network once served workings above Penwyllt Quarry. This tramway can be accessed from the railway trackbed at SN 854151 and repays exploration. It used a series of zigzag reversals to gain height, and these can still be followed uphill to its summit, where the N&BR can be seen below. There is also an incline at SN 854151.

Just south of Rhayader on the Cambrian Railways' line from Moat Lane Junction to Three Cocks Junction, a contractor's railway of 1894 branched off for the Elan Valley where four large reservoirs were constructed to provide Birmingham with water. The main features of this railway are its constant climb and this steep-sided cutting, known as Devil's Gulch. (Bob Morgan)

Rhayader–Caban Coch (near Elan Village)–Craig Goch: C, W, UP, DR, 9m, SN 966678–SN 926647. This trail uses a short section of the Cambrian Railway's Mid-Wales line out of Rhayader before turning west at Elan Junction (SN 963671) on to the trackbed of the 1894 contractor's railway. The line starts to climb markedly after Caban Coch, where the first of four large dams in the Elan Valley is encountered. The trail reuses the whole of the contractor's railway, which was used to transport materials for the construction of these dams at the turn of the nineteenth and twentieth centuries.

Talybont-on-Usk–Ffos y Wern: W, UU, DT, 7m, SO 116226–SO 108152. The Brynoer Tramway originally constructed as a feeder to the local canal, then the Brecknock & Abergavenny, now better known as the Monmouthshire & Brecon. The tramway continued beyond Ffos y Wern to Trefil Quarries (SO 120133) at the head of the Sirhowy Valley; this section is easy to trace, but part of the trackbed has been taken over by a minor road.

Talybont-on-Usk–Torpantau Tunnel: W, UP, DR, 6m, SO 108210–SO 057171. This is most of the Seven Mile Bank on the Brecon & Merthyr Tydfil Junction Railway, now part of the Taff Trail. Diversions at either end account for the 'missing mile'.

Spend and Save

Earlsheaton Tunnel received its official opening on St Valentine's Day 2013, when a dusting of snow adorned the area. At £1.3 million, the work was not cheap, but Lynnette Evans, the Cycling Officer for Kirklees Council, explained that the road alternative was steep, heavily trafficked, and not at all cycle-friendly. She continued: 'The disused railway provides a level route and passes many residential areas so it will give people an opportunity to make their journeys more sustainably.' And safe, of course. (Peter Martin)

Money alone sets all the world in motion.

Attributed to Publilius Syrus

In the seminal 1960s science fiction series *The Prisoner*, Patrick McGoohan's character asks a question of a supercomputer code named 'The General', which is being used to brainwash the residents of the sinister village in which he has been imprisoned. The machine accepts his encoded microfilm, but soon its tape reels are spinning, smoke begins to emit from its fan vents, and finally The

General short circuits and bursts into flames. Picking up the twisted microfilm from the molten wreckage, the chairman of the village demands to know what the prisoner's question was. He replies: 'It's insoluble, for man or machine … W. H. Y. Question mark.' Why? The reaction on social media of some motorists to the provision of improved facilities for cyclists recalls The General's demise. The car is an extremely useful machine, and this is not an anti-car book; but who in the twenty-first century has not stood on the pavement of an urban road and despaired of ever getting across for the sheer volume of vehicles? Imagine how difficult it is for a young cyclist to negotiate a right-hand turn in such a traffic flow.

Cycling in the UK has enjoyed many boosts in recent years. The strained economy has made cycling a good-value transport choice; more extreme weather events have made people think more carefully about their mode of travel; the continued roll-out of traffic-free trails has provided more places for people to walk and cycle safely; ever more urgent advice to 'get active' as a means of combatting obesity is making people at least think about giving up sedentary lifestyles; and the success of the country's cycling Olympians such as Bradley Wiggins, Chris Hoy and Chris Froome has inspired a new generation to 'get on their bikes'. (It must be emphasised that walking has also benefitted from the new trails, and offers similar benefits.)

But an old problem has returned to cycling. When Sustrans was founded in 1984, the number

of fatalities and serious accidents affecting cyclists on Britain's roads had reached a peak; something needed to be done. Since then, national government, local government, Sustrans and, through their campaigning, the Cyclists' Touring Club have driven down the number of cyclist fatalities from a peak of 345 in 1984 to just over the 100 mark in 2015. Unfortunately, serious injuries have proven more intractable, and they are affecting young cyclists disproportionately: they fell steadily from 1984 to 2004 (from 6,250 to 2,174), but have been rising steadily since. And these figures count just the incidents that make it into the official record. The Royal Society for the Prevention of Accidents reckons that there could be 'two or three times as many seriously injured cyclists and double the number of slightly injured'. It appears that many cycling accidents are not reported to the police, even when hospital treatment is required. The type of road also has a bearing on accident rates: in 2013, rural roads carried 30 per cent of cycle traffic but accounted for 58 per cent of cyclist fatalities. This unhappy combination demonstrates the value of the 'classic' railway path, which reuses a closed rural line and thus gets walkers and cyclists off rural roads.

Like all road traffic accidents, those involving cyclists (and walkers) are a huge drain on public resources. The obvious costs are attendance by police, ambulance and paramedics; hospital care, including subsequent physiotherapy; the economic cost of a blocked road; and follow-up visits by police, e.g. to obtain statements from non-local witnesses. After that come other costs like damage to property and another really big one – the loss of the victim's economic output. Each year, the Department for Transport publishes 'A valuation of road accidents and casualties in Great Britain', which sets out the accident costs to be used in the appraisal of new transport schemes. This report and the various tables in it allow a value to be placed on the reduction in accidents believed to be achievable by a new road. The individual figures are eye watering: in 2012, each fatality was reckoned to cost on average £1,917,766, each serious injury £219,043, and each slight injury £23,336. The one thing that can be sure is that all of these figures will have increased in the years since.

A formula like this needs to be included in the cost–benefit analysis for new rail trails. There is no doubt that they are expensive: the new bridges over the River Stour at Fiddleford Mill and Hodmoor cost in excess of £500,000, but now villagers in the upper Stour Valley have a traffic-free means of reaching Sturminster Newton and Blandford Forum. The users include children travelling to and from local schools. What is the immediate value of those children not being at risk of a road traffic accident when cycling on the A350, as they would have to do if the railway path did not exist? And what is the longer-term value of those children developing a cycling habit and needing fewer resources from the NHS during their lives because they become active individuals and do not develop into obese adults?

The more one looks at this subject, the more benefits begin to appear. Local economies along the routes of trails, especially the longer ones, are beginning to notice increased spending from an increased passing trade. At Warmley, the village's old station on the Bath to Bristol path now supports a café, which positively bustles at weekends. The Camel Trail in Cornwall has its own Camel Trail Tea Room near Nanstallon, successfully trading for over twenty years, and that's before one takes account of the cycle hire businesses now established at Bodmin, Wadebridge and Padstow – towns where, forty years ago, it was impossible to hire a bicycle at all. Parsley Hay in Derbyshire used to be the junction station where the LNWR's lines to Ashbourne and Cromford diverged; now it's home to a cycle hire centre from where railway paths head off in three different directions. Admittedly, this business is run by the

The North Dorset Trailway, which will eventually reuse the former Somerset & Dorset Railway from Stalbridge to Corfe Mullen (with onward trackbed connections to Wimborne Minster and Poole), features a number of signs like this. They're not expensive to install, but can make a lot of difference to a rural business. Incidentally, the Old Ox Inn is in Shillingstone; why not give it a try? (Author)

The Padiham Greenway reuses parts of the L&YR's former line from Rose Grove to Blackburn. In Padiham, a railway embankment used to run between these two rows of houses, cutting out light, giving the area an industrial feel and no doubt depressing property values. Sustrans and Lancashire County Council took the bold decision to remove the embankment, and this is the result – a new and popular local facility which not only connects communities, but also won an award in 2011 from the European Greenways Association for being an 'exemplary initiative'. (Author)

Peak District National Park, but one hopes it makes money for them.

The passing trade, whether walking or cycling, spreads out from a railway path into the places that the railway used to serve, or often couldn't serve because the next station was 2 miles away. The family man is likely to put all he needs in the family car – the wife, the kids and a picnic; and there's nothing wrong with that because bringing up a family is not cheap, and the economics of the family car often defeat those of the bus or train – especially when four tickets have to be purchased. However, the self-powered travellers on these trails tend to travel light and spend more time and money in the communities through which they pass. The beneficiaries are not just the obvious cycle hire centres, but also pubs, cafés, local shops, B&Bs, farms which can accommodate campers, local visitor attractions, and so on. In 2012, the Market Research Group at Bournemouth University published an 'Impact Analysis of the North Dorset Trailway', the under-development rail trail which will eventually

run from Stalbridge near the Somerset border down to Poole. At the time the report was published, the Trailway was only half complete, but already it was generating around 80,000 trips per year, including events arranged by walking, cycling and running clubs which brought larger than usual batches of users into the area. Some of the walking groups used local bus services so that they could ride out and walk back along the old railway – a type of activity which helps to support rural public transport, especially during the warmer months.

Shortly after Bournemouth University's MRG reported on the North Dorset Trailway, the Trans Pennine Trail Office at Barnsley reported that, during 2012, the Trans Pennine Trail had attracted 966,000 users (including 227,000 cyclists) who had spent around £800,000 in the local economy. In 2013 Transform Scotland, the national alliance for sustainable transport in Scotland, published *The Value of Cycle Tourism: Opportunities for the Scottish Economy*. This concluded that, 'taking the economic contribution from the mountain biking and leisure cycle tourism sectors together, the combined value is between £236.2m and £358m per year'.

This is not the place for a detailed analysis of all the academic reports which have been produced on this subject, but it does seem clear that significant economic and health benefits are available from rail trails as part of a wider programme of improving facilities for walkers and cyclists – not forgetting the others who benefit, such as families with children in prams and buggies, and those who depend on a mobility scooter. The National Cycle Network is the over-arching framework which holds all of this together, its great advantage being that it takes over where a railway path ends and provides a safe route into a town or city centre. (The BR Property Board easily sold much old railway land within urban areas, which is why so many rail trails start and end at the edges of places.)

In 2016, the Chancellor of the Exchequer announced more investment in new roads, but in England committed no significant funding for the development of walking and cycling. The Infrastructure Act of 2015, one of the final pieces of legislation passed by the Coalition government, offered a ray of hope, but as from a distant star. It was intended to expedite infrastructure projects by improving the funding, management and planning processes; it also included clauses that allow the government to create a Cycling and Walking Investment Strategy (CWIS) in England, or vary an existing strategy. The very idea of such a thing was a significant development, but its implementation was badly timed and its funding level was miserly. Previous funding for walking and cycling in England finished at the end of March 2016, at the very time when the public consultation on England's first CWIS was about to start; publication of the final CWIS was scheduled for 'summer 2016', with the roll-out set to begin some time after that. For Sustrans, that timetable presented an unfunded black hole of at least three months, and probably longer – time enough for experienced path design and development teams to need laying off, with a consequent loss and dispersal of expertise. Additionally, the CWIS provided funding at just 15 per cent of the previous level,

which was too low to make a real impact, and put England significantly out of step with other countries in the British Isles. Behind the grandiloquent name, the CWIS was a lightweight scheme whose real purpose was to slash investment in health-enhancing and life-saving projects in order to support the government's austerity policy. When one considers how much money pours from the public purse as a result of road traffic accidents involving walkers and cyclists, this is clearly a false economy. (Will some future government please give a future CWIS proper funding and credibility?)

In order to bring about material change in people's travel habits, a continuous plan and funding strategy are required with content and real money behind them to allow planners, politicians and the 'supply chain' to take decisions to support the plan, and implement it. England's first CIWS was important, but it was extremely disruptive to have a hiatus

This is the new bridge which spans Millmead Road in Bath on the day of the official opening of the city's Two Tunnels Trail, 6 April 2013. It was not cheap, but delivers 'grade separation' which keeps walkers and cyclists on the trail separate from road traffic. Note the extensive tree planting on the embankment faces. (Author)

while it started up, combined with a massive funding cut. The situation was very different in Scotland and Wales. To take Scotland as an example, in 2016–17 the Scottish government set a provisional budget for sustainable and active travel of £62 million, up from £57 million in 2015–16. It also had policies in place to direct and guide this spending, such as the 'Cycling Action Plan for Scotland' (2010–20), the 'National Walking Strategy' (2015–20) and the 'Long Term Vision for Active Travel in Scotland' (2020–30). In England, by contrast, only a small group of big cities had funding thanks to 'Cycle City Ambition Funding' and Transport for London's work in the capital; but if you didn't happen to live in Birmingham, Bristol, Cambridge, London, Manchester, Newcastle, Norwich or Oxford, you were out of luck.

Railway paths cost money; the National Cycle Network costs money; and a properly funded Cycling and Walking Investment Strategy for England *would* cost money. However, they deliver important returns – improved health, reduced numbers of costly accidents affecting walkers and cyclists, and a reduced dependence on fossil fuels which, to say the least, are heavily implicated in changing weather patterns. Then there are the economic benefits, which are being experienced along the routes of the longer trails, and which can be expected to spread as the range of cycling, and especially recreational cycling, extends. Funds invested in a new trail will not in themselves save the village post office, shop or pub; but they will gradually bring more passing trade from which benefits will flow. Reports, such as that undertaken in 2012 by Bournemouth University into the impact of the North Dorset Trailway are already showing this.

The car has helped to create a national retail structure where virtually everything can be situated remotely on the edge of a community: that's great for distributors because their lorries have to spend only ten minutes or so off the motorway, but it obliges everyone else to travel – usually by car – to the point of distribution. Most of our supplies used to be centred in *communities*. The out-of-town relocations that we now live with are the result of a collective 'dictatorship of supply', justified by traffic-clogged town and city centres, which we have accepted passively. It may be too late to turn back all of this, but perhaps we can stop it getting any worse, especially outside the urban areas. For those of us who live in the urban areas, we can all walk or cycle to a local shop, café, pub, library, cinema, tourist attraction, etc. We need a government that will promote safe ways to do that by both planning in a timely manner, and funding to an appropriate level, so as not to disrupt the supply mechanism.

One final thing remains to be said on the subject of 'spend and save'. The benefits will be difficult to quantify – how can anyone prove when a railway path has saved a life that would have been lost on the alternative road? – but this spending will save lives.

USEFUL WEBSITES

www.bing.com/mapspreview?FORM=MMREDR
This very useful free service offers a range of mapping tools, including Ordnance Survey maps (in both Landranger and Explorer formats), street maps and various actual views (aerial, bird's eye and street view).

www.branchline.org.uk
The Branch Line Society UK is a national organisation established in 1955 for the 'study of railway infrastructure and history of networks'. This rather dry description disguises the fact that the BLS organises some first-rate rail tours and occasional walks over disused trackbeds.

www.camra.org.uk
Camra is the Campaign for Real Ale, which publishes the national *Good Beer Guide* from its St Albans head office, leaving its regional branches to publish local guides. All of these publications offer a convenient way of identifying good pubs when you are out exploring in unfamiliar parts of the country.

www.disused-stations.org.uk
Disused Stations is an offshoot of the website of an organisation called Subterranea Britannica, which is concerned with underground Britain – everything from caves to once secret wartime bunkers via tunnels and mines. Nick Catford is one of the leading lights in 'Sub Brit', and this fascinating and well-informed website reflects his love of Britain's lost railways.

www.forgottenrelics.co.uk
The 'Forgotten Relics' website is a labour of love by Graeme Bickerdike, who has produced a high-quality and endlessly fascinating resource about Britain's network of closed and forgotten railways. Keep an eye on this (and the Railway Ramblers' website, below) for the latest developments.

www.johngrimshawassociates.co.uk
John Grimshaw & Associates is a design consultancy that specialises in drawing up proposals for cycling and walking projects which 'would make a real difference in the [travel] opportunities for local people'. What this doesn't say is that the practice focuses on delivering projects that have proved intractable in the past. John Grimshaw was the founder of Sustrans (see below) and has been developing traffic-free, multi-use paths since 1979.

www.nationalrail.co.uk
The National Rail journey planner. If you can, book in advance to get the best value tickets.

www.ordnancesurvey.co.uk
The Ordnance Survey's website. Includes an online shop for both standard and customised maps. The 'OS Maps' service will make the organisation's entire mapping available online for a modest annual fee (under £20 in 2016).

www.railwayramblers.org.uk
Railway Ramblers is the UK's specialist club for exploring disused railways. Its members made significant contributions to the information and photographs in this book.

www.railwaypaths.org.uk
Railway Paths works in conjunction with Sustrans (see below) and owns a significant portfolio of ex-railway property, which the former British Rail Property Board had not disposed of prior to the privatisation of the railways, completed in 1997. It finds new uses for supposedly unwanted railway infrastructure, and restores it.

www.sustrans.org.uk
Sustrans is the cycling charity behind the National Cycle Network and has done more than any other agency in the UK to put abandoned railways to constructive new use. The company also publishes high-quality printed maps for its routes, such as NCN62 (the Trans Pennine Trail), which appears frequently in this guide as it follows various old railways across the spine of the country from Hornsea to Southport. Sustrans also has an excellent online map service at www.sustrans.org.uk/map, which gives to cycle trails the prominence normally reserved for motorways. As one would expect, this online mapping shows everything in the NCN, as well as local authority routes such as the Meon Valley and Test Valley routes in Hampshire. Maximum zoom goes down to street map level, complete with street names.

If you enjoyed this book, you may also be interested in ...

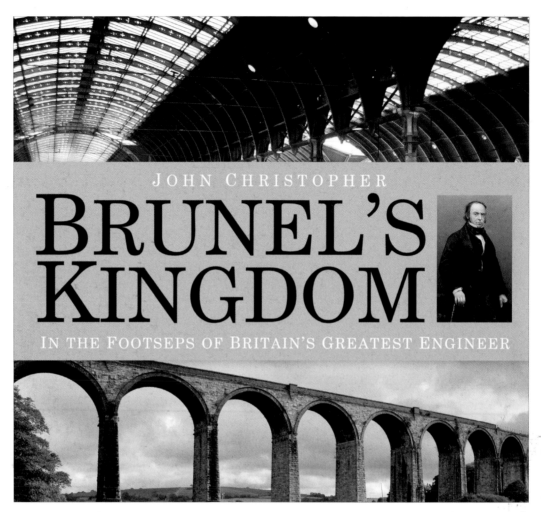

JOHN CHRISTOPHER

BRUNEL'S KINGDOM

IN THE FOOTSEPS OF BRITAIN'S GREATEST ENGINEER

978 0 7509 6306 0

The History Press

The destination for history
www.thehistorypress.co.uk